D0846986

Joe could see into people. They felt he really knew them. He told me he had a dream to spread the Fifth City ideal of community throughout the whole world. That motivated me to carry on. Joe was a powerful symbol. I called him the Dean of the Iron Men.

~**Ruth Carter**, Director of Fifth City Preschool, Chicago

Dr. Mathews' insights into facilitative leadership, partnership polity, and systems change shaped the conceptual framework for my organization's service to national and international education agencies.

~**Marilyn R. Crocker**, Ed.D., President, Crocker & Associates, Inc., Maine

Whenever Joe was present, things took on greater meaning for me, and consciousness greater depth.

~**Vinasithamby Dharmalingam**, journalist, Malaysia

The Mathews' talks inspire me to see my classroom as sacred space and my students as Those Who Care for the Not Yet.

~**Leah Early**, teacher, Nevada

The tools for transformational living in the midst of the everyday is Joe's enduring gift to me.

~**Lela Jahn,** CFP, owner, wealth management firm, California

Joe Mathews broke through the medieval teaching of Christianity and showed me the meaning and concreteness of the cross and empty tomb today.

~**Cristian Nacht**, businessman, Brazil

We learned to be global citizens and to care for humanity from our only guru, Joe.

~**Vinod and Kamala Parekh**, trainers, India

After three degrees and seventeen years in my profession, Joe Mathews gave me the tools that allowed me to more effectively re-mythologize the Gospel for my students.

~**Clarence H. Snelling**, Jr., Ph.D., Professor Emeritus, The Iliff School of Theology, Colorado

His ability to articulate and demonstrate the meaning and relevance of the "Great Teachings" to everyday life has been the basis for my approach to leadership, teamwork, and corporate culture.

~**Raymond Spencer**, Chairman and CEO, Kanbay International Inc., Chicago

There was awe in Joe's' life and awe in his writings.

~**Brian Stanfield**, Institute of Cultural Affairs, Australia

I first met Joe when he came to visit the Ethiopian Patriarch, where I was serving as the Secretary General of the Ethiopian Orthodox Church. He had a piercing look when he talked with individuals, and we took him very seriously. He talked of being interested in the church, and of wanting churchmen to become aware of their responsibility in the modern world.

~**V. Rev. L. L. T. Mikael N. Taffesse**, The Ethiopian Orthodox Church of Medhane-Alem

Joe found and expanded on individual greatness for the greater good.

~**Sandra True**, nurse administrator, and **Robert True**, physician, NYC

Joe Mathews was a master pedagogue. He remains an exemplar of effective teaching for me.

~**Neil Vance**, Senior Lecturer, University of Arizona

Joe helped me realize that living a deeply human life is living a deeply spiritual life.

~**Larry Ward**, business owner, clergy, and Director of the Lotus Institute, North Carolina

The 21st century is in desperate need of Joe's words of challenge and healing. I will always cherish my years of study and work with him and his team as we attempted to facilitate human development around the globe.

~**Robertson Work**, Principal Policy Advisor, Decentralized Governance, United Nations Development Programme (UNDP)

Bending History

BENDING HISTORY

Selected Talks of Joseph W. Mathews

General Editor: John L. Epps

Editorial Guild:

John P. Cock, George R. Holcombe,

Betty C. Pesek, M. George Walters

resurgence publishing

Published with Permission:

The original materials used in this publication are copies of written documents provided by Betty C. Pesek, Archivist, and taken with permission from the Joseph Wesley Mathews Archives, and recorded tapes contributed by Charles and Doris Hahn and Amy and Frank Hilliard. Permission for use of the written documents was granted by Joseph Wesley Mathews, Jr., and James J. Mathews, the heirs of the Joseph Wesley Mathews Estate. All editing of those materials is the responsibility of the editors of this publication and in no way is intended to represent the views or opinions of those who contributed originals or copies of the materials. Contact by e-mail:

Info@ResurgencePublishing.com

Cover design by Tara McDermott

ISBN 0-9763892-0-7
Printed in the United States of America

Dedicated To . . .

the citizens of Fifth City: Chicago;
O:E in dispersion;
and the archangel of the archives.

Formal remarks made at Washington, D. C., April 4, 2003:

"[I]n 1955 [I] went to the University of Texas from Yale and there I met Joseph Mathews. . . . He and I became close friends and colleagues. He brought to that campus a spiritual depth and enthusiasm. . . . There he was at a largely secular campus of 25,000 . . . students, and he created something of a religious revival. But it wasn't the "tub-thumping" revival, or one characterized by "evangelism." . . . It was rather [a] spiritual revival as he pushed students to new depths of intellectual search on spiritual issues. He had a following hard to imagine, and it took only two or three years for him to [help] develop it into the Christian Faith and Life Community. He took the germ of that idea with him through many parts of the world as he developed [a] movement.

"If we had had a structure in the Methodist Church or even in Protestantism that had the rigor of the [Roman] Catholic hierarchy, Joseph Mathews would probably have been treated first with hostility, as was St. Francis, and then later admitted into the fold as one who was the great revivalist of spiritual life in our time."

~Dr. John R. Silber
Boston University President (1971-96; 2002-03)
Chancellor (1996-2003)

Acknowledgements

This book is clearly not the work of one person. Many have played significant roles in bringing it to press. While it is not possible to name them all, some deserve special mention. First, of course, would be those who recorded these talks when they were given and who preserved the tapes through several generations of technology. Perhaps Bob Hummer could represent that group.

Thanks go to David Dunn who arranged for the tapes – some on 7-inch reels – to be transferred into electronic soft copy. Then a special tribute goes to Karen Bueno and Clare Whitney who typed the RS-I lectures into word processing format. Typing a lively lecture from a recording requires a level of persistence and patience rarely attained, and these two did it well.

To the team – George Walters, George Holcombe, John Cock, and Betty Pesek – go special thanks. Your enthusiasm, confidence, and wisdom, along with your familiarity with Joe, made it possible.

Special thanks go to Betty, who for twenty-seven years has served as "guardian" of Joe's files and who has no plans to relinquish that role, even though it may take a different form.

Thanks also go to our spouses – Ann, Carol, Wanda, and Lynda. You not only shared with us the experience of hearing many of these talks, you also graciously supported (and put up with) us while we were pulling them together.

Then there are many whose insights contributed significantly to Joe's formulations. There were such people as Fred and Sara Buss, Joe and Anne Slicker, David and Donna McCleskey, Joe and Carol Pierce, Bill and Marianna Bailey, Joe and Marilyn Crocker, Neil and Faith Vance, Jim and Judy Wiegel, Jon and Maureen Jenkins, Frank and Amy Hilliard, Gene and Ruth Marshall, Doris and Charles Hahn – the list is too long to name. Perhaps they can represent all the people in and around the Order: Ecumenical whose journeys and struggles and breakthroughs gave rise to many of the insights in this book.

One other group deserves special mention. We called them the "Guardians," meaning by that term those in the established structures who lent their support and wisdom to what we were doing. Representative of this large group of people can be the North Shore Cadre, a group of people who lived in the North Shore area of Chicago and who supported Joe in ways too numerous to mention. This group includes Anne and David Wood, George and Georgianna McBurney, Betty and Martin Pesek, Jim and LaVerne Phillips, Betty and Sheldon Hill, Priscilla and Rodney Wilson, Mary Warren and Don Moffett, and Len and Nicki Dresslar. Their service was substantial. They helped keep Joe in touch with how the structures of society operated and gave him insights into how effectively to operate as a "structural revolutionary."

Finally, none of these people should take the blame for this book. The final responsibility has to be that of the general editor, the role I've played with a huge sense of gratitude.

John Epps
Kuala Lumpur, Malaysia
2004

Contents

Section IV: New Form of the Religious

Foreword

By James K. Mathews, Ph.D., Bishop of the United Methodist Church, missionary to India, son-in-law of E. Stanley Jones, author of ten books, and younger brother of Joseph W. Mathews

Ever since I was asked to write a foreword to this collection of "talks" or speeches by my brother Joe, I have been searching my memory about what it was that helped make him what he was. Events from his early years do indeed give some hint about this subject. Some of these I shall try to record here in the order in which they came to me.

Others have often made the point that Joe Mathews did not leave much of a paper trail – in the sense of formal writing. On the other hand, he saw to it that extensive notes, drafts, and outlines were preserved in abundance.

Somehow when he took a pen in hand, his style became cramped and stiff. There were, of course, exceptions, as in the case of his essay "The Time My Father Died" and a few others. When he turned to speaking in public, however, he immediately became loose and lucid. This was his medium. There is good reason for St. Paul's assertion: "Faith comes from *hearing*" (Rom. 10:17).

I hesitate to liken Joe to Winston Churchill, but I recall hearing that when the latter arose to speak in the House of Commons, the word would quickly spread, "Winnnie's up!" and the chamber would become instantly crowded. It was somewhat like this with Joe.

This aptitude manifested itself very early in Sunday School, in public school, or even at home. When it came to reciting verse or "speaking a piece," Joe excelled. Let me recall a little poem he used to repeat with great gusto:

Of Father George and Martha too,
I'm proud as I can be;
For they were parents of this land
Of which I'm part, you see.

We all ought to honor them,
For it is very sure, I am:
That if there'd been no Father George,
There'd be no Uncle Sam!

No claim can be made for that being great poetry, but when voiced by Joe, it would open up the wellsprings of patriotism! Incidentally, be showed a lifelong interest in good poetry, ranging from the Psalms, the Browning's, e.e. cummings, and D.H. Lawrence, among others.

While we were growing up there was a barn on our property, not uncommon even in town during horse and buggy days. The barn lent itself to "theatricals" of all sorts. Since ours was a large family, as was true also of our neighbors, casting was never a problem. Some presentations were our own composition. At times our undertakings were more ambitious. How well I recall Joe's role in a selection from *As You Like It*.

We were fortunate later in attending the outstanding Senior High School in Mansfield, Ohio. The teachers were of superior quality and always alert to encourage promising students. Joe excelled in English and in Public Speaking. In fact, he rated very high in statewide oratorical competition in Ohio. In turn, he encouraged his younger siblings, Alice and myself, in the field of public address.

It was also during his high school years that Joe's gifts in acting were uncovered. He successfully tried out for Sheridan's *The Rivals*. No one who saw him in the role of Captain Absolute – clothed in red-coat regimentals and all – could forget his prowess as an actor. He also played the leading role in a play – popular on Broadway in the 1920's – *Rollo's Wild Oats*.

After having been graduated from high school he did not immediately go on to college but was active in a local drama group. Among other plays he had a principal part in *Witness for the Prosecution*. This led to a tryout at the Cleveland Playhouse. One of the judges on that occasion was the well-known character-actress (this feminine term was still used in those days) Marie Dressler. She recommended that Joe go to Hollywood and try out for the movies! The details of that story are told in my forthcoming biography of my brother.

In a word, Joe did not become a movie actor, although there always remained about him something of the actor – so no waste there. Very often I have thought about another man from the Middle West who went to Hollywood about the same time. He *did* get into the movies and ended up living in a prominent residence in Washington, D.C. His name was Ronald Reagan.

Perhaps I should mention at this point that Joe took up the habit of cigarette smoking while involved in drama. One part called for this and he was determined to master the "stage business" related to the practice. In this endeavor he succeeded, but he never succeeded in breaking the tobacco habit, though at times he tried. He tolerated my complaining to him about this, although he thought my admonitions arose out of some sort of "moralism." In my view, his addiction hastened his death but the Creator at no time has entrusted me with control in such matters.

Meanwhile, my brother ended up in Los Angeles in 1932. It was the year of the Olympic Games in that city. The churches mounted a program at that time called the "Olympiad of Religion." Some of the finest preachers in the country took part. Among them was Bishop Arthur J. Moore of the Methodist Episcopal Church, South. His message and delivery were always compelling and convincing. Joe responded to the Gospel and this proved to be the most transforming moment of his journey. The direction of his life was completely changed. All else ensued from this. He returned home later that summer and told the story to me. I, too, responded and was changed, and though we had always enjoyed a close relationship, from then on we became Colleagues in the Spirit in a most profound way.

It goes almost without saying that Joe learned from Bishop Moore and sometimes imitated his manner of preaching. He sought out other great preachers of every stripe and learned from them. Later, while he was in seminary in New York, he and I literally feasted on the sermons of the leading preachers of the day. Nor did he neglect learning from the outstanding camp meeting preachers of the time whose very hallmark was earnestness. All of this left a lasting impression on Joe. His speaking was always dramatic, always emphatic, and always passionate. Invariably, too, he expected response and he usually got it.

It was in the autumn of 1932 that I first recall hearing him preach. His text I have forgotten, but not his topic: "Presume Not That I Am What I Was." It dealt, of course, with his spiritual awakening and the change in his life's direction. It is hardly surprising that the title came from Shakespeare, specifically from the Second Part of *King Henry the Fourth* (5.05.56). To this day I can hear him "ringing the changes" in this oft-repeated testimony – the story of his conversion.

It was about this time that both of us became well acquainted with a renowned Methodist preacher who was regarded one of the greatest orators of his day. His name was John Wesley Hill – a superb master of old-style oratory. He encouraged both of us in public speaking – in fact he "took us in hand" to school us in clear enunciation. How many times we were caused to repeat the tongue-twister: "The rat ran over the roof with a piece of red liver in its mouth." "Master that phrase and they will catch your every word – even in the back row," he would admonish.

Joe and I were together in college for two years. We studied together in seminary for one year. We preached together in the summer of 1935 in southwestern Virginia. This was evangelistic preaching – revival meetings, but much more. We would also call on every family in the towns and then in the surrounding farmers' homes. In town we would walk; for the countryside we would borrow horses. As we expressed it at the time: "we walked until we could not stand up and we rode until we could not sit down." But the people came in droves. During the mornings we would teach Bible and every evening we would preach – alternately. Our message was the same but our manner was different. Joe would declare the wrath and judgment of God and then I would proclaim the love of God. Between us we developed a kind of "divine pincer movement" which proved highly effective, for the people did respond.

During the following summer – 1936 – Joe and I were engaged together in a modern version of the "Lollard Movement" (14th century preachers related to John Wycliffe in bringing the Bible to people in the language of the people). In northern Ohio we organized some thirty Bible study groups in, say, twenty communities. We drove an old Essex car, each teaching separate groups of 20-35 persons every week. We did extensive charting methods, which Joe was later to develop into a fine art. We did not so much lecture to the classes as to "draw the message out of the participants" who were exposed directly to one or another books of the Bible. About 700 people altogether were involved. To our surprise, we discovered twenty years later that some of these groups still continued!

Thereafter our paths parted for some years – Joe to pastorates in the United States, followed by chaplaincy in the Army in Word War II; I to India as a missionary and also four years in the Army. After the war we were reunited, so to speak, and continued our close affinity to the end.

Some readers may conclude that too much emphasis has been placed here on Joe's speaking skills. To this the only response is that this volume is, after all, a collection of his public addresses. His dramatic skills were not a façade but instruments to communicate vitally world-transforming truths.

It may also be rightfully asked what transformed Joseph Mathews from a more or less conventional preacher to the radical churchman he became. There can be no doubt that it was Joe's war experience, which literally shocked him into drastic change, for firsthand he was confronted with the brevity of life and, therefore, of its profound finality and seriousness. He was not an "armchair" but a "frontline" chaplain. In the successive and severe battles in the Pacific he saw hundreds of the soldiers he served literally obliterated in a second's flash. In burying them he was inevitably deepened and thereafter never ceased to explore the depths of human existence. He pondered: "What have I to say to people who are doomed to death?" He concluded that his theological preparation was utterly inadequate.

It was for this reason that he enrolled in Yale Divinity School. For the first time in his life he was freed for a period of the need to support himself as he learned. The G.I. Bill of Rights and the labors of his wife, Lyn, paid expenses. He immersed himself in uninterrupted study as never before. He felt the demand upon him to bring the message to the people in a fresh way, acceptable to modern minds.

Meanwhile, Joe sat under or was introduced to the world's finest theological minds. These included the contemporary theologians: the Niebuhrs, Tillich, Bonhoeffer, Bultmann, Barth; and the historical ones, Wesley, Luther, Aquinas, Augustine – the whole array.

Finally, he was convinced that modern theology had done all the theological groundwork for church renewal. For him the task was to help work out the concrete pragmatic application that these insights demanded.

Always he was focused on the Christian message, but this had to be available for all. "God works in a mysterious way" but his wonders serve the present age in every place and every person.

Introduction

By John Epps

May I have the honor of introducing you to Joseph Wesley Mathews (1911-1977), or Joe, as he was known in his lifetime.

Joe might be characterized as a Protestant prophet, as a Methodist maverick, or as a religious revolutionary. He was all those things and many more. He was one whose presence impacted everyone he encountered. His great gift was to focus that presence on whatever situation in which he found himself. When Joe tied his shoe, that shoe knew it had been *tied.* When he wished you "Good morning," you knew full well that you had been *greeted.* However one attempts to characterize the man, intensity would be a dominant trait. No encounter was casual for Joe Mathews, and no one he encountered was unmoved.[1]

The articles in these pages were mostly talks given in the framework of the Order: Ecumenical, the group that formed the staff of the Ecumenical Institute, and later, the Institute of Cultural Affairs. From 1962 until his death in October of 1977, Joe was Dean of the Order: Ecumenical. We were a group of families, covenanted to live corporately under the disciplines of poverty (detachment), chastity (single-mindedness), and obedience (engagement in mission). This was a group, at one time numbering 1700 around the world, dedicated to renewal of the church in service to the world. Prior to 1973, work focused on the religious life and service to the church; afterwards the focus shifted to renewal of local communities and organizations as a pilot for the church's mission of service. Joe led the charge on both fronts, the religious and the secular.

Since these talks were often delivered to the staff, they sometimes have peculiar phrases and jargon that the group used to enhance communications. The editors have attempted either to remove the jargon or to make the terms clearer to the reader. The message is relevant far beyond the confines of the group that first heard it, in part because the group saw itself as experimental, "guinea pigs" if you like, on behalf of the larger society.

Joe's passion for authentic human living caused him constantly to probe religion, sociology, philosophy, theology, and the arts for insights, which he used in profound and moving presentations. But the presentations were not the aim: Joe sought authenticity not for himself but for everyone, whether or not they shared his worldview, philosophy, or religion. Human authenticity, not spiritual insight, was his aim. When his insights were developed and presented, they

[1] For a biography of Joe W. Mathews, see the forthcoming work of his brother, Bishop James K. Mathews.

frequently became the grist for methods and "spirit exercises" that allowed people to explore them personally.

Theologically, one can find the root of Joe's thought in the works of his graduate professor at Yale University, H. Richard Niebuhr. With few exceptions, Joe's theology is a practical grounding of Niebuhr's insights. According to Joe, major theological breakthroughs had occurred in the works of Barth, Bultmann, Tillich, Bonhoeffer, and the Niebuhr brothers. Their works accomplished the intellectual accommodation of the Christian faith to the 20th century scientific, secular, and urban worldview. While there was rational clarity about the faith, its existential impact was virtually unexplored. Joe saw his task to be clarifying concepts of faith in life experience.

Yet in that clarification, Joe was profoundly corporate. Often he would pose an insight to a group and encourage extensive discussion – sometimes over a period of months – until it was refined, polished, and shaped into a communicable form. Hence, few of his speeches were Joe's alone in their substance. He drew from the insights and experiences of a wide variety of people and shaped them into content that we all owned.

What Joe brought was oratory. Joe was a speaker. When you heard a Joe Mathews lecture, you were changed. You may not have liked it, or may not have understood it, but you certainly had to come to terms with it. Whether on a rostrum, behind a pulpit, across a table, or one-on-one in a hallway, Joe let his considerable passion focus on his tongue. He could, and frequently did, animate, illuminate, and illustrate the most profound concepts while alternatively intriguing, challenging, and castigating his audience. The man's oratory was awesome.

Part of it was his willingness to use whatever language seemed most appropriate to the topic – not necessarily to the audience. He used shock value to great advantage, and the most pious of people listened with considerable discomfort at his army-like profanity while expounding on religion. Far from bothering him, he was delighted to expose "little old ladies of both sexes."

After you finished listening to a Joe Mathews talk, your worldview was different, and you typically were left with a decision of how to embody that difference.

Joe left a limited legacy. Most materials were in the form of speeches or talks or lectures. In this book, in their written and edited form, they omit most of the rhetorical flourish that marked their delivery. You cannot simply transcribe and publish a good speech. Asides, personal names, expletives, stutters, pauses, growls, cackles, and sighs all fall victim to the editor's pencil.

But Joe's content was deeper than oratorical fanfare. It gave form and voice to profound insights into authentic humanness developed by a sensitive and disciplined body of people for whom Joe was the spokesperson. This content is worth knowing and it is valuable knowledge. Although it came from a particular time and place, it has universal implications. We ignore it at our peril. There were several consistent themes that are apparent in his works, and I would like to say a word about them as part of this introduction.

1. Authentic living consists of total expenditure on behalf of all in one's particular situation.

Joe was not one who held back or who tolerated others who did. Life is meant to be lived fully, not hoarded, and that living meant active engagement in the major issues of the times. Once in a vocational retreat, a student asked Joe what would be a significant vocation. His reply was to ask the student to name the three most important issues in the world. The student gave his response, to which Joe replied, "If, when I come back next year, you're not doing something about those, then you're living in sin!" Vocation is expending your life addressing what you find are the important issues of the world. But it is not simply addressing an issue or a set of related issues that constitutes human authenticity. The only thing worth addressing is the whole thing – the world and all its issues. And even that is finite and fleeting. So, ultimately, it's God that you serve, but you can do that only through service in and to the world.

While addressing the major issues was of primary importance, so also is the *way* you address them. Joe had little patience for the "protest" approach which is ineffective, in part because it depends on someone else to correct the situation. The approach Joe advocated and demonstrated was one of demonstrating with your own life the solution, and then advocating that solution to the appropriate social structures. He referred to this as the approach of *structural revolution.*

Personal risk and rewards were not high values to Joe; being effective was. And this meant using every ounce of energy and creativity you can muster to address the real needs you face. He understood that you have one life that is fleeting; attempts to hold onto that one life simply don't work. He would have regarded the current spate of efforts towards self-development (whether they be spiritual or physical or mental) as misguided at best and perhaps idolatrous. The sole reason for developing your capacities is not so that you can be more fulfilled; it is so that you can be more effective in addressing the issues. Joe went so far as to study ancient strategists, Sun Tzu from China and Musashi from Japan, in order to learn effective ways of addressing contemporary issues.

One might suspect this approach meant a kind of perpetual seriousness, but Joe understood that people need rituals, celebrations, and times of discontinuity to sustain effective and creative engagement. He felt that once you select your point of engagement, you go for it with all you've got. If you get any more, you throw that into the fray as well.

It was the big picture that was worth living and dying for, not just a simple little cause. He could be quite caustic when anyone began to take her/himself too seriously. What matters is the "last fat lady," to use an expression Joe borrowed from J. D. Salinger's *Franny and Zooey*. One community doesn't matter; what matters are *all* communities in the world. Put another way, you give yourself in bringing life to this community so that it becomes a sign of possibility for others. In fact, Joe demonstrated this approach in initiating Human Development Projects in each of the world's time zones. Each was to become a demonstration of possibility for others in its zone, and so a unit of care in a global network.

But you cannot go for the "big picture" directly; it can only be addressed in the particular local situation. Abstract causes held no appeal for Joe, and, in fact, were manifestations of what he regarded as "the liberal heresy." You can only engage the world from your particular standpoint, but to be responsible you must engage *the world* from that standpoint.

"Expenditure" in this definition of authenticity carries with it a large degree of self-consciousness. You *decide* what you're going to do with your life; you don't let circumstances decide for you. It's an ambiguous decision made with wracking deliberation in total uncertainty. As a result, you find yourself standing over nothing with a hundred-ton crane on your shoulders, to use a couple of Joe's favorite metaphors. As you decide to pick up the weight of the world, there is no assurance that you're doing the right thing, and this very uncertainty is part and parcel of authentic living. You're always up against sheer mystery.

This means that you have a peculiar and passionate nonchalance about what you are doing. On the one hand, it doesn't matter. It's insignificant compared to the whole. On the other hand, it is the means through which you address the whole and so is crucially important, even though it will definitely pass away. You may recognize this as the paradox of radical monotheism as laid out by H. Richard Niebuhr.[2] Joe called this lifestyle many things: "cruciformity," "the resurrected life," "profound humanness," and many other phrases you will find in these works. People who practice it are, variously, "the church," "those who care," "the league," "the spirit movement," "the secular-religious," "the guild."

In all cases there is the double paradox of 1) giving your life in order to find it, and 2) engaging the particular to address the universal. While these can be easily footnoted from the New Testament, Joe's means of authenticating his message was with his life, not with an external authority. As he often quoted (from St. Paul), "Our only weapon, our sole defense, is a life of integrity."

Maintaining that posture of integrity – passionate nonchalance, effective local engagement, and global responsibility – does not come easy. It requires a disciplined spirit life to keep the perspective and stay "on the Way." This brings up the second of Joe's underlying themes.

2. Spirit exercises sustain you on the journey of authenticity.

Human authenticity is a continuing journey, a progression through numerous stages, with various pitfalls. It is a journey of consciousness and engagement,

---

[2] See his *Radical Monotheism and Western Culture* (New York: Harpercollins College Division, 1972) for a complete description of this paradox.

combining *knowing* and *doing* in a perpetual drama of development, disillusion, decision, and destiny. Joseph Campbell chronicled the journey as it was described by various ancient cultures in his classic *The Hero with A Thousand Faces.* Joe's efforts attempted to give a contemporary expression to the topic of human authenticity. While he never put together a comprehensive narrative describing the complete journey, he provided detailed and moving accounts of various landmarks along the trail.

The journey begins with some form of "awakenment," when you find yourself up against final and ultimate Mystery, received by Being, and responsible for the world. This often comes as a religious experience, but there is nothing religious about it. It can occur with equal profundity in community meetings or business consultations or personal relations in which you confront your own negation of the given situation and choose to engage responsibly. Religion is the mythology and dramatization of these profoundly human dynamics.

In the midst of this work, Joe stumbled onto what he considered to be one of the most significant findings of his career: the Other World in the midst of this world. Following H. Richard Niebuhr's insight from 1942, that "mankind lives in two worlds, and whenever he attempts to reduce life to either one alone, something goes seriously wrong,"[3] Joe found a way to describe that Other World that was both consistent with the scientific worldview and illuminative of human experience. We live, basically, in two dimensions, the surface and the depth. The surface is the world of ordinary experience; the depth is our state of being as we live on the surface. Our ordinary experience sometimes becomes transparent to the depths wherein lies significance and meaning.

As was typical of Joe's work, he pursued this insight and mapped out 64 distinct states of being that constitute the Other World in the midst of this world. They are grouped into four elements of topography which he labeled "The Land of Mystery," "The River of Consciousness," "The Mountain of Care," and "The Sea of Tranquillity." Each was related to a type of experience you have on the journey of authenticity.

Living as awakened, you sometimes experience another phase – "sanctification" was one term Joe used to describe it. In this phase his descriptive terms were "universal benevolence," in which you fall in love with the world; "radical integrity," in which the responsibility for the world drops on you; and "endless fulfillment," in which you find paradoxical joy in your given situation. None of these terms means quite what you would expect – each contains both misery and elation.

In the interplay between these phases you find yourself experiencing the "dark night of the soul," (humiliation, weakness, resentment, and suffering); the "long march of care," (rootlessness, ineffectiveness, weariness, and

---

[3] "Towards a New Otherworldliness," H. Richard Niebuhr, *Theology Today*, 1942.

unfulfillment); and "hope beyond hope" (ghostliness, ceaselessness, nothingness, and salvific presence). Each of these dynamics was carefully delineated so that anyone could recognize it in her/his experience.

Even with all these marks along the trail of authenticity, you cannot simply let things happen. It is exceptionally easy to lose your way. In fact, culture conspires to make it difficult to follow the way of authenticity. Commonly accepted values of sufficiency, self-preservation, and comfort intrude into the journey, making it difficult to stay "on the Way."

Hence, Joe spent a great deal of time, energy, and creativity working out "spirit exercises" that could sustain people on the journey. Each of them could warrant a book of explanation and practice. The point here is to note that Joe was thoroughly involved in the development and practice of spirit exercises. He found them essential for keeping yourself reminded of your decision to live the life of authenticity.

But what was it all for, if personal authenticity was not a goal worthy of pursuit in itself? This brings up the third major theme in Joe's works: primal community.

3. Primal community is the sociological manifestation of human authenticity. While much of Joe's creativity went into matters of spirit, he was no less concerned with sociological reality. In fact, his lifelong grievance with the established church was its irrelevance to the major social issues confronting the world. His initial effort with the Ecumenical Institute was to provide a laboratory to discover how the church might effectively serve society in its local setting. The two faces of Joe's work were a "new religious mode" and a "new social vehicle."

As a pilot project, the Institute located in the West Side ghetto of Chicago and set to work serving the needs of the area. It quickly became evident that any effective work would need to be in a limited geographical area, and a section was delimited and named "Fifth City." This location became a lifelong passion for Joe, and he was laid to rest with a handful of Fifth City soil in his urn.

But as a pilot project Fifth City had to yield insights and wisdom applicable to other situations, and indeed it did. In all future human development project consultations, principles were presented that came from the experience of the Institute in Fifth City. In the economic arena, principles were: 1) imaginally isolate the community from the larger economy; 2) bring money in; 3) cut the outflows; 4) circulate the money rapidly; and 5) re-relate to the larger economy. Culturally, the principles were: 1) define a limited geographical area; 2) deal with all the people; 3) address all the issues; 4) identify the underlying contradiction; and 5) use symbols as key. Once when questioned about these principles, Joe remarked that prior to our efforts in Fifth City and elsewhere, these things were not known. Now they may be commonplace and even obvious because lives were invested in specific efforts to make them known.

4. Human authenticity is the birthright of every person in the world.

Throughout his life, Joe exhibited a passion for the dispossessed. In his later years when he was able to visit rural villages in third world countries, he found among residents a dignity, depth, practical intelligence, and passion waiting to be released. He came away greatly impressed and clear that authenticity is not exclusive to those of the Christian persuasion or of those with adequate economic resources. He articulated this insight powerfully in a talk entitled "Transpadane Christianity." While this may seem self-evident to persons raised in a multi-cultural setting, most of us tend to regard those with dramatically different cultures and values as less than fully human.

This, for Joe, constitutes bigotry. Speaking personally, he regarded his deepest and most entrenched prejudice to be "Christian bigotry," thinking and acting as though Christians had an exclusive right to authenticity. That is *not* the case, and, while Christian mythology spells out the dynamics of authenticity, the capacity for it resides in everyone. The job for Those Who Care is to bring it out. Joe made numerous disparaging comments about those who insisted everyone had to "say the Boy Scout Oath like I do" (meaning to verbalize Christian poetry) in order to be fully human. For him, the Christian poetry points to realities that are not restricted to one form of poetry. It was far more important to manifest in your life those dynamics than to speak about them. Authentic living consists in manifesting profound humanness, whatever poetry you use to express it. It is to be welcomed and celebrated wherever it is found. Joe engaged in extensive research to articulate the dimensions and dynamics of profound humanness in secular, non-Christian terms.

Rational clarity, however, was not the point. Communication of that clarity was, and in his unique way Joe made his point through telling a story. It was the story of walking through the fields near Maliwada, a village development project in Maharashtra, India. The fields were spotted with wells from which villagers drew their water. As Joe put it:

> They have those big wells, some of them twenty to thirty feet across, others six to eight feet across, and in my imagination I was afraid of falling down those wells. As a matter of fact, vertigo overcame me, and I looked in one of those things and thought, "If you don't get out of here, Mathews, you're going to jump." I was walking with old men: we were an old Muslim, an old Hindu, and an old Christian. We spread out as we were walking in the fields and simultaneously each one of us fell down a separate well. There we met a table of common consciousness. We three fell down into consciousness. Those wells we fell down were our own historical poetry. I fell down through a hole in Christian poetry, and another fell down through a hole in Hindu poetry, and

> another through a hole in Muslim poetry. And when we hit the water table of consciousness, we didn't need to speak Hindi, or Marathi, or English together. We just looked into the deeps of one another's eyes.

Despite the research, Joe himself never left the Christian poetry in his personal expressions. Nor did he expect others to leave their particular poetry in talking about the profound. He only believed – and deeply believed – that down beneath the poetry lies reality which we all share. Surely, he said, we should be able to relate positively to it and therefore to each other.

Meet Joe the Man

The Time My Father Died

By Joseph Wesley Mathews

Sometime past noon, November ninth the last, our telephone rang. It was for me, person-to person. My oldest sister, Margaret, was calling.

"Joe, Papa just died!"

We children never called him Papa while we were growing up. He was mostly "Dad." But in the last decade or so, out of a strange mellowing affection, we started, all seven of us, referring to our father as Papa.

My Papa dead! – just seven days before he was nine-two.

Within the hour I began my journey to my father. I find it difficult to express how deeply I wanted to be with him in his death. Furthermore, he had long since commissioned my brother and me to conduct the celebration. My brother unfortunately was out of the country and I had quiet anxiety about executing it alone.

The late afternoon flight was conducive to contemplation. I thought of the many well-meant condolences already received.

"Isn't it fine that your father lived to be ninety-two?"

"It must be easier for you since he lived such a long life."

Certainly I was grateful for such comments. But I found myself perturbed too. Didn't they realize that to die is to die, whether you are seventeen, forty-nine, or one hundred and ten? Didn't they know that our death is our death? And that each of us has only one death to die? This was my father's death! It was no less significant because he was most of a hundred. It was his death. The only one he would ever have.

The family had already gathered when I arrived in the little New England town. We immediately sat in council. The first task was to clarify our self-understanding. The second was to embody that understanding in the celebration of Papa's death. Consensus was already present: the One who gives us our life is the same that takes it from us. From this stance we felt certain broad implications should guide the formation of the ceremony.

> Death is a very lively part of life and no life is finished without the experience of death.

> Death is a crucial point in the human adventure that somehow transposes to every other aspect of life.
>
> Death is to be received in humble gratitude and must ever be honored with honest dignity.

Together we concluded that the death of our father must be celebrated as a real part of his history, before the final Author that gave him both his life and his death, with integrity and solemn appreciation.

The very articulation of these lines of guidance worked backward laying bare our own inward flight from death. They also made more obvious the efforts of our culture to disguise death. I mean the great concealment by means of plush caskets, white satin linings, soft cushions, head pillows, Sunday clothes, cosmetics, perfume, flowers, and guaranteed vaults. Empty of symbolic meaning, they serve but to deceive – to simulate life. They seem to say, "Nothing has actually happened. Nothing is really changed." What vanity to denude death! All our pretenses about it only strengthen its power to destroy our lives. Death stripped of meaning and dignity becomes a demon. Not to embrace death as part of our given life is finally not to embrace our life. That is, we do not really live. This is the power of unacknowledged death. I ponder over the strange smile on faces of the dead.

To symbolize the dignity of our father's death, the family thought to clothe him in a pine box and to rest him in the raw earth.

I remembered the men of the war I buried. There was great dignity in the shelter – half shrouded, in the soiled clothing, in the dirty face, in the shallow grave. I say dignity was there. Death was recognized as death. Death was dramatized as the death of the men who had died their own death.

A sister and brother-in-law were sent to make arrangements. They asked about the coffin. A pine box was out of the question. None was to be had. The undertaker, as they called him, explained that caskets ranged from one hundred to several thousands of dollars. Interpreting the spirit of the common mind, our emissaries asked for the $100 coffin.

"What $100 coffin?" replied an astonished undertaker.

"Why the one you mentioned."

"Oh no, caskets begin at $275."

"Did you not mention a $100 coffin?"

"Yes. Yes. But you wouldn't want that. It is for paupers. We bury only the paupers in the $100 coffins."

This thought racked the psychic foundations of my sister and her husband. They retreated for further consultation. None of the rest of us, it turned out, was emotionally prepared for the pauper twist. Actually, the tyranny of the economic order over us was exposed. Our deepest emotions of guilt, love, sorrow, regret were all mixed up with this strange tyranny. In short, we could not move forward with our decision until we first agreed to set up a small memorial for Papa that would be used for charity in the little community.

By this time, assuming that no one would want to put his father away as a pauper, the undertaker had placed Papa in the $275 casket. Having recovered some equilibrium we protested. He was understandably upset by our stand and insisted that we come to his showroom. We all went together, including Mama, who has been weathering the storms of life now for more than fourscore years. Caskets of all kinds filled the place. We asked about the pauper's coffin.

"We keep that outside in the storehouse." Anticipating our next request he hurried on. "No, I can't bring that into my showroom."

In the back I saw a wooden rough box which reminded me of the pine coffin. We talked, the undertaker and I. He was really a very sensitive man. Certainly he had a living to make. When I offered to pay him more for the other expenses of the funeral, he refused. But he mellowed a bit. He remembered when he lived in upper New York state as a little boy. His grandfather had been an undertaker too. Grandfather had used rough pine boxes out in the country to bury people in. In his recollecting he found a kind of meaning in our decision for the pauper's coffin. He even brought it into the showroom where Mama and the rest of the family could see it.

Immediately it was opened and another mild shock came. The pauper's coffin was exactly like any other coffin – pillow, white satin, and all. Except the white satin wasn't really white satin. It was the kind of shiny material you might buy at the ten-cent store. Everything was simply cheap imitation. We had hoped for something honest. Despite the disappointment, we took the pauper's box. And Papa was transferred to his own coffin.

I did not want to see my father until I could have some time with him alone. Several hours before the funeral I went to where he waited. I can scarcely describe what 1 saw and felt.

My father, I say, was ninety-two. In his latter years he had wonderfully chiseled wrinkles. I had helped to put them there. His cheeks were deeply sunken; his lips pale. He was an old man. There is a kind of glory in the face of an old man. Not so with the stranger lying there. They had my Papa looking like he was fifty-two. Cotton stuffed in his cheeks had erased the best wrinkles. Make-up powder and rouge plastered his face way up into his hair and around his neck and ears. His lips were painted. He . . . he looked ready to step before the footlights of the matinee performance.

I fiercely wanted to pluck out the cotton but was afraid. At least the make-up could come off. I called for alcohol and linens. A very reluctant mortician brought them to me. And I began the restoration. As the powder, the rouge, the lipstick disappeared, the stranger grew older. He never recovered the look of his ninety-two years but in the end the man in the coffin became my Papa.

Something else happened to me there with my father in his death. Throughout childhood, I had been instructed in the medieval worldview. This by many people who were greatly concerned for me: my father, my mother, my Sunday school teacher, yes, my teachers at the school, and most of my neighbors. They taught me the ancient Greek picture of how when you die there's something down inside of you that escapes death, how the real me doesn't die at all. Much later I came to see that both the biblical view and the modern image were something quite different. But I wondered if the meeting with my father in his death would create nostalgia for the worldview of my youth. I wondered if I would be tempted to revert to that earlier conditioning in order to handle the problems of my own existence. It wasn't this way.

What did happen to me I am deeply grateful for. I don't know how much I'm able to communicate. It happened when I reached down to straighten my father's tie. There was my father. Not the remains, not the body of my father, but my father. It was my father in death! Ever since I can remember, Papa never succeeded in getting his tie quite straight. We children took some kind of pleasure in fixing it before he went out. Though he always pretended to be irritated at this, we knew that he enjoyed our attention. It was all sort of a secret sign of mutual acknowledgment. Now in death I did it once again. This simple little act became a new catalyst of meaning. That was my Papa whose tie I straightened in the coffin. It was my father there experiencing his death. It was my Papa involved in the Mystery in his death as he had been involved in the Mystery in his life. I say there he was related to the same Final Mystery in death as in life. Somehow the dichotomy between living and dying was overcome.

> Where is thy victory, O death?

Death is indeed a powerfully individual happening. My Papa experienced his death all alone. About this I am quite clear. I remember during the war I wanted to help men die. I was never finally able to do this. I tried. Sometimes I placed a lighted cigarette in a soldier's mouth as we talked. Sometimes I quoted to him the Twenty-third Psalm. Sometimes I wiped the sweat and blood from his face. Sometimes I held his hand. Sometimes I did nothing. It was a rude shock to discover that I could not in the final sense help a man to die. Each had to do his own dying, alone.

But then I say death is something more than an individual experience. It is also a social happening. Papa's death was an event in our family. All of us knew that a happening had happened to us as a family and not just to Papa. Furthermore, the dying of an individual is also an internal occurrence in the larger communities of life. Indeed it happens to all history and creation itself. This is true whether that individual be great or small. The inner being of a little New England town is somehow changed by the absence of the daily trek of an eccentric old gentleman to the post office where he stopped to deliver long monologues on not very interesting subjects to all who could not avoid him.

Perhaps we don't know how to feel these happenings as communities. Maybe we don't know how to celebrate them. But they happen.

We wanted to celebrate Papa's death as his own event but we wanted also to celebrate it as a social happening. Most of all, we wanted to celebrate Christianly. But this is not so simple. The office of the funeral suffers a great malaise in our day. Perhaps even more than other rites. There are many causes. The undertaker, in the showroom episode, spoke to this with deep concern. His rather scathing words disturb me still.

"Funerals today have become no more than disposal services!"

"What of those conducted by the church?" I ventured.

"Church indeed! I mean the church," he said.

His professional posture was here set aside. Pointing out that most funerals today are held outside any real sense of Christian community, he spoke of the tragedy of keeping children away from death. He spoke of adults who sophisticatedly boast of never having engaged in the death rite. He spoke of the overall decrease in funeral attendance. He especially rued the emptiness of the rites because they were no longer understood. And he caricatured the clergy as the hired disposal units with their artificial airs, unrealistic words, and hurried services.

"What we all seem to want nowadays" he said, "is to get rid of the body as quickly and efficiently as is respectably allowable, with as little trouble to as few folk as possible."

These solemn words were creatively sobering. The funeral embodied the full office of worship. We who gathered acted out all three parts. We first confessed our own self-illusions and received once again the word of cosmic promise of fresh beginnings. Then we read to ourselves from our classic scriptures recounting men's courage to be before God and boldly expressed together our thanksgiving for the given actualities of our lives. Thirdly, we presented ourselves to the Unchanging Mystery beyond all that is and corporately dedicated our lives once more to the task of affirming the world and creating civilization.

The point is, we did not gather to console ourselves. We did not gather to psychologically bolster one another. We did not gather to excuse anybody's existence or to pretend about the world we live in. We celebrated the death of my father by recollecting and acknowledging who we are and what we must therefore become. That is, we assembled as the church on this occasion in our history to remember that we are the church.

In the midst of the service of death the "words over the dead," are pronounced. I had sensed for a long time that one day I might pronounce them over Papa. Now that the time had come I found myself melancholy beyond due. It was not simply that it was my father. Yet, just because it was my father, I was perhaps acutely sensitive. I mean about the funeral meditation, as it is revealingly termed. Memories of poetic rationalizations of our human pretenses about death gnawed at my spirit. Some that I recalled actually seemed designed to blanket the awareness that comes in the face of death, that death is a part of life and that all must die. I remembered others as attempts to explain away the sharp sense of ontological guilt and moral emptiness that we all experience before the dead. The very gifts of grace were here denied, whether by ignorance or intent, and the human spirit thereby smothered into nothing. I remembered still other of these meditations even more grotesque in their disfigurement of life – undisguised sentimentalities offering shallow assurances and fanciful comforts. How could we shepherds of the souls do such things to human beings? Perhaps after all I was not unduly depressed.

Coincidental with these broodings, my imagination was vividly assaulted by another image. It was a homely scene from a television western. A small crowd of townsfolk was assembled on Boot Hill to pay last respects to one that had lived and died outside the law. A very ordinary citizen was asked to say "a few words over the dead." He spoke with the plainness of wisdom born out of intimate living with life as it actually is. Protesting that he was not a religious man, he reminded the gathered of the mystery present in that situation beyond the understanding of any one or all of them together. Then he turned and spoke words to the dead one. He spoke words to the family. He spoke words to the townsfolk themselves. In each case his words confronted the intended hearer with the real events and guilt of the past and in each case he offered an image of significance for the future. There was comfort in his words. But it was the honest, painful comfort of coming to terms with who we are in the midst of the world as it is. It impressed me as deeply religious, as deeply Christian.

For my father I took this pattern as my own. At the appointed place I too reminded the assembled body of the Incomprehensible One who is the ground of all living and dying. I too announced a word to the assembled townsfolk, and to my family, and to my father.

I looked out at the members of the funeral party who represented the village where my father had spent his last years. They were sitting face to face before one another, each caught in the gaze of the neighbor. In that moment, if I had never known it before, I knew that a community's life is somehow held before it whenever it takes, with even vague seriousness, the death of one of its members. I saw in its face its failures and fears, its acts of injustice, callousness, and irresponsibility. I saw its guilt. I saw its despair. They would call it sorrow for a passing one. But it was their sorrow. Indeed it was, in a strange way, sorrow for themselves.

In the name of the church, I spoke first of all this that they already knew yet so desperately needed to know aloud. And then I pronounced all their past, remembered and forgotten, fully and finally received before the Unconditioned Being who is Lord both of life and death.

I looked out at my family. There was my mother surrounded by her children and her children's children. What was going on in the deeps of this woman who had mixed her destiny with that of the dead man for the major share of a century?

What of sister Margaret who knew so well the severity of her father? What of the son who had never won approval? Or the son-in-law never quite received? What of the one who knew hidden things? What of the rebellious one? What of the specially favored? What of Alice? What of Arthur? What of Elizabeth? I knew as I looked, perhaps all over again, that the sorrow at death is not only that of the loss of the cherished and the familiar. It is the sorrow of unacknowledged guilt, postponed intentions, buried animosities, unmended ruptures. The sorrow of the funeral is the pain of our own creatureliness, of self-disclosure, and of self-acknowledgement. It is the pain of turning from the past to the future. It is the pain of having to decide all over again about our lives.

In the name of the church, I spoke of these things written so clearly upon our family countenance. And then in fear and joy I pronounced all our relations with Papa and one another as cosmically approved by the One who gives us our lives and takes them from us once again.

I looked at my father. And I knew things in a way I had not known them before. It wasn't that I knew anything new. But my knowing was now transposed so that everything was different. I knew his very tragic boyhood. I knew the scars it engraved on his soul. I knew his lifelong, agonizing struggle to rise beyond them. I knew his unknown greatness. I knew his qualities next to genius that never found deliverance. I knew his secret sense of failure. I knew things he never knew I knew. I knew the dark nights of his soul. I knew . . . well, what I knew was his life. His spirit's journey. That was it. It was his life I knew in that moment. It was frozen now. It was all in now. It was complete. It was finished. It was offered up for what it was. This was the difference made by death.

In the name of the church, I spoke his life out loud. Not excusing, not glorifying, I spoke just of his life as I saw it then. And then I pronounced it good and great and utterly significant before the One who had given it to history, just as it was. Not as it might have been, not as it could have been abstractly considered, not as I might have wanted it to be or others felt it should have been, not even as Papa might have wanted it altered. I sealed it as acceptable to God, then, just as it was finished.

The celebration ended in the burial grounds.

The funeral party bore Papa to his grave. There was no drama in the processional. It was just empty utility. The death march, once explosive in symbolic force, had lost its power. I allowed myself to be swept along in silent frustration. I was sad for Papa. I had pity for those of us who bore him. I grew angry with myself.

The sun had already fallen behind the ridge when we came to the burial ground. It was on a remote New England hillside (they call it a mountain there). I remember clearly the sharp, cold air and how the very chill made me feel keenly alive. I remember also how the dark shadows dancing on the hills reminded me of life. But I remember most of all the clean smell of God's good earth freshly turned.

I say I smelled the fresh earth. There was none to be seen. What I did see is difficult to believe. I mean the green stuff. Someone had come before us and covered that good, wonderful raw dirt, every clod of it, with green stuff. Everything, every scar of the grave, was concealed under simulated grass. Just as if nothing had been disturbed here. Just as if nothing were going on here. Just as if nothing at all were happening. What an offense against nature, against history, against Papa, against us, against God!

I wanted to scream. I wanted to cry out to the whole world, "Something is going on here, something great, something significantly human. Look! Everybody, look! Here is my father's death. It is going on here!"

The banks of flowers upon the green façade only added to the deception. Was it all contrived to pretend at this last moment that my father was not really dead after all? Was it not insisting that death is not important, not a lively part of our lives, not thoroughly human, not bestowed by the Final One? Suddenly the great lie took on cosmic proportion. And suddenly I was physically sick!

This time I didn't want to scream. I experienced an acute urge to vomit.

A sister sensitively perceived all this and understood. She pushed to my side and gave me courage. Together we laid aside the banks of flowers. Together we rolled back the carpet of deceit. God's good, wonderful clean earth lay once again unashamedly naked. I drank it into my being. The nausea passed.

Mind you, I'm not blaming anybody. Not anybody, really, save myself. I just hadn't anticipated everything. I have no excuse but I was taken by surprise, you understand. And I so passionately wanted to celebrate Papa's death with honesty and integrity and dignity – for his sake, for our sake, for God's sake.

We lowered Papa then in his pauper's box deep into the raw ground. Then began the final rites. There were three.

I lifted up the Bible. It was a sign. We were commemorating Papa's journey in the historical community of the faithful. However distantly, however feebly, however brokenly, he had walked with the knights of faith, Abraham, Amos, Paul, Augustine, Thomas, Luther, Wesley, Jesus. By fate and by choice these were his first companions of the road. I recalled aloud from their constitution that I held in my hands. The heroic formula from Job is what I meant to recite: "Naked I came from my mother's womb, and naked shall I return; the Lord gave, and the Lord has taken away; blessed be the name of the Lord." What came from my lips were the words of Paul. "If 1 live, I live unto the Lord; if I die, I die unto the Lord; so whether I live or whether I die, I am the Lord's."

I lifted up a very old, musty, leather-bound volume of poetry. This too was a sign. We were ritualizing Papa's own unique and unrepeatable engagement in the human adventure. Papa was an individual, a solitary individual before God. It was most fitting that a last rite should honor this individuality. Such was the role of the volume of hymn-poems. From it Papa had read and quoted and sung in monotone for as long as any of us, including Mama, could recall. The words I joined to the sign were from this collection. The author was a friend of Papa's.

> God moves in a mysterious way, his wonders to perform;
> He plants his footsteps on the sea and rides upon the storm;
> Blind unbelief is sure to err, and scan His works in vain;
> God is His own interpreter and He shall make it plain.

The third sign celebrated the fact that Papa was a participant in the total wonder of creation and that his life and death were good because creation is good. What I mean is that Papa was God's friend. My last act was to place him gladly and gratefully on behalf of all good men and women everywhere in the hands of the One in whose hands he already was, that Mysterious Power who rules the unknown realm of death to do with him as he well pleaseth. I ask to know no more. This I symbolized. Three times I stooped low, three times I plunged my hands deep into the loose earth beside the open pit, and three times I threw that good earth upon my Papa within his grave. And all the while I sang forth the majestic threefold formula,

> In the name of the Father and of the Son and of the Holy Ghost.

And some of those present there for the sake of all history and all creation said, "Amen."[4]

---

[4] Printed in *Motive* magazine of the Methodist Student Movement of the Methodist Church, January-February Issue, 1964, and printed in *i.e.* (newsletter of the Ecumenical Institute: Chicago, August 1964). This is a finished writing of his reflections that gives insight to Joseph the speaker as well as Joseph the man. One senses the power of his address at the two services he describes.

Section I

Joe's Theology

Commentary by John Epps

Talks:

The Christ of History (booklet form, 1969)

Three RS-I Talks (mid to late 1960s)
The Christ Lecture
The Freedom Lecture
The Church Lecture

This Is the Time of Sanctification (1972)

The Barefoot Jesus (1977)

Endlessness (1972)

SECTION I: JOE'S THEOLOGY

Commentary

By John Epps

Joe Mathews understood that his task as a practicing theologian was to uncover the human meaning – the "so what" – of Christian doctrines. His theological works are an attempt to clarify in a direct and powerful manner the human issues they address and to pose the decisions they require. He was very clear that the required decisions are not about intellectually assenting to abstract propositions. They are life decisions – personal decisions about innermost attitudes, perspectives, and actions. Consequently, Joe's aim was to recover Christian doctrine and poetry as illuminative of profound human living in the contemporary world.

For Joe that world was characterized as in the midst of a cultural revolution. In his schema, the globe underwent a political revolution in the 18th century, an economic revolution in the 19th century, and the 20th was the time of a revolution in culture, the way in which people perceive and relate to their situation. This revolution created globally a mindset that was unabashedly scientific, urban, and secular. This posed a challenge to theology since science did away with the two-story universe assumed by scripture and tradition; urbanity rendered obsolete the rural imagery used in earlier times; and secularity found awe and meaning in the midst of ordinary life rather than in a special religious realm. Joe regarded this mindset as given, the context within which the Christian *word* must be grasped if it is to have any relevance or even intelligibility.

To address this challenge, Joe looked for the human experience that both gave rise to religious longing and was addressed by Christianity's insights. He found it in the consciousness of one's own contingency. The awareness of one's approaching death forces a search for security, a search continually frustrated by reliance on temporal objects or causes. This experience, made evident to Joe in his time as a combat chaplain during World War II, is the phenomenological basis of his theology. Other features of human experience will be evident in the writings to follow. The major point here is that Joe attempted to relate all his interpretations of Christian doctrine to profound experiences in human life.

Philosophically, Joe was indebted to Heidegger and Sartre, the existentialists. Theologically, Joe derived many of his formulations from Barth, Bultmann, Tillich, Bonhoeffer, and the Niebuhr brothers, Reinhold and especially H. Richard – anchors of the Neo-Orthodox approach. That said, one has to give due credit to his reliance on John Wesley, both in style and substance.

Joe found Wesley to be a religious revolutionary and said as much in his dissertation. He also found Wesley's emphasis on sanctification illuminative of a stage in the journey of profound living that was largely ignored by more recent theologians.

Finally, one would have to characterize Joe's theology as constructive. He was not out to criticize the church or religious doctrines. In fact, on his deathbed he said to a trusted Roman Catholic friend, Msgr. Jack Egan:

> We tried to get the established church to see that it's not about peddling abstract dogma, but about awakening humans to life and significant engagement in the historical process, so that they might truly experience the glory of life through the intensification of consciousness and the intensification of engagement. The hope that is God's hope belongs to humanity. The joy that is unspeakable is of the Lord. The peace that passeth understanding is ours – on loan from God, of course. I hope the church breaks through its provincialism of defending church members to concern for all humanity – which will save the church and purify it.

Joe sought to find the meaning in the church's doctrines and, more importantly, to make that meaning accessible to everyone. Despite his unflinching insistence on demythologizing all religious language without reservation, he none the less continued to use "God-talk" throughout his life. It seemed to him to have irreplaceable power in expressing the human's ultimate relationship. But he was quite clear that the language was to be taken seriously as poetry, and not to be taken literally as if it were scientific.

The talks presented in this section provide, if not a complete exposition of his theology, at least an introduction to Joe's approach and major themes.

"The Christ of History" is an early classic (published earlier by John Cock, with an extensive commentary[5]). It stands here as a fine example of both explaining the various layers of tradition in our statements about Jesus and in reaching the heart of the Christian message as it relates to human life.

Three Religious Studies-I lectures are published here for the first time (Brian Stanfield has written a secularized version[6]). Many of us delivered them in the course taught to thousands of church groups around the world. We added our own embellishments and illustrations, but the basic structure and content were Joe's. What's presented here are the lectures as Joe delivered them. Methodists might draw the analogy between them and Wesley's "Standard Sermons."

"The Christ Lecture" clarifies the happening in life in which the possibility made manifest in Jesus as the Christ confronts each of us.

"The Freedom Lecture" focuses on the "spirited" life for which responsible freedom is the major defining category.

---

[5] John Cock, *The Transparent Event* (Greensboro, N.C.: Transcribe Books, 2001).

[6] Brian Stanfield, *The Courage to Lead* (Gabriola Island, Canada: New Society, 2000).

"The Church Lecture" presents an understanding of the People of God as mission on the leading edge of history, standing precariously between the "no longer" and the "not yet."

"The Barefoot Jesus" is Joe's later reflection on the paradigm of profound humanness. As you will note, its source is three-fold: scripture, the movie "The Gospel According to St. Matthew," and Joe's own experience. It is a powerful presentation of the shape of authentic life.

"This is the Time of Sanctification" explores another level of profound living that follows one's initiation into the process of justification.

"Endlessness" represents Joe's take on our ultimate destiny. Delivered in response to the death of his son John, in a traffic accident, it is a powerful representation of Joe's uncompromising commitment to the contemporary worldview (When you die, you're dead, period!) and his recovery of the human meaning of doctrines about everlasting life.

These seven talks will both illumine your life and call you into question. Read them with care.

The Christ of History

The Everyman Christ

The need to "make sense" out of our sufferings and actions is deeply human. Apparently people everywhere and in every time have sensed themselves as pilgrims looking for a way to really live in this world. In the language of the poet, EVERYMAN quests after some light, way, truth, door. More or less awarely, people search for a bread or *word* of life. They dwell in the hope that some tomorrow will bring a delivering power, an illuminating story, some saving event, a final blessedness. When that day comes, so they dream, then surely in some way the essence of life and the living of it will be different. All peoples have forged signs and symbols of this human characteristic. For the Hebrews of old, one such image was the coming "anointed one," the Messiah, translated into the Greek as "the Christ."

This Messianic hope of EVERYMAN is born out of his experience of the limitations of existence. His encounter with the unknowns, ambiguities, sufferings and deaths of this world discloses his insecurity. This primordial anxiety breeds the Messiah image. Watch him, as he is thrown up against his finitude, become a seeker after some truth which will overcome the unbearable incomprehensibles of life. Watch him search, however subtly, for the justification which will alleviate his sense of insignificance. Watch him relentlessly strive for a peace which will somehow blot out his lucid awareness of the tragic dimension of life. One senses in this spectacle a creature vainly striving to rise above his creaturely limits. Finding his givenness burdensome beyond bearing, he dreams of discovering some other kind of a world. Indeed he already has a different world for he literally exists in his present hopes about the future. Thereby he escapes his actual life in the Now. His very meaning is his anticipation that some tomorrow will render his situation quite different. On that day the ultimate key will come clear; the final excuse for his existence will emerge and true contentment will bathe his being. Then shall he truly live, so he imagines, delivered from this present world of uncertainty, unfulfillment, and anxiety. Such a life-quest is an experience, I submit, that all of us are quite privy to. People dwell sometimes very explicitly, most times quite vaguely, in great expectations of that which will relieve them of the necessity of living their given life in the present situation. This great hope, whatever its form, is the CHRIST OF EVERYMAN.

The Jesus of Nazareth

The New Testament age opens with the Jews, like EVERYMAN, expecting the Christ. Of course, they were doing so out of their concrete historical memory. The Christ-quest is always tied to specific life situations. It was into this particular Jewish yearning, around the beginning of the first century, that one Jesus intruded. It might have been, in an abstract sense, Herman of Hebbronville or Jones of Smithville. But it was not. It was this fellow Jesus of Nazareth in Galilee. Very little detail is directly known about this man. But as all of us do, he lived a life and died a death. It was, to be sure, *his* life that he lived and *his* death that he died. This is most important for it was in the midst of these very definite historical occurrences, as they disturbed the hopes of Israel, that the New Testament happening of Christ took place.

Perhaps the core of the issue could be put something like this: a very specific man lived a very specific life and for that specific life died a very specific death. Somehow in these concretions the deeps of human existence became exposed. A man got born, lived his life, and experienced death even as you and I. Yet there was a plus. Not a metaphysical plus, but what might be termed a plus in specifics. I mean he lived a life essentially like that of anyone else, save he seemed to *really* live his. However one chooses to account for it – special mutations of genes, unusual neurotic tendencies, peculiar environmental influences, unique occurrences of lucidity – is all quite beside my concern at the moment. Here was one who apparently not only lived, but *lived* his living. He appropriated his life as an unqualified gift and bore it as a significant mission. The *givenness* of creaturely living appeared to him to be the very meaning of it. Indeed, he kept saying that what everyone is looking for is very much AT HAND.

EVERYMAN, here in Jewish guise, was understandably disconcerted by the style of this unknown and everyday stranger. The very point is that Jesus collided with the lives of all he encountered. He invaded, broke into, and penetrated their worlds, leaving them painfully unsettled. To the proud he seemed humble and they were threatened. If men hated life, he loved it. To those who hung desperately onto living, he appeared nonchalant about it all. If they thought of life as detachment, he was utterly involved. If their living was a bondage, he was too obviously free. Where men were other-directed, he was independent. When they were confidently self-determining, he seemed lost in loyalties. To conservatives he was manifestly revolutionary; he impressed the radicals as a reactionary. Obviously, the life of such a human being would be in jeopardy. When people's lives are audited to the quick, either they must re-do their lives or destroy the occasion of the audit. Jesus was executed.

Death comes to all. So it had to come in some fashion to Jesus of Nazareth. The specifics are what concern us. A life that was in some way *really* lived drove people to destroy it. Let this be said again. Precisely because his living somehow exhibited the way life actually is, people felt he had to be removed. Rulers saw him as a danger to society. The hierarchy feared him as a menace to religion. The strange irony here uncovers a tragic inversion in human history. There is yet another important concretion. The man of Galilee embraced death as he embraced life. Call it the slaughter of the innocent or the miscarriage of justice; call it murder or mistake; call it social expediency or the intervention of fate; however, and whatever, he took unto himself his death without malice as a part of the givenness of his life. Not that he sought death. But when it came, and as it came, he died it as significant. In consequence, there was a compounding of disturbance. His dying as his living was disquieting.

In some such fashion did the life and death of an unknown, Jesus of Nazareth, protrude into the history and the hope of Israel, and therefore into the life of EVERYMAN. But this is not yet the end, nor even the finally important aspect of the tale.

The Jesus-Christ-Event

In the midst of the happenings surrounding Jesus, some individuals were seized by a radically new possibility for living in this world. Incredible as it was to the many, a few actually raised the question of Christ in connection with Jesus. This moves us to the heart of the matter. To really hear this question is to sense an absolutely unbelievable twist in the Christ symbol. The very life-image of the Jews, their very existence, their very history, was cut to the marrow by the question Is Jesus the Christ? Quite understandably they reacted to it as scandalous. Because it was a scandal, crucial decisions had to be made. Here are the keys to the New Testament Christ-happening: scandal and decision.

The scandal is clearly manifest in the broad picture. The EVERYMAN-CHRIST for the Jews was concretized in the anticipated coming of a mighty king or cosmic figure that would fulfill the corporate dreams of Israel. Patently, such a figure Jesus was not. He came a helpless babe in a feeding trough. He left a pitiful personage on the state gallows. This have to do with Messiah? How ridiculous! Indeed, in the light of the sacred hopes, it was blasphemous.

Now the offense of the Jew is the offense of EVERYMAN. The question about Jesus insinuates an unmitigated revolution in human self-perception. The distressing implication is that life is not in the future, it is in the present; it is not in some other circumstances, it is those at hand; it is not to be sought after, it is already given. Obviously this cuts across the notions to which every person has attached her/his being. The one who seeks to escape the present situation as meaningless must certainly be outraged by the hint that the final meaning is to receive that very situation. Those who look to tomorrow to solve the riddle will surely feel affronted before the intimation that the ultimate solution is living the Now. This is the elemental scandal in the Jesus question.

The point needs to be underlined. If the self-understanding which broke into history surrounding the living and dying of one Jesus is to be designated by the term "Christ," then very evidently a radical eruption has occurred in history through a complete inversion of the Christ symbol. This is not just an addition to or an alteration of life. The total image of life is disputed. In truth, it is literally turned upside down. That is, the scandal is cataclysmic and universal. Concisely, what we shall call the JESUS-CHRIST mortally assaults the EVERYMAN-CHRIST.

The JESUS-CHRIST fronts people with the awareness that there is no messiah and never will be one, and furthermore, that this very reality is the Messiah. This must not, however, be understood as an intellectual abstraction. It is rather a happening that meets people in the midst of their living. Indeed, the fronting is experienced as death itself. For to receive the JESUS-CHRIST is to put an end to my Christ quest; it is to surrender my very life stance; it means that I must die to my very self. Or better still, my self must die. The threat of the JESUS-CHRIST is now unmasked as the threat of death. The scandal, as experienced, is that I must choose to die.

The drama of this deciding unto death permeates the New Testament. This is certainly to be expected. For decision is a rudimentary component of the New Testament Christ Happening and a necessary consequence of the Christ offense. Those seized by the scandal of the Jesus question could not avoid an answer. One way or the other they had to decide. Life decisions are always compelled by the disturbance of life modes. But the choice was not apprehended as just *another* choice. It was understood as the *elemental* one, and this precisely because the above scandal was the ultimate assault upon the world of EVERYMAN. In short, the great and final divide of all human decisions is located in the strange New Testament question Is Jesus the Christ?

The response demanded and the only one that could be demanded was a simple yea or nay. There is no possible third option; no middle ground; no perhaps. Not even a delay is thinkable. For not to decide here is still to decide. At any other point, several alternatives, in principle at least, are offered. Such is not the case here. The scandal is either embraced or it is rejected. Though repudiation has a thousand faces, yes, a thousand times a thousand times, all are but some form of re-entrenchment in the EVERYMAN-CHRIST. This extreme dimension becomes clearer when one remembers that *for the New Testament people the Christ decision was transparently an election for or against life itself.* The negative answer was at bottom a rejection of human existence as it is constituted. The acknowledgement of the scandal, on the other hand, is a full and free affirmation of the significance of the creaturehood of humans. *When the human situation is nakedly exposed there are but two choices: to affirm life or to negate it.*

Perhaps it appears incredible that such fathomless deeps of mankind and history are caught up in so very concrete a decision. Yet this is exactly the way things are in this dimension of existence. As the search for meaning is always concrete, so necessarily is the offense to this meaning historically rooted. And therefore the ensuing decision must likewise be grounded in the very particular. Though at base the New Testament people were deciding about their own stance and destiny, yet, because Jesus was the occasion of the question, externally it took the form of deciding about him: Is Jesus the Christ? What do you say? Is your CHRIST, JESUS-CHRIST? or the EVERYMAN-CHRIST?

One final concern before the summation. The JESUS-CHRIST-EVENT has been depicted at one and the same time as both death and life. This draws together the entire twist. It is unmistakably plain that the early Christians conceived of and experienced this happening as the very fullness of life. They sensed after themselves as the blind who now see, as the deaf who have been given to hear, the bound set free, the maimed made whole, the dead who are alive. The death involved in encompassing the scandal was discovered to be life itself. There is no addition here, no subtle way out. Any addendum would be a cancellation of the event. The choice to give up our illusions and false hopes and hiding places is the death of choosing the scandal. This very death is life, they insisted. *To die is to live*. To use their figures, it is like being born all over again. It is like the healing of a mortal illness. It is like being forgiven a big lie at the heart of our being. It is like a resurrection from a tomb.

The dying to the life-quest becomes itself the very bread of life. Surrender of the demand for final truth becomes quite the truth about things. Capitulation to the secret that there is no way out becomes the very door and way to being. This is the end of the road of self-understanding. There is no beyond it. There is no need. For one can now freely live in his negations, learn in his perpetual ignorance and walk in all his given creatureliness. In brief, the decision to die is at the same time an election to life. The JESUS-CHRIST is life abundant. As it was in the beginning, is now and ever shall be.

Now to the recapitulation: the JESUS-CHRIST is an historical event. It is a radical revolution in the interior history of people proceeding from an absolute reversal in human self-understanding. Originally occasioned by Jesus of Nazareth, it is first of all the experience of an offense. This offense is grounded in an actual disaffirmation of our creaturely phantasms which issues in a new possibility of living our bestowed existence as a great benefaction. It is, secondly, the decision to receive the offense and embrace the ensuing possibility as our own. This entails a dying to ourselves as defined by our mirages, which very death is experienced as the very life we were mistakenly searching for. Such is the radical transfiguration of the JESUS-CHRIST-EVENT.

The early Christians' pronouncement of it contained an inseparable promise and demand. The demand is to die. That this very dying is life is the promise.

The Christian Story

Our task is not finished. Any serious dialogue on the Christ symbol must of necessity consider the Christian story, so-called. In and through the JESUS-CHRIST-EVENT an historical community broke into time. The church and the event are actually but two sides of one historical occurrence. Those to whom the event happened constituted the church. Like every historical people the church forged a life-apologue or meaning story by which it communicated to itself and to others that the event which created it was rooted in ultimacy. What we have termed the Christian story became, therefore, along with the event and the church, an integral component of the total historical complex.

The cosmic tale has a universal and definitive agency. Both the social body and the comprising individuals are contingent upon it. As insinuated above, it is the vehicle by which the interior history is transcendently grounded, comprehensively appropriated and significantly communicated. To say it again, it freights the universal dimension to self-understandings and life missions. In fact, all intentional being and doing, all self-conscious existence is finally interwoven with one or another cosmic-meaning drama.

Such stories are conspicuously penetrated by the relative and arbitrary: not in their inner meaning but in their form. Yet once the story is devised, there is a certain absolute quality about even the form. In principle, the detail could have been quite different at its creation. And any time thereafter its basic intent can be expressed in other ways. But once the original dramaturgy is complete, that production is the prototype. It remains prototypal as long as the historical community remains. The early Christians formulated their classical tale out of the relative stuff of their specific Hebrew memory, the unique worldviews of their time, and whatever figures emerged from the collective unconscious. It was a work of expansive conception and consummate artistry. Through it the church continued to grasp for themselves and transmit to others the finality of what had occurred in their midst. This is to say, it endured as irreplaceable.

The story is a strange metamorphic tale of two symbols: the cross and the empty tomb. These basic New Testament emblems pervade the drama from the beginning to the end. The truth of the matter is they play the stellar role. Uncommon and fantastic as it may sound, the leading character of the Christian story is none other than the biform symbol, cross and open sepulcher, indicating and embodying the reality of the crucifixion that is resurrection, the death that is life. To say it another way, the principle player is the meaning-word that people may dare to be fully human, living freely among the uncertainties, ambiguities and anxieties of creaturehood, in gratitude, concern and creativity. The hero, in brief, is not Jesus, but the JESUS-CHRIST-EVENT.

In brief synopsis, the story develops as a dramatic extravaganza in three sweeping acts executed on two stage levels. It opens on the upper stage representing the cosmic, universal, transcendent dimension of life. It moves next to the historical, temporal, human level on the lower stage. Finally, in the third act the movement returns once more to the cosmic gallery. Each of the three acts is a spectacle in itself. Yet all are bound together into one majestic movement by two transitional scenes between the acts.

The time and place of act one is the beginning of the beginnings. Exciting awesomeness is the overarching mood. The JESUS-CHRIST-EVENT, disguised as a most curious lamb which is alive though dead, is the principle figure on stage. Here, before the foundations of the world, a slain lamb is sitting very much alive on the very throne of thrones alongside the creator. Indeed the lamb is portrayed as the creator himself calling all things into being. Without him no thing that comes to be comes to be. Passing to the third and final act of the play, the scene is very much the same. It is again on the cosmic level with the slain lamb occupying stage center. The difference is that it is now the ending of the endings. All things have passed away. The lamb, alive-while-dead, is once more seated on the throne. This time he is playing the role of the unconditional judge presiding over the finale of history. In sober awe all things come forth to account and no thing is judged save by the judgment of the lamb.

Embracing the middle act are two transitional scenes. Their theatric function is that of getting the lamb on and off the historical stage where the second act is performed. The entrance into temporality of the JESUS-CHRIST-EVENT figure cannot of course be like any other entry. Heralded by angelic hosts, he arrives born of a virgin. If the play were being composed today the advent might well have been by way of a space rocket fired out of nowhere. In this case, the lamb imagery conceivably would be replaced by that of a strange little creature from beyond the time-space continuum. The important point is that the cosmic figure invades history on a mighty mission. When the mission is accomplished he departs the temporal, not of course as others do, but through ascending in an effulgence of glory again to the upper level.

In the second act, the interest is in the cosmic mission. The central character is still the JESUS-CHRIST-EVENT. Camouflaged in the first and last act as the slain lamb, it is here disguised as a man. In this double concealment the cosmic figure submits to the ordeal of finitude. He meets and straightforwardly engages the twin forces of death and the devil: that is, the temptation to illusion and the anxiety of creatureliness, which drives us into the clutches of illusion. He engages the forces of EVERYMAN-CHRIST and destroys their power by boldly withstanding their subtlest wiles. He enters the very den of death and emerges from the grave the unchallenged conqueror. In a mighty invasion the JESUS-CHRIST-EVENT has overcome the hosts of the foe on the plains of history, pushed to the fortified place and bound the strong man, leading humanity forth from its bondage and slavery unto the glorious freedom of life. The sign and power of the cross and empty tomb are engraved for all time upon the fact of history. Cosmic permission to live has been epiphanied. Mission accomplished, the lamb returns to that realm from whence he came, the manifest victor to rule as sovereign lord and only judge forever and forever. What a play!

It must be underscored that this drama is in no sense a web of metaphysical statements. Nor is it an aggregate of religious doctrines to be believed. It is a story. Its task is to hold before the reader, in a comprehensive, precise, and constraining fashion, the stance of life. One is moved therefore not to ask whether the dramatic images correspond to "objective realities," but whether the life meaning they embody corresponds to the way life comes to us as persons.

When it is received as the truth-story it is, the axial point is quite plain. Though the point is singular, it peradventure ought to be put several ways. First of all, the JESUS-CHRIST is presented not as just a way of life, but the final and only way. The story announces both the cosmic permission and the cosmic requirement to live after this style. Second, it is clear in the play that the JESUS-CHRIST is the way real life has always been from the very beginning of human existence, and will always be to the very ending. Third, the JESUS-CHRIST is a removal of the false veils we have drawn over life as it is. It is in no wise a superimposition upon life. The transfiguration is a restoration, not a novelty. Lastly, the JESUS-CHRIST tells us nothing we do not somehow know. The meaning of being human is that we were constituted to be human. This is what we were given to be. This alone shall be our judge.

The compendium is this: the JESUS-CHRIST IS LORD in every sense of the word. Everyone, it is plain, bows his/her knee to some life image. Before one or another self-understanding under the general canopy of the EVERYMAN-CHRIST, s/he utters the submissive word: My Lord. The early church was quite clear about this. She was also transparent concerning the location of her own obeisance and confession of allegiance. Her earliest creedal formula, JESUS-CHRIST IS LORD, is an abbreviation of the whole cosmic tale. It is at once a subjective decision and an objective state of affairs. The story of the cosmic Christ – his pre- and post-existence, his virgin birth and ascension to heaven, his historical life, death and resurrection – are all signs and symbols of this lordship.

In all of this the primitive church was calling upon herself and everyone everywhere to live boldly in the JESUS-CHRIST, confidently sure that this is the way things are, ever have been, and ever will be. There is but one objective, everlasting, unchanging life truth, namely, the living of life as a gift is the meaning of living life. Put it liturgically: the JESUS-CHRIST IS LORD.

The Eschatological Hero

Intimately related to the Christian story, yet not synonymous with it, is still another component of the Christ construct. It is the image created by the primitive Christians of a hero of faith or a cultic exemplar. The hero was first etched upon the common memory of the community. In time he became universally public as the central literary figure in the Four Gospels. One must not be misled here. This cultic man is not Jesus of Nazareth. Nor is he the cosmic figure sketched above. Neither is he simply a representation of what we have termed the JESUS-CHRIST Happening. One must rather say that the Christian paragon is a masterfully artistic combination of them all.

Every historical community has its cultic figures. They are the models of the corporate self-understanding in the collective imagination. Such representations inform the liturgical dramas through which the group recollects who it is. They are the "universal" categories which provide the everyday common sense. They are the generalized other in the conscience that prompts and judges action. They are the master signs through which the active and passive emotions are usefully illuminated. In sum: the archetypal persons are the keys of concretion in the corporate worship dramas, the corporate lifestyles and the corporate practical wisdoms.

It is most understandable, then, that the early church was inspired to create such a hero. His paradoxical nature has already been indicated. He eats and weeps and experiences deep struggles of the spirit. Yet he also withers trees with a glance, does disappearing feats and quite actually rises from the grave on page twenty-five or so of the record. Succinctly, the Christian hero is the JESUS-CHRIST-EVENT embodied at the same time in both the temporal Jesus and the cosmic lamb.

This complex of paradoxes needs a closer look. To begin with, the hero is a man of this world, plus or minus nothing. He was born and he died. In between, he is portrayed as experiencing life's gamut of joys and sorrows, failures and successes, knowns and unknowns. Furthermore, he struggles, as humans must, to assume his posture toward his creatureliness. The stance he embodies, however, is not that of the EVERYMAN. He elects to live entirely within the JESUS-CHRIST faith, deciding and acting only in the style of the death that is life. The Christian prototype, to employ a formula, is in the first instance the historical-JESUS-CHRIST-man.

The other pole of the hero's individuality is likewise a fusion. In this case, the ingredients, like those in the Christian story, are the cosmic dimension and the JESUS-CHRIST-EVENT. This is the figure that stills storms, turns water to wine, casts out demons, and raises up dead men. He signifies the wholly other, the utterly absolute, being in itself. Use any symbol of ultimacy, the beginning and the end, the first and the last, he is it. At the same moment, he is the JESUS-CHRIST-EVENT that takes place in time. His own death and resurrection are presented as the master sign. The wonders he performs and the oracles he utters are likewise symbols of the Christ Happening. Actually, his total existence is an unbroken nexus of signs pointing to crucifixion that is the resurrection. In terms of our schemata, the archetypal hero is the cosmic-JESUS-CHRIST-figure as well as the historical-JESUS-CHRIST-man.

The picture is still not complete. The whole emerges only after the polarities in the two formulae are totally amalgamated into one. A diagrammatic statement of this amalgamation would look something like this: the cosmic-historical-JESUS-CHRIST-man-figure. Authentic human existence and ultimate cosmic significance coalesce in the JESUS-CHRIST-EVENT. Here is the bare skeleton on which was shaped the most remarkable personality in the literature of any people. The paradoxes are made to completely cohere in the characterization of that strange personage who moves through the New Testament Gospels. It is a work of consummate artistry. In one paragraph he moves from the very human business of dispersing crowds and enjoying a moment alone to his stroll across the lake. Wonder-filling as this is, the reader is not surprised. There is no jarring. The player is exactly in character, so to speak.

In literary flesh and blood, the gospel hero is first and last a man of mission. Being and doing are consolidated in him. His single-minded vocation is exhibited in a two-fold activity of living life genuinely, authentically – as a man of faith in the midst of the world – and announcing to all others the possibility of such living. This is patent in both poles of his individualization: cosmic and historical. To use our earlier figure, he walks freely out across the anxious, uncertain, ambiguous waters of life. At the same time, he beckons others to do likewise. On the temporal side, the same pattern is discernible. With utter intentionality, the hero lives as the free person. He humbly opens himself to what is given; gratefully receives himself in what is given; and benevolently involves himself on behalf of what is given. He is liberated to be thankful for life; to love this world of neighbors; to be directed toward the future. This is to say, he is free to live life. And while he is busy living, he simultaneously declares to those about who have ears to hear the good news that they too can live in the freedom of the JESUS-CHRIST-EVENT.

Within the cultus, the name of the hero came to be Jesus Christ. This is frequently abbreviated just to Christ. And sometimes, perhaps more of the time, he is simply called Jesus. This is the Jesus of piety. To caution once more, he is not Jesus of Nazareth, but rather Jesus of the holy literature, the Jesus of the liturgical experience, the Jesus of the common life. As such he is the most vividly alive, the most finally significant, the most always present personality in the existence of the cultus. There are, of course, a host of other companions who live in the collective memory. Jesus Christ is the primordial one. The many titles bestowed upon him are indicative of this: Lord of Lords, King of Kings, Son of Man, Son of God. No designation or mark of honor is too high or high enough to articulate his status for the people who bear his name. This raises a question about the adequacy of the term "cultic hero." The representational Jesus very obviously is the cultic or prototypal figure of the people who live in the CHRIST-EVENT. Yet the church knew him to be more: not just the cultic hero but the final or eschatological hero. That is, he represents the way things are for everyone. He is the paragon of man as Man.

This eschatological hero is then the portraiture of what human living actually is. He is an unqualified delineation of the human style of life. He is a model of faith-filled living. A model is a design of the way things are. It is a construct of the manner in which things are understood to function. In dealing with subjects rather than objects, as in the case at hand, where the model is a personage, perhaps the "exemplar" would be a more fitting term. The Christ hero is a model or exemplar of what is going on where unmitigated human living is taking place.

The terms "ideal" and "example" have been intentionally avoided for fear of distracting connotations. To be sure, since a model is necessarily a totally unbroken and unfragmented representation, it might be labeled "ideal." But it is not ideal in the sense of disclosing some ought-world of precepts and virtue through which we can escape our humanity. It is not ideal in the sense of some moral goal toward which people strive for the sake of meaning and significance. All this would be merely a subtle form of the EVERYMAN-CHRIST that builds illusions about the human situation in seeking for truth, perfection, and peace.

The Jesus model is the JESUS-CHRIST made flesh. It is a dramaturgical embodiment of that life stance or posture. To follow in the steps of the representational Jesus is not to imitate his words or reproduce his deeds. It is to be and do as a free person in our concretion as he depicted this stance in the concretions of his role. It is to walk out across the uncertain, ambiguous, anxious deeps of my life in gratitude, humility and compassion, with the sure confidence that this very walking is the meaning of life. The Exemplar is an ever present indicative word in the memory of a people, that to live is to live in the Christ event, and an ever present imperative word that continually calls them to it. In this sense, it guides their thoughts and deeds, their words and feelings. It is the context in which and out of which they forge their concrete actions.

The New Testament writers think of their Jesus hero as the pioneer who blazes the way; the elder brother who goes on before; the first fruit of a mighty harvest to be reaped. The followers then see themselves as the second wave of explorers, the younger brother, the latter harvest, yet as embodying the same life, traveling on the same way, participating in the same mission. As he lived his life as the meaning of his life, and announced the cosmic permission for all people thus to live, so the church understands that she can and must go and do likewise. As Luther said, the Christians are to be little Christs.[7]

---

[7] This published writing by Joseph Mathews came from his talks. "The Christ of History" was first printed in booklet form in the *Image*: *Journal of the Ecumenical Institute*: *Chicago*, Number 7, June 1969. The copy here is found in John P. Cock's *The Transparent Event*: *Post-modern Christ Images*, pp. 108-22, with interpretive chapters following.

Three RS-I Lectures:

Christ, Freedom, and Church

Three talks by Joseph Mathews at Religious Studies I seminars, mid to late 1960s

The Christ Lecture

The Christian Self-understanding of Death and Resurrection

Genuine Humanness is Dependent upon Symbols

We are cripples at being genuine human beings before one another. You and I can be pigs without the use of symbols, but to be persons we are utterly and completely dependent upon symbols that mediate our deeps. For example, I have resorted to an ancient formula: "Grace be unto you and peace, from God our Father and the Lord Jesus Christ. Amen."

Prologue I. You must understand that you alone can live your own life. My friend Luther stood in his pulpit one day and said something like this to his people: "When I got born-ned, you were not there. When you got born-ned, I was not there. When you get die-ded, I'll not be there, and when I get die-ded, you'll not be there. Everyone of us must do our own getting born and getting died utterly alone, because everyone of us has to live our own life.

Prologue II. St. Paul once said to all of creation: "As I follow Christ, as I live an authentic existence, so you must follow my pattern and live an authentic existence. As I reflect Christ," he said, "you reflect me." That, I wish to say to you, is exactly my stance. As I follow Christ, you follow me. As I grow with authenticity and integrity, you follow me. That's what I mean to say to the world, that everyone must do his or her own living and his or her own dying. Alone.

Prologue III has to do with what we're doing here. But before I start, I have poetry which D. H. Lawrence and I wrote together for you. He never actually produced these things I produce out here, so we're a team.

As we live . . .

I wish I were an actor, rather than a ham [laughter], but I tell you, words just fascinate me. Have you ever noticed those good four-letter Anglo-Saxon words have whole universes in them? You have? Oh, I didn't think that you were that kind of a girl [laughter]. It's that word "live." How do we say it in such a way that those four letters, you know, just breathe meaning? This is one way:

> As we live, we are the transmitters of life.
> And when we fail to transmit life, life fails to flow through us.
>
> That is a part of the mystery of sex, it is a flow onwards.
> Sexless people transmit nothing.
>
> And if, as we work, we can transmit life into our work,
> life, still more life, rushes into us to compensate, to be ready
> and we . . . [revel at life] through the days.
>
> Even if it is a woman making an apple dumpling, or a man a stool,
> if life goes into the pudding, good is the pudding,
> good is the stool,
> content is the woman, with fresh life rippling in to her,
> content is the man.
>
> Give, and it shall be given unto you
> is still the truth about life.
> But giving life is not so easy.
> It doesn't mean handing it out to some mean fool,
> or letting the living dead eat you up.
> It means kindling the life-quality where it was not,
> even if it's only in the whiteness of a washed pocket handkerchief.
> ("We Are Transmitters," *The Complete Poems* . . . , p. 449)

You like that poem? Wouldn't you like to have that power? Every time you moved your hand to touch another being, a new life they never dreamed of – well, you've got to be *alive* to do that. So unstop those ears. Unblock that tongue.

I love poetry, don't you? Another friend, this one named John, but I don't know his last name. He and I wrote a little bit of poetry that I want to read next.

> Sometime later came one of the Jewish feast-days and [Joshua] went up to Jerusalem. There is in Jerusalem near the sheep-gate a pool surrounded by five arches. . . . Under these arches a great many sick people were in the habit of lying; some of them were blind, some lame, and some had withered limbs. (They used to wait there for the "moving of the water," for at certain times an angel used to come down into the pool and disturb the water, and then the first person who stepped into the water after the disturbance would be healed of whatever he was suffering from.) One particular man had been there ill for thirty-eight years. When [Joshua] saw him lying there on his back, knowing that he had been there for a long time, he said to him, "Do you want to get well again?" [long pause]

"Sir," replied the sick man, "I just haven't got anybody to put me into the pool when the water is all stirred up. While I'm trying to get there somebody else gets down into the water first."

"Get up," said [Joshua], "pick up your [life] and walk!" (Jn. 5:1-8, JBP)

The Christ Event

I want to deal first with the Christ Event, and second with the Christ Story, and third with the Christ Drama. Yesterday I was attempting to talk about life in terms of what I call the edge of life. And I came at that in terms of the two ways in which anyone meets it, and that's in terms of the overwhelming emptiness of life, and then the overwhelming fullness of life.

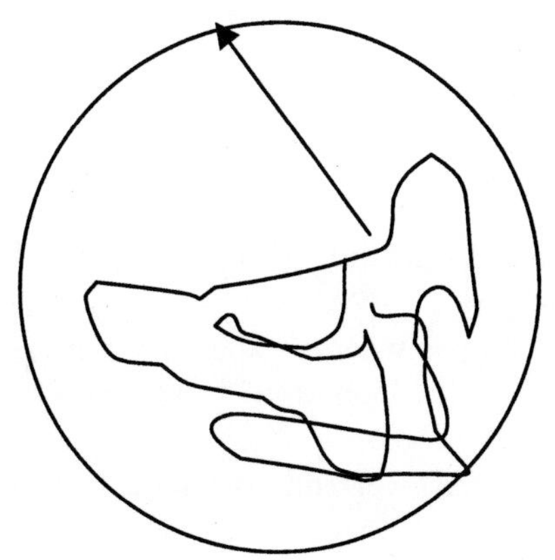

Figure 1-1: The Edge of our Lives

Let this little circle represent all of those structures of the civilizing process in which we find ourselves. Yesterday I talked about that life situation wherein you and I get shoved to the very edge of life. Within this circle there are all kinds of complexes, or little games. The person, who knows what you and I know, knows that everyone lives by faith in some god, in something that bestows significance on life. If it isn't Mama, then it's Goldwater or Liberalism. And if it isn't Liberalism, it's the Methodist Church. And if it isn't the Methodist Church, it's something else.

Fifty years ago, people raised the question as to whether or not there's a God. That kind of a question is as anachronistic as anything can be. You can always spot a person who's either fleeing from life, or who is naïve when he or she raises the question Is there a God? The kind of a universe in which you can raise that question hasn't existed for a long time. The problem in the spirit of humans today is that we're aware that there are so damn many gods we don't know what to do with them. That's our problem. Therefore, the spirit question of life is Which god is God? Which God am I going to get myself born before and get myself died before? Which one of the not-me-nesses in life am I finally going to live my life before? That's the question, not whether there's a God.

Finally, all other gods fail. Do you remember that time when Mama collapsed off of the pedestal for you, or hasn't she yet? I can remember the time when it happened for me. Mama sent me to the door to tell somebody who was knocking that she wasn't home. And it finally dawned on me, "Mama's a liar! Waaaa!"

This is an amazing thing when the god called Mama cracks. She is delivered from the phony universe we stuck her in, because, mark you, my Mama was a creature, not a god. The worms got Mama like they got Plato and Kant. When this "Waaaa!" happens, then you've got a genuine hunk of flesh and blood you can relate to, called Mama.

It doesn't always happen so dramatically. Being an upright Methodist clergyman, to say nothing of having been conditioned in a moralistic type of childhood, I used to hide from my Mama that I smoked. And it became finally ridiculous, because Mama knew that I smoked, and I knew that I smoked, and I knew that Mama knew that I smoked, and Mama knew that I knew that she knew that I smoked. I was going along one day driving Mama in the car, and I said to myself it's now or never.

"Mama, you're pretty old aren't you?

"Yes, son."

"You're not going to live too much longer, are you?"

And she said, "Well, likely not."

I said, "Isn't it time you and I really become human beings before one another?"

She looked at me, you know. She never knows what to expect from me. So I said, "Now, over in that glove compartment are my cigarettes. I think you ought to be the one to hand them to me."

She looked at me seriously and then reached over and got them. I tell you, Mama and I were new people after that.

Do you grasp what I'm saying? Shall I rehearse the death of another god? When you finally become aware that the Methodist Church wasn't always here, and will not always be here, and when you see that, it's already gone. It's already gone. It can no longer be the meaning of your life. The cr-aa-ck has taken place. The pedestal is broken. And when you see that the United States of America wasn't always here and isn't always going to be here, it's already gone. Cr-aa-ck!

Which is to say that I'm working up here to the edge of this circle. You see, everything that is, is in that same predicament. Everything passes away. Even your most favorite theologian passes away. Down at Perkins Theological Seminary, once a year they ought to get all the theologians up on the stage and have them turn sideways, and then strip stark naked before their students, so all can see our pot bellies and our flabby muscles, so they will never take us seriously ever again. We are only human beings that the worms will eat as they have eaten every theologian before us.

That's what I'm talking about by the edge of life where lucidity breaks in. Question: What are you up against? Nobody has ever known what he or she was up against. A student said, "Well, I'm just up against the great question mark. I'm just up against what the hell? I don't know." Any name you put on it, that's it. The great Mystery, huh? And in that awareness you become aware that your basic relationship that constitutes you as a person is the relationship to the great unknowable unknown.

Now, this isn't some kind of doctrine. It's not some kind of philosophy. It's just the way life is. At this point, the only real decision anybody ever had to make is *How are you going to live your life and die your death?* You get but one chance, not two. If I'd been God, I'd have given everybody two times around so they could have played with the first and come back sober for the next one. But you know that's not the way life is.

It's exactly at this point, and only at this point, that the question of God in depth is raised. If you're sitting around here nursing off of Mama, Methodism, Plato, Tillich, Mathews, Goldwater, Kennedy; if you're nursing any of those gods, you have never raised the question of God. Not of G-O-D. And only at the point where the question of God is raised for you is the Christ *word* relevant. The gospel of Jesus Christ has no meaning when you stand anywhere else. But when you stand at the edge of the circle, at the edge of your being, then you become aware of the relevance of what we symbolically call the *word.*

The Event

Let's see if we can ground this in life experience. My wife is literally the wrath of God upon me because she knows where my gizzard is. I mean, if the gizzard in a person is the illusion-making faculty, she knows more about my illusions than anybody in this universe. At times she sticks a knife into my gizzard. That's why she's the wrath of God upon me.

But the wrath of God is always God's love. Not that God's love comes sometimes and his wrath comes sometimes, or his mercy comes after his wrath. No, no, no. His wrath is his mercy. That is, you haven't the slightest chance of being other than who you are until some over-against-ness in life takes you and shakes you till your teeth rattle. Only when you die do you live.

I say my wife is the wrath of God. She's always calling into question my illusions. I remember a student who said that he came home to his wife after having a great theological dialogue over in the library with some of his buddies. He came waddling home in the image of being a really-with-it theologian, only to be met at the door by his frau, who pulled out her hatpin and stuck it into his illusion (POP! like a balloon) as she reminded him he was not a really-with-it theologian but a thirty-minutes-late babysitter.

Do you understand? When these negations move in, sometimes in these negations I am hurled out to the edge where I see the "No" of life. But not always. And especially as I grow more sophisticated and more lucid, it's increasingly hard to get to me. You see, the moment somebody moves in on your life, you have to kill 'em to protect yourself. But there're laws against literally slitting wives' throats – they put you in electric chairs and things like that – so us subtle people, we learn how to destroy and kill with kindness.

I had a group of students out to my house one night, and we were just sitting around, and I was just scintillating all over the place. Lyn, my wife, stood up and started out of the room, saying, "Joseph, I will see you in the kitchen." Now, when Mama – I mean my wife – calls me "Joseph," I feel guilty to begin with. I know I've done something wrong. So, without knowing how I was threatened, I was already sharpening my knives as I moved toward the kitchen. I quickly spoke first, "Lyn, you can't do this to me. Tomorrow I'm their professor. I've got to stand up and be their professor. You can't humiliate me by ordering me around in my house like that."

She said, "Joseph, you know women were given weapons. They've used them all their lives and they're effective. And sooner or later, if you're going to live with one, you're going to come to terms with that fact."

But I have other ways. "Well, I don't care what I did, you've done worse" (laughs). I see that you understand what I'm saying. You understand that when someone destroys your illusions you strike back.

When you are not able to destroy the intrusion in your life, you're thrown out here (in the circle) to the very edge where you see the collapse of the collapse of the collapse. There you stand utterly naked without any justification, without any excuse for having showed up in history.

The Seizure

It's at that point that the *word* becomes relevant. This *word*, it came to me in terms of what happened to me. First, I experience it as a seizure. Second, I experience it as an offense. And, third, I experience it as a decision, a deadly decision, I might add. What I mean by that is that in those moments, a word breaks out of my latent memory into my active memory and addresses me. It's a word like, "Joseph, you're significant." Now, mark you, I'm standing there naked as a jaybird. Caught. Unveiled. And that *word* moves in. "Joseph, your life is utterly significant."

And I say, "Who, me? How could you make that kind of a statement?"

"Your life is utterly significant."

Wesley said that it was something like this: you carry within your mind an abstract idea that God so loved the world, and that in a situation like this your name appears on that word. It's like, "Joseph, your life is significant."

That's what I mean by "seizure." It becomes relevant. And as a matter of fact, at this point it becomes the only relevant word. You are filled with the awareness that if that isn't *the word*, then by god, there isn't any word! At that moment, you don't care when that *word* broke into history. It might just as well have come from the braying of a jackass in 1846 on the south slope of the Alps. Do you understand that? At that moment there isn't any question of who first said that *word*, because that's the only *word* that can ever have meaning. What Nietzsche saw very clearly is that if that isn't *the word*, then either spend the rest of your life (and I'm gonna swear real hard because you swear down in your guts when you take this stance) saying, "This Goddamn universe!" Or else you conjure up a new rosy illusion like the characters in "The Iceman Cometh," in which you pretend that you don't know what you damn well know, and then the cussing comes out through the form of colitis, ulcers, migraines, tics, eccentricities, slobism. Do you understand what I'm saying? At that point, wherever that *word* came from, it is the lone *word* that has relevance. That's what I mean by seizure.

The Offense

But there's a sneakiness in this seizure. Let's say that here I am seized by that *word* as that which pronounces possibility for my existence. That *word* is the kind of a word that is an utter offense. It strikes you and knocks you outside of yourself so that you are able to see old Joseph over there being seized, and yet here is Joseph seeing Joseph being seized, and seeing that it's a scandalous seizure. The reason why it's scandalous is because of intellectual and emotional, emotional and intellectual, insecurity raised to the nth power.

When you are seized, the scandal that causes the gap is first the intellectual scandal of "Who said so?" Now, I've already pointed to that in a way. But now you are facing it head-on. Here I am seized with the only *word* that has relevance, and now I want three good reasons. This is what it means to be a rational creature. But you see, at this time, none of this helps. If I say, "Tillich says so!" at this point I know damn well that the worms are going to eat Paul Tillich as well as me.

It doesn't do any good to say, "My dear friend Luther says so!" Because, hell, Luther, he got eaten too. It doesn't do any good to say, "The Bible says so," because that's exactly the problem. And certainly it doesn't do any good to say "My eschatological hero, Jesus, says so!" Because who in the hell is Joshua to say this?

If I give you three good reasons why "A" is better than "B," you aren't interested. You're interested in where in the wide world does a guy get three good reasons?

You are at the point of decision. You make a kind of decision. A person that stands at this point is the one who will step out beyond any cynic, out one step beyond any skeptic, a person who in principle is aware of every doubt possible in the whole universe. Maybe one day you're going to see that the Christian faith is not to take care of those neurotics who can't handle their neuroses. The Christian faith is that self-understanding that shoves a person to the limit beyond which there is no more truth. That's what I'm trying to articulate.

The emotional insecurity is the other side of the coin – this person who dares to stand here and say "yes" to that *word* knows that no Mama can ever be a womb again, that no political cause can ever give security again, no religious institution can offer everlasting security, no friendship can take away the anxiety. At this point you have to become a "Goddamn liar" if you're going to get any significance out of any of those authorities. Said theologically, at this point you have to build a lie that is damning to God, as you hide behind illusions that are known to be illusions. That's the emotional insecurity.

Some of you look surprised that bourgeois philosophy is dressed up in Christian terminology: that Christianity is a matter of security. No! That's the Christianity that denies God. The person of faith seized and offended by this *word* is out over 70,000 fathoms of insecurity for the duration of being.

That's the offense. That's why nobody ever heard this *word* save his or her life collapsed, or he or she hit bottom.

The Decision

And then the third part of the analysis of the dynamic of faith is the decision, a decision out over nothing. I mean the kind of decision that doesn't have three good reasons for deciding anything. I mean the decision that has nothing as a basis for deciding. I mean the kind of decision in which the decision itself is the gamble of your own existence, remember, that only goes around the clock once. It's the kind of a decision when you use pure guts to make your decision.

Let me be very clear: the *word* never comes to a person as truth. Good Lord, no! That's the problem. The *word* comes to you as *possibility*, which is a question, which forces you to answer the question as to whether or not you're going to live in the deeps of humanness, or whether you're going to live in the lying, secure shallows. The *word* does not come as a truth. It comes as possibility, which is a question that addresses the very depths of your life and world. And you have to answer that question. And you have to answer it out over nothing. And the cost of it is your whole being. It's that kind of word.

It's as if the person of faith picks up every doubt in the universe. This is why that person out-skepticizes the skeptic. The skeptic knows nothing that the person of faith doesn't know. The tragic hero knows nothing, the most lucid stoic knows nothing, the atheistic existentialist knows nothing that the person of faith doesn't know. The person of faith knows emotional insecurities. The person of faith can be surprised by nothing. This person internalizes every insecurity, even somebody pushing the atomic bomb button – every insecurity in the universe.

Now, let me see if I can get a little more flesh and blood on that *word*. It's been said in history so many ways, for example, that word of Augustine, which was "All that is, is good." He knew damn well that anybody with two ounces of sense knew that this world isn't good. "All that is, is good" is a confessional statement.

Trees talk to me. I used to have an office down in Austin, Texas, and the students at the university would come in and talk to me and pour out their troubles. I tell you, the students at Texas really had bellies full of problems. I'd sit there and I'd listen to them like I'd never heard things like that in my whole life, until it got so painful that all I could think of were my own problems. And when I got to thinking about my own problems, I'd sort of turn away, just a little bit, but pretend to listen. But I wasn't hearing a thing they said. I was just consumed with my own problems.

And then I'd look out the window, and across the street there was a tree. That tree was a friend of mine. It was a strange old tree. In Texas they have hurricanes, and some of the limbs of this tree were knocked off, and there was a great big gash down through its psyche, I mean its trunk. And that black stuff was smeared on it to patch it up. I knew it wasn't long for this world and the students would come by and they would pay no attention to it. Even the faculty members would walk right by that tree, my old friend, and literally ignore it. But in these circumstances that tree used to speak to me. Augustine went around and asked all the little flowers if the meaning of life was in them, and in those days, a lot of flowers could talk, and they said, "No, it's not in me."

This tree talked also. He'd start out, he'd say, "Hello, Joseph." He'd always call me Joseph. He'd say, "Hello, Joseph." And I'd say, "Hello, tree." And the tree would start in saying, "Look. I'm accepted in this universe," and I'd say, "What?!? You mean with all those stubby old limbs of yours?" And he's say, "Yes, I'm received in the universe." And I'd say, "With that great big gash through your psyche, that you're never going to get over, and you're going to carry . . . ?" And he'd say, "Yes, I'm received, even with that big gash in my psyche." And I'd say, "You mean even though everybody pays you no attention?" He'd say, "Yes, I'm received." I'd say, "How do you know that?" And the tree said to me, "Look." And sure enough, I'd look. And whatever was sustaining everything else in being was sustaining my friend the tree in being! Just as it was! And then the tree would be sneaky. He'd turn it around on me. He'd say, "You know, Joseph, you're received in this universe." I'd say, "What do you mean? You mean this guy that can't even stand the pain of listening to this poor student?" He'd say, "Yes!" "You mean this guy who never was quite what his Papa wanted him to be?" "Yes!" "You mean this fellow who never quite made it like his brother made it?" "Yes!" "You mean this guy who's done all of these horrible things that you know damn well. . . ?" "Yes!"

And I'd say, "How do you know?" And he'd say, "Look." And sure enough, I looked down and there I am, and whatever is sustaining anything in this universe is sustaining me. Whether anyone likes me or not.

You know, whether you like me or not, whether my Mama cares for me, whether or not my wife likes me, whether or not I approve of myself. By whatever finally is going on in this universe, Joseph Wesley Mathews, as he is, not as he might have been, not as you think he ought to be, not as he might like to be, but exactly as he is, is pronounced utterly received. That's John 3:16. That's the *word* that seizes you as possibility. But you see it's not your *word* until you say, "I *am* the one who is utterly approved in this universe!" And then, that *word* is the *word* of my life. It's the anchor of my existence, and if you ask me, "Who says so?" Then I say, "I say so!" And only after I say, "I say so!" do I say "We say so!" Which means Mrs. Bigbottom and I down at First Methodist. Which means Luther and I, which means Paul and I, which means Amos and I, which means Bill sitting over there and I.

That's the Christ Happening. And our fathers had many wonderful parables by which they spoke of it. They said, "All my life I was maimed, but didn't think I was maimed. I thought I was a two-armed and a two-legged man, but I only have one arm and one leg. All my life I was maimed. And lo, in this Happening I am whole. All my life I've been blind," is what they said, "Oh, I thought I could see. But I was blind. And now I see. All my life I've been deaf. Now I hear. All my life I've been tongue-tied. And now I can speak. All my life I've been in chains. And now I am free. All my life I've been a cadaver. I've been dead. And, lo, now I am alive. I've been resurrected from the dead."

And the strange irony is that what I've described is nothing short of death in the deepest meaning of "death." Here I die to all of those illusions which seemed to give me life. And when I die to those illusions and become nothing, out over 70,000 fathoms, in my nothingness I discover I am approved by the cosmos. When I die, it is then that I discover this is my life and that I've had my life from the beginning. But I did not know I had my life, and therefore, I did not live.

Listen! The Christ Happening isn't something that took place 2000 years ago. The Christ Event is something that happened back in the beginning of time and it happens now in your life. And there's nothing religious about it. There is nothing pious about it. There is nothing dogmatic about it. It's as human as going to the toilet.

The Story of Our Life

Your next question, and mark you, this is your next question. Your next question is, "How can these things be?" "How can these things be?" When you and I step back from this Happening and try to think and talk about it, we become aware that we cannot speak to ourselves about how these things can be, save we tell the *story* of our lives, which is the story of the community in which we live when this happening has become the Happening in and through which we define ourselves in history.

Let me tell you the story that the church knows. When you come to us as the church and ask us to talk about how this can be, you find us lying like sailors. That is to say, these people who say they have embraced their insecurity you find to be the most insecure people you ever saw. They lie like sailors. They begin to give you three good psychological reasons why this is true and three good philosophical reasons why this is true. And yet, when you yank the rug out from under them each time, which you have to do, because they're so insecure, these people, when you drive them into the corner, and finally you get them squatted down there with their heads between their knees and their hands over their heads, they'll finally say, "All right! All right! All right! I'll tell you the story of my life!"

And when they do, they tell a story something like this: One time we were not. We did not be. And then a configuration of happenings – the center of which was one Joshua – happened. I say, a configuration of occurrences occurred, after which here we be. You see that? They say, "At one time in history we had no being, and after a configuration of circumstances, here we be!"

It's sort of like the Revolutionary War. If you ask us who we are and we finally tell the story, and we say, well, one time we were not, and after a conflux of circumstances that we loosely refer to as the Revolutionary War, after which, here we is! Here we is.

"Jesus Christ" is not the first and the last name of a character. The term "Christ" is a title like "Mr. President," Harry Truman. So you have "Jesus" plus "the Christ" equals this Happening or Event, because this Christ is the significance for human existence. What I'm trying to say is that in and about some Joe Blow, about whom we know next to nothing, a new significance in terms of grasping what it means to be a human being got belched into history.

I said that when you stand on the edge it doesn't make any difference how that *word* came into history. But scientifically, apparently, and that's what you always have to say, this self-understanding, this possibility for being human, broke into history in and about the character named Joshua – one Jesus. But what broke into being was the self-understanding, which is to say, the Christ Self-understanding, or the possibility of the Christ Happening happening in history. And out of this happening, these people wove a tremendous story.

The Christian Story

And I want to retell you that story. I've never read a story like it. Maybe that's because it's my story. I mean, it's the story behind all of the stories in life that give meaning to my being Joseph Wesley Mathews.

And the story goes like this. You've got to go back and get their stage setting. Amy Sample McPherson wrote an opera, and there were three stage levels: Earth, Heaven, and Hell. I went to see it, and it was rather a phenomenal thing. Anyway, on this stage there are two levels. The lower level represents the civilizing process, or history, if you please. The upper level represents the cosmic, in the poetic sense. It represents the ultimate. It represents the final meaning of life.

These strange people of the church, to whom this thing happened – this new self-understanding, this awareness that they had divine permission to be human beings with all of the creatureliness that that meant – these people built two basic symbols. Those two symbols, in my opinion, are the *omega* – that's really the empty tomb – and the *cross*. Which is to say, that when we die, I mean die to all of our pretensions about life, we discover we've been resurrected, that we're alive. That we live! That we're really human beings.

To put it in another way, our fathers never separated these two symbols. This was what happened in history, those two symbols of death and resurrection. They told their story to try to say to themselves and the world that this is not just another happening, but it's the final happening of humanness.

What a story! First of all, they took these two symbols and put 'em up on the cosmic level, and then shoved the cosmic level in the play back to the beginning of the beginning. To get this little episode in the play, you have to go back to those primordial moments. You know, the Jews in the first chapter of Genesis have a great picture of it. You remember in the little play there, they waddle old Yahweh out on the stage and have him hurl out a little bit of isness, and at the end of the day he steps back and says, "It's good." And then they waddle him out a second day and have him throw out a little more isness, and he says it's good again. And when he wraps it all up – it took seven days to get through that little dramatic episode – when he got all the isnesses going, he stepped back and said, "It's very good." What a play!

You see the scene. Old Papa sitting on the throne back here in this scene, that means the ultimate up-against-ness in life, and guess what's sitting on his lap? Well, it's a little baby lamb. Now, just to be sure that you don't get this mixed up with any antiquated literalism, it's a lamb. I want you to understand that that lamb represents this symbol, right here, that if a person dies to any pretension or illusion, s/he lives. That's what it represents. And to be sure that you get that symbolism that they used, this little lamb as it hops along, said "Baa, baa, baa." Now you've got the picture in the play we're rehearsing. And this little lamb, which was the Lamb of the world, back in the primordial moment, was sitting on the lap of the Papa. What a play! And guess what! In this play the little Lamb is the one who hurled into being all isnesses. Therefore, our fathers were saying that this self-understanding is the cosmic self-understanding that was there from the very beginning, whatever that means mythologically. And you and I haven't the foggiest, for that was millennia ago when they were using all those mythological concepts and symbols.

Let's go to the other act of this play. I tell you, this ought to be on Broadway. We've been talking about the pre-existence of the Christ Happening. Now we go to the post-existence. When the play wraps up, and history is all rolled up, whatever that means, you've got the old Papa, of course, sitting on the throne. But guess who's on his lap. Why, the little Lamb is there. And guess who is the one who gets to say whether this whole play was good or bad. The Lamb gets to do that in the play. It's the Lamb that was slain before the foundation of the world, it's the Lamb that's still dripping with blood, it's the Lamb who decided what the play was about, and it's the Lamb who decides whether the play was good.

Do you understand why, for me, it's a matter of utter life and death that I'm washed in the blood of the Lamb, or that I'm given cosmic permission to live in the Christ *word*? There is nothing religious about it, nothing supernatural about it, nothing philosophical about it, nothing dogmatic about it – just the way life is.

There are a couple of tremendous little transitional scenes in the play. First of all, they had to get the Lamb into history. They had to get him into human form so that he didn't say, "Baa, baa, baa," but so he could say, "I am the way, the truth, and the life." They had to get the eschatological hero into history. They did it through that tremendous scene, the Virgin Birth. Wouldn't you like to orchestrate that scene? If it'd been in our day, it wouldn't have been that. We sure wouldn't have done it with the Virgin Birth. Maybe we'd use a flying saucer. He wouldn't have been a little old Lamb, he'd have been a little old Green Man from Mars.

But we didn't write the play. It was written long ago. That's the play, with the Lamb. Anyway, here he was hurled into being on a Virgin. Grace rode a Virgin. This is to say, you could no more get along without the Virgin Birth in the play than you could fly to the moon.

Then they had to get him off the stage of history. I like the way they did that – a lot of drama in it. You know, when I was a little boy, I lived in Ada, Ohio, and I went to Sunday school one day to see that strange picture of the Ascension. They've got this guy about halfway up in the picture? He's on his way. I came home that afternoon and went out to the edge of Ada, to a little knoll, and you may think I was crazy, but anyway, I tried it; but I never got off the ground, except maybe a little jump. This is a tremendous scene in which the hero goes out. The meaning of existence beats the wrath of the worms, and he's the only one that beats the wrath of the worms.

The Meaning of the Story

Now, the real question is, what does this play mean for Joseph Wesley Mathews? The self-understanding that bought my ticket, in the cosmic sense, was Jesus. In the earliest creed they said, "Jesus the Christ, Our Lord." And it was the Lord. This community bowed its knee before this self-understanding. And the Virgin Birth pointed to the Lordship, the early scenes to the Lordship, the Ascension to the Lordship, the post-existence to the Lordship. It all pointed to "Jesus Christ is Lord."

But what does that mean to this unique, unrepeatable fellow in the 20th century? It means that when I dare to receive the negations of my life and appropriate afresh the *word* that I am received; when the *word* intrudes in the flesh of my concrete situation, when the incarnation takes place for me, in that moment I become aware of grace.

From the beginning that *word* was over my life even though I never knew it. My whole memory is reconstructed, including the times that my Papa beat the daylights out of me for not shelling beans as fast as my brother. Do you understand how that scarred my being? And can you understand how I'm not over it yet? And can you understand that something has happened, because at least I can talk about it to myself? Can you understand that I am enabled to say that which is obviously *not good* is nevertheless *very good*? That it's mine! That all my life I have been an utterly approved man. And at this moment I know it. And not only do I have a memory, I have a capacity to anticipate, that is to say, shove out into the darkness of the future.

When I'm able to receive my life as significant, then I am able to grasp, first of all, that I haven't the slightest idea of what the future is going to be. I may be dead in five minutes. I may have one leg tomorrow. But there is one thing I am sure of, that the cosmic going-on-ness of this world pronounces my life approved! Approved, under any circumstances. This is to say, if I show up tomorrow as a one-legged man, I shall be accepted in the universe as a one-legged man, and dare to live my one-legged-ness to the hilt. And if tomorrow I am given the gift of my death, I shall grasp the fact, that dead, as well as alive, my existence is approved. And therefore I can pick up my death and die it.

That's what this strange story means. This is why this is *the* story, this is *the* play, without which history is not in the deepest sense history. This is why this is *the* story without which no human being, in the deepest sense, is ever a human being. This is to say the story isn't true because it's better than some other story. You see the joke of that, don't you? This is the story that is the last story. I mean, there's no place else to go. This is the end of the road of meaning. I mean, this is the final *word* on humanness. Before God, in Christ, one discovers in that *word* is our cosmic permission: if we die we live. Therefore, we can stand exposed in the white-hot insecurity of nothingness itself.

In the third act, therefore, we are able to pick up our lives and plunge them into the deeps of concern for the whole civilizing process. I remember "A Raisin in the Sun," a great movie. But they left out the punch line of the play. That was when the African Negro man asked the American Negro girl to marry him and go back to Africa. With amazing lucidity, the Negro girl reminded him of all the uncertainties, all the contingencies, of all the inhumanities, of all of the tragedies, all the dyings that awaited them if they went to Africa. And then she turned to him and asked him, "What's your answer to all these questions?" His reply, "I intend to live my answer."

So I say to you, the Christ Happening, the Christ Story, the Christ Drama in worship is that which gives me final permission to be the living embodiment of answers that I hurl into the face of the questions coming at me from the universe. That's what it means to be a Christian. But most of all, that's what it means for any person in this century to be a person of faith.

The Freedom Lecture

Biblical Faith and the Ethical Revolution

Grace be unto to you and peace, from God our Father and the Lord Jesus Christ. Amen.

The Christ Happening Is in This World, Now

You probably have noticed that the way I come at life is always to begin with the "is" and not with the "ought." Each person and each authentic community forges their "oughts" out of the concrete "ises." In terms of theology, my mind always goes this way.

You and I do not present Christ to the world. Christ *is* already Lord of this world. Our job is to pull off the mask. At the very depths of personal and social going-on-ness is the Christ Happening. That is the way it was in the beginning, is now, and shall be at the end. There's nothing religious about it, there's nothing Christian about it, there's nothing pious about it. The self-understanding that I point to with the Christ Happening is what it means to be a human being. The problem is, most of us have blinders on as to what it means to be a human being. Or we do not see that Christ, or what we point to with that symbol, is the Lord of this world.

I see my task in life, whether I do it with skill or not, is simply to pull the mask off of our eyes, that we may see, in the very depths of the great human adventure, that there is one – only one – eternal, unchanging, never passing truth and happening, and that's the Christ Happening.

A Radically New World

Our subject today is *Freedom*: *the biblical faith and the ethical revolution.* I have to come at it in this fashion: you and I are living in a radically new world, and the Christ Happening is to be found right in the midst of this world. That's where it's always been. If we're looking any place else other than in the midst of the scientific revolution, the urban revolution, the secular revolution, we haven't the slightest chance of seeing the Lordship of Jesus Christ. We have to begin by looking hard-headedly at the actual world, for Christ never rules over any of our dream worlds. He only rules over the actual world we're in. We begin there, and then we try to say to ourselves the meaning for us of this Happening of happenings.

The Style of the People of Faith in this New World

I want to deal with the style of life that issues from that Happening and place it in the context of the new image of the church in the 20th century. Before I do that, I have two bits of poetry. One is from my friend D. H. Lawrence:

> Those that go searching for love
> only make manifest their own lovelessness,
>
> and the loveless never find love,
> only the loving find love,
> and they never have to seek for it.
> ("Search for Love," *The Complete Poems* . . . , p. 661)

And now from my friend Paul:

> Oh, you dear idiots of Galatia, who saw Jesus Christ the crucified so plainly, who has been casting a spell over you? I will ask you one simple question: did you receive the Spirit by trying to keep the law or by believing the message of the gospel? Surely you can't be so idiotic as to think that a man begins his spiritual life in the Spirit and then completes it by reverting to outward observances? Has all your painful experience brought you nowhere? I simply cannot believe it of you! Does God, who gives you his Spirit and works miracles among you, do these things because you have obeyed the Law? Or because you have believed the gospel? Ask yourselves that. . . . At one time when you had no knowledge of God, you were under the authority of the gods who had no real existence. But now that you have come to know God, or rather are known by him, how can you revert to dead and sterile principles and consent to be under their power all over again? Your religion is beginning to be a matter of observing certain days . . . [or believing certain ideas]. Frankly, you stagger me, you make me wonder if all my efforts over you have been wasted! . . . *Plant your feet firmly therefore within the freedom that Christ has won for us*, and do not let yourselves be caught again in the shackles of slavery. . . . *It is to freedom that you have been called*, my brothers [and sisters] (Gal. 3: 1-5; 4: 8-11; 5: 1; 5:13 – JBP).

What a poet. If you, along with Augustine and myself, can allow yourself to say that "All that is, is good" – which is to say there is one God and not two – then you'll understand how I am persuaded that if this one God is "wroughting mighty wroughts" in the midst of the historical going-on-ness of our time, then one God is at the same time upheavaling creation and its people.

Faith vs. Ethics: the Real Problem Is Faith

I want to go to that individual now who's standing in faith. The category in and through which the style of life that flows out of faith is delineated more adequately than anything else is the category of *freedom*. My friend Luther made use of it, and Wesley made use of it, but he meant something a little different than most people mean. Certainly Paul made use of it. Now, you could use other categories, but I think this is the primary one. The person in Christ is free. Period. Paul was very clear the fruit of the Christian life was un-divorced from faith. That is, to be a person of faith is to be a free person, and to be a free person is to be a person of faith. I don't become a person of faith and then go out to be free. A person of faith is a free person. The Christian has always understood that the basic problem is not the ethical problem, but is the faith problem. It is the problem of deciding who you are going to be.

We've got to put a little content on that. I like to think of freedom as the freedom to be *lucid*, the freedom to be *sensitive*, the freedom to be *exposed*, and the freedom to be *disciplined.*

The Free Person of Faith has the Freedom to be Lucid

The person of faith is delivered unto lucidity. This is to say that the person of faith knows everything that there is to be known, minus nothing. I repeat, the person of faith knows everything that there is to be known, minus nothing – a person of utter lucidity.

You remember the picture by Camus in the *Myth of Sisyphus*? He has Sisyphus pushing the rock up the hill, his shoulders are dug into it, his muscles tensed, his face furrowed with strain. He's dripping with perspiration as he edges that rock of life up the hill. And when he gets it up the hill, he steps back and watches it roll back down again. Camus says this is the moment of the pause in which one becomes utterly lucid about one's lucidity – utterly lucid about just the way life is.

The person of faith doesn't have to kid himself any more about his showed-up-ness in history. He knows damn well that he just showed up. He just appeared, without any consultation on his part. He showed up a male and not a female, or she showed up a female and not a male. His color was white, or her color was black, slant eyes, or straight eyes, my neurotic problem, or yours. The free person dares to see that what is, is what is.

The free person doesn't have to lie about death, but knows that one day they're going to stick her in a hole in the ground, and that the worms are going to eat her. That's all she knows for sure. She doesn't have to conjure up some Platonic scheme of a body with a soul in it with three parts, the appetitive, the irascible, and the rational, the bottom two of which rot away in the ground because they are so intimately connected to that body, and that the rational part floats up to heaven when she dies and defeats death. But she doesn't need this kind of a rationalized escape. She can face life as it is. She's liberated to be lucid about herself. She knows she's going to die with a warped and scarred psyche. She also knows that her very scars are her gifts, and that her problem isn't that she's scarred, but it's having guts enough to pick up those scars and shove them into history. She says, if you take my neurotic pattern away from me, you take my gifts as well.

The lucid person understands his neighbor. He knows that his neighbor is an S.O.B. before he ever meets him, and he doesn't have to go around pretending otherwise. My neighbor knows that I know things about him that he wouldn't tell his own mother, and yet he never told me a thing. If he's a lucid man, he doesn't have to go around kidding himself. He doesn't have to go around pretending anymore. He knows that everybody lives in an illusion and that it's possible to pick up your tent and move out of the illusion once it's disclosed. This is the lucid one. This is the person who is in faith, who is stamped with the approval of great God Almighty, the one who understands that the great human venture is going on in God's world, and that God loves us and pronounces all creation good, including us.

The Free Person of Faith has the Freedom to be Sensitive

Secondly, the free person in Jesus Christ is the one who is sensitive. I'd like to use the word "love," but that word has been abused. The one who is in Christ dares to be present to every situation. The French have the term "disposabilite," one who dares to give himself to the situation, to be sensitive to it with the filed down finger tips of the safecracker, who can feel what's going on way down inside the lock. This is the one who dares to be present with the third ear. He or she doesn't pay any attention to any questions that anybody asks, but pays attention to the context out of which the question is asked. He or she doesn't pay any attention to what someone says but pays attention to what that person is most trying to reveal and conceal at the same time in what is said. The sensitive person dares to care about another person down deep in the spirit dimension of that person, where the real problems are. This is what I mean by sensitivity

The sensitive person takes a washrag and wrings the last drop of meaning out of it. The ancient Hebrews were clear about this when they saw that the divine activity was not only on the upbeats of life, but also in the downbeats of life. Getting an "A" in a course or getting an "F" in a course are equally significant. Having a good sex night with your wife is no more significant than having a bad sex night with your wife. Not only those great successes but those failures have meaning. Not only the "yea's" of life but also the "nay's" of life resound with the eternal "yes" said over existence. Not only getting born, but getting died is significant. Who is to say which is prior to the other, as Calvin would put it?

Camus used the figures of *the lover, the actor*, and *the conqueror. The lover*, as the free person, is the man who loves every woman he meets to the hilt, and when he finishes he leaves her so that he can be ready for the next woman, ready to love her to the hilt. Now, if you've got Puritan morality in your veins as I do, you like to hasten on to say that he's talking about life situations. This is a person who takes every situation as it comes and squeezes every bit of meaning out of it, then lets it go to be ready for how God is confronting him in the next situation. He then moves into that situation and wrings it out.

You don't have any more lifetime than you have right now in this room. You never had any more and you never will have any more. One of the great tragedies of life is that we don't experience most of our lives. We don't stand at attention. Think of the living that you and I have done since we got up this morning and did not have selfhood enough to stand at attention long enough to take it into ourselves. We were at a worship service. There's a lot wrong with that worship service, but what was wrong with it was just as important as what was right with it. The person of faith dares to be sensitive. She marches through life at attention, as the one who loves and does not lose her soul to any moment. Yes, yesterday was given. Tremendous. But tomorrow is at hand. I move on to embrace it.

The free person is *the actor*. He plays many roles in life. My gracious, I'm just amazed at the number of roles I play. Being the husband of Lyn is not an easy role, but it's an exciting one. But Lyn isn't the meaning of my life. However, that's my role, and I live it to the hilt, but I don't lose my soul to it. I'm also a clergyman. I tell you, in our day that's a hard role to play. What does it mean to authentically create the role of a clergyman? I am the clergyman of the 20th century. I say, let every clergyman be exactly like me. That's what it means to play a role to the hilt. Now, granted, there have been many Hamlets played, but a man who did not say to himself, "Mine is the greatest Hamlet," didn't know what he was doing. And he never came off with it. That's what I mean, you play your role to the hilt without losing your soul to it.

You play many roles, and they're complex roles, and you play each one as if it's the only role you have, while at the same time you're wholly detached from it. Luther called this a holy nonchalance toward life. An utterly serious attachment that makes the pharisee think you're a pharisee, and an utter nonchalance that makes the pharisee think you're a libertine: this is the person of faith who's never boxed in. About the time you pigeonhole him over here, he's over there. It's that kind of a picture. He's giving himself with all that he is to the other in any given situation. This is the one who really cares about life. He cares about people. He is the concerned one.

And Camus said that the free person is *the conqueror*, the one who sees that life has a billion causes and stands before them all. This is to say with Paul, everything is permitted, and yet not everything is expedient. He meant you just have to choose. Everything is permitted and yet you have to choose. That's frightening, because you know that when you stand before that woman and say "yes" to her, you are saying "no" to all the rest. And so it is in choosing a vocation, the overwhelmingness of possibility.

With some little narrow god I don't have much of a problem. However, the person of faith has insecurity, for everything is good and everything is permitted.

The person of faith dares to launch into a cause, knowing that that cause is not going to save his soul, that that cause is not going to save history's soul. They tell me that even the pyramids are beginning to round off. He sees that every cause in the world is finally a ridiculous cause, because if bodies in the sky collide and earth isn't anymore, then our human history isn't anymore.

He's like the man who sees that ten thousand years from now somebody is going to pick up a broken cup handle, take it to the archaeologist who's gonna say, "Mmm, that comes from those people who came roughly between Ramses I and Einstein." And anyone who doesn't see that, and embrace it, doesn't know what it means to love. This is the person who is sensitive. This is the one who cares. This is the one who creates for some other reason than feeling good about a job well done or life well lived.

The Free Person of Faith has the Freedom to be Exposed

The person in faith has the freedom to be exposed. By exposure I mean the one who dares to act and takes within herself the risk of acting. She acts without any appeal. Finally, no one has any three good reasons that justify any act ever done.

If I decide that this criterion is going to approve my act, my question is How did you decide upon that criterion? Every moral deed is finally without any appeal. This is what Paul meant when he said that a man is only justified by faith. The free person is the one who dares to risk himself without ever again seeking any unambiguous knowledge that he did the right thing.

And he's the man who lives with the consequences of his act. This is to say you never do anything in which you know the consequences beforehand. The person of faith takes into himself the consequences, whatever they may be, before he does his deed. Therefore, after the deed he does not say that's the fault of my having a neurotic Papa, or that's the fault of that campus chaplain who advised me to marry this slob. No. He takes responsibility for his own actions, his own existence.

I tell you once again, I came out of a family where my Papa was neurotic. Am I the product of a neurotic father? No! I am Joseph Wesley Mathews. I am responsible for every ounce of me. That's what it means to be a free man in Jesus Christ. It wasn't that I married some old shrew and therefore became this mouse. I resent it when someone says that women castrate men. Now, mark you, they do that, but when you find a man who excuses himself as castrated by his wife, hell, he had all sorts of possibilities and decided to be castrated. He's accountable if he is sexless. This is the free man. He blames nobody or no-thing. No external circumstances have anything whatsoever to do with my life. I am my life. That's the freedom that's in Jesus Christ.

The Free Person of Faith has the Freedom to be Disciplined

And lastly, this person is free to be a disciplined one. I don't mean by disciplined those schedules that a freshman puts up in his room about when he's going to brush his teeth or when he's going to get up in the morning. I don't care when he gets up. I'm interested in what he does when he gets up.

By discipline I mean the one who's taken upon himself to be himself in the civilizing process. This comes to me in the form of the indicative and the imperative. The Gospel of Jesus Christ strikes me as the indicative. That's just the *word*. Joseph, you are loved of God. But when I receive that indicative as the indicative of my life, it becomes the imperative of my life. That is to say, I shall be what I am. I am a forgiven man. Therefore, I will be a forgiven man in every life situation. I am a received man. Therefore in every life situation I will be the received man. This is to say that I can receive you. Do you understand that? It is not an imperative that comes from the outside. It's my imperative, the one I put on myself. I shall be what I am. I shall ever become what I be.

The person of faith is set free to be the utterly disciplined person. In the great indicative of the gospel, I expect you to expect to find me, wherever you meet me, under whatever circumstances, standing as a free man. I must expect you and all of history to expect to find Joseph Wesley Mathews as the free man he is and has decided to be.

Now, whether you find me that way or not, that's beside the point. I'm not even talking about that. That all people shall always expect to find me a free man, that's what I mean by discipline. I must always be, and mark you, it's a twenty-four-a-day job, a life-long job. I'm the one who disciplines myself, demands of myself, demands that history demands of me that I be standing here giving myself for the civilizing process.

You're never going to decide how I give my life. I alone decide. But you must always demand that my life be given.

Let's pray. Prayer is the most horrifying human activity in the world. Whatever else it is, it means you come to terms with who you are and have decided to be. You may have thought you gave up private devotions because they didn't have any meaning. Today that's not the real problem. You know now you have to come to terms with your freedom to be in every moment.

Oh Thou, who dost ever remain the naught that intrudes in our life as the only fullness, have mercy on us. Amen.

The Church Lecture

The Dynamical Understanding of the People of God

The Theoretical Task – Clarifying Our Understanding of the Trinity

Our task, the theoretical task of the church in our day, is to get stated in clear terms what we mean by the Trinity – God, Christ, and Holy Spirit, what we have been talking about up till now in the seminar – so that the 20th century person can understand it and choose to live out of that profound understanding. That's our basic task. Your job and my job are not done until we are able to get that said so that it gets communicated to "the last fat lady" in the back of the audience. Now, we are ready to consider "church."

Before I start on what we mean when we say "church" in the 20th century, I want to again read a bit of poetry. Right now I think this is the greatest poem ever written. Tomorrow I'll decide that something else is the greatest poem. You see, it is my business to decide what is the greatest poem ever written.

II
I was so weary of the world,
I was so sick of it,
everything was tainted with myself,
skies, trees, flowers, birds, water,
people, houses, streets, vehicles, machines,
nations, armies, war, peace-making,
work, recreation, governing, anarchy,
it was all tainted with myself, I knew it all to start with
because it was all myself.

When I gathered flowers, I knew it was myself plucking my own flowering.
When I went in a train, I knew it was myself travelling by my own invention.
When I heard the cannon of the war, I listened with my own ears to
    my own destruction.
When I saw the torn dead, I knew it was my own torn dead body.
It was all me, I had done it all in my own flesh.

III
I shall never forget the maniacal horror of it all in the end . . .
I anticipated it all, all in my own soul
because I was the author and the result
I was the God and the creation at once;
. . . it was a maniacal horror in the end.

I was a lover, I kissed the woman I loved,
and God of horror, I was also kissing myself.

I was a father and a begetter of children,
and oh, oh horror, I was begetting and conceiving in my own body.

IV
At last came death, sufficiency of death,
and that at last relieved me, I died. . . .

V
God, but it is good to have died, to have been trodden out,
trodden to nought by the sour, dead earth,
quite to nought,
absolutely to nothing,
nothing. . . .

For when it is quite, quite nothing, then it is everything.
When I am trodden quite out, quite, quite out,
every vestige gone, then I am here
risen and setting my foot on another world
risen, accomplishing a resurrection
risen, not born again, but risen, body the same as before,
new beyond knowledge of newness, alive beyond life,
proud beyond inkling or furthest conception of pride,
living where life was never yet dreamed of, or even hinted at,
here, in the other world, still terrestrial
myself, the same as before, yet unaccountably new.

VI
I, in the sour black tomb, trodden to absolute death
I put out my hand in the night, one night, and my hand
touched that which was verily not me,
verily it was not me.
Where I had been was a sudden blaze,
a sudden flaring blaze!
So I put my hand out further, a little further
and I felt that which was not I,
it verily was not I,
it was the unknown.

Ha, I was a blaze leaping up!
I was a tiger bursting into sunlight.
I was greedy, I was mad for the unknown.
I, new-risen, resurrected, starved from the tomb,
starved from a life of devouring always myself,
now here was I, new-awakened, with my hand stretching out
and touching the unknown, the real unknown, the unknown unknown.

("New Heaven and Earth," *The Collected Poems of D. H. Lawrence*, pp. 256-59)

Now this bit of gospel poetry:

> Never think that I have come to bring peace upon the earth. No, I have not come to bring peace but a sword! For I have come to set man against his own father, [If you feel a little bourgeois, and want to leave, feel free, and come back when I have finished.] a daughter against her own mother, and a daughter-in-law against her mother-in-law. A man's enemies shall be those who live in his own house. Anyone who puts love for father or mother above his love for me does not deserve to be mine, and he who loves son or daughter more than me is not worthy of me, and neither is the man who refuses to take up his cross [that is, lay down his life, in case you've got that wrong: neither is the man who is not willing to lay down his life] and follow my way. The man who has found his whole life will lose it, but the man who has lost it for my sake will find it. Whoever welcomes you, welcomes me; and whoever welcomes me is welcoming the one who sent me. (Mt. 10: 34-40, JBP)

This is the 49th year of the radical renewal of the church in the 20th century. This ought not to come as any surprise that the church has a new operating image, for Calvin long since said the church is never without historical manifestation; but it is never synonymous with any historical manifestation.

Master and Functional Images of the Church Throughout History

In the history of the church there have been great master and functional images. In the ancient church, she saw herself as the eschatological congregation that put the limits of temporality before all mankind and promised that if in the everydayness of their lives they would live before those radical limits, they would discover in the here and now what Life is, with a capital "L."

The second great operating image of the church was forged in the medieval period. The church grasped itself as the super-agency that welded together every facet of the structures of humanity that disclosed the final meaning of their existence. She promised humanity that if in the midst of the everydayness of their lives they would live before the final meaning of that life, they would discover what Life – spelled with a capital "L" – is all about.

The Reformers' image was that of a priestly/prophetic community that held before all of humankind the propensity to live in the illusion that hid us from the actualities of life. She promised humans that if they would come to terms in the midst of the everydayness of their life and deal with their illusions about themselves, new possibility would be theirs, which would be Life – with a capital "L" – from the bottom up.

Now, to continue my oversimplification, each of these images was perverted. The first one ended up in the desert; the second one ended up in ecclesiastical tyranny; and you and I are the living embodiment of the perversion of the third great image.

Here we have to slow down just a bit. It seems to me that this happened about a hundred years ago in America at the close of the Civil War, when the new science impacted our nation, as it had not impacted it up to that time. In the midst of that impact the church lost its courage to understand itself as significantly engaged in the civilizing process. When you and I lose that kind of a sense of significant engagement, we have to conjure up some kind of pseudo-image of significance. The one the church brought into being in our time was that of the defender of the status quo.

It reminds me of that ancient Greek myth: out on the edges was chaos, then the area of the irrational, the area of the unexpected, the area of change. Humanity with its rational capacity built a little island of security in the midst of that irrationality and then put a dyke around it to keep out change, and then created a class of people called dyke walkers, sometimes known as clergymen, whose job it was to see to it that no change poked through that dyke. If any trickle came, they stuck in their finger or their arm, or, if necessary, their head. That's the picture of the church, as she became the defender, the knight in shining armor defending the status quo.

I have the idea most of you are still trapped in that kind of morality, and not only trapped in it, but you still think you have to defend it. There's a kind of irony in it. The Lord is sneaky – instead of attacking the dyke, the Lord moved in the 20th century down underneath that island and shook it until its teeth rattled and the church was left with its sword drawn to defend it. And guess what, it looked around and it hasn't got a damn thing to defend anymore.

Being trapped, it moved to the second stage that we call the sick, sick, sickness of the church. That was turning in upon itself so that we became a group of crippled characters huddled together, trying to waddle to the grave propping one another's psyches up. That was the end of the road of the detachment of the church from significant engagement in the world. I do not mean to belabor this. I only want to point very quickly to three indications of this sickness.

Three Sicknesses in the Church Today

One of our sicknesses in the church today has to do with *doctrinalism.* Whenever any person or group of people no longer has a sense of creative involvement, they become the defenders of a body of truth. That is to say, whenever you have to defend God, you can be damn sure it's not God that you are defending but some little reductionistic concept in your mind out of which you are trying to suck some kind of meaning. God is that goingonness, that thereness, which has no need of defense and cannot be defended. If you get yourself worked up about little old atheists here and little old atheists there, you can be sure that you are not concerned with God in any way whatsoever, but some abstract concept that you think is of importance and comfort to you.

Also, by defending doctrine I'd point to the way we use, or don't use, the term "Christ." Whenever you sense you are defending Christ, you can be sure it is not the Christ Happening you are talking about but some abstract category. And some of you are almost ashamed to use the word "Christ." All Christ ever meant for you was some kind of an abstract concept which now you grasp is as empty as it was in the beginning. Therefore, your rebellion against that term has nothing whatsoever to do with the reality that term has pointed to in history. That reality has no need of your defense or anybody else's, and cannot be defended. That's the happening that judges you. You never judged it and you never could judge it. And whenever you find it necessary to defend the church, you can be sure that it is not the church you are defending. It cannot be defended, and has no need of it.

The second manifestation of our sickness is *institutionalism.* I didn't say "institution." Mark you, there are young squirts running around who are attacking the palaces as if the evil is in structures. What are they talking about? There isn't such a thing as social existence without structure. There is no such thing as a marriage without structure; there isn't any friendship that is not structured. Structure is that in and through which two or more people do something in history. If we don't want to do anything in history but to waddle off into some phony work to handle the salvation of our shriveled-up soul, then we start beating structures over the head.

"Institutionalism" is something quite different. Institutionalism is a set of structures without a sense of mission. The function of the structures comes to be the maintaining of the structures themselves. That's a perversion, whether it's in a fraternity or in your family. Since you couldn't find a womb any place else, you may have made your family into a womb. That means you've got institutionalism in your family. We Methodists need to listen to this. We need to listen hard. We know more about how to keep wheels within wheels within wheels going and well oiled, I suppose, than anybody in the world. Part of what I am screaming is this: the creative, awakened, young clergymen across this country are not shooting their guns in the right direction, and therefore they are wasting their efforts.

The last thing has to do with *communityism*, and Lord, I almost hate to talk about this. Navel-gazing is not what the body of Christ is all about. Sometimes I think that when I worked in Austin, and we had a college house for students at the University of Texas, we made a big mistake putting the term "Christian" out in front – Christian Faith and Life Community. We told the students coming in that "this isn't a womb." They said they understood, but they didn't understand. That word "Christian" gave them the wrong idea. "Christian" meant to them a bunch of old ladies who made gentlemen's agreements that they would like each other and agree not to do naughty things. About the time some creative tension was about to bring something useful into being, the little old lady put on a band-aid and said, "Woo, woo, if you just got to know each other better you'd see that you agree." I always wanted to say, "Bullshit." When you understand Christian love as having a nice feeling toward a fine Christian person, then you've gotten turned inward. You're more concerned with being a loving animal than you are with loving your neighbor. And because we weren't the only sick part of society, there were little old ladies of both sexes outside the church. They brought into being the vocation of group dynamics, wherein one glows with the fact that they are liked by other people. The church picked this up, this kind of raw barbarity that destroys humanness. This is the end of the road of community. That's what I mean by the sick, sick, sickness of the church.

A New Operating Image: The Church is Mission

But, thank God, the church is forging a new operating image in our time: *mission*. Not that the church *has* a mission, but the church *is* mission. If all of us were suddenly on Mars today, we wouldn't have a mission; we would be the Mission of Earth to Mars. The old image of the church was that she had a mission, or many missions. The new image of the church is that she *is* mission. Not *a* mission in civilization but *the* mission to civilization. The church is not in competition with anybody. The church is the mission to the civilizing process. The tragedy is that we haven't put much content on that yet, but the content is coming clear.

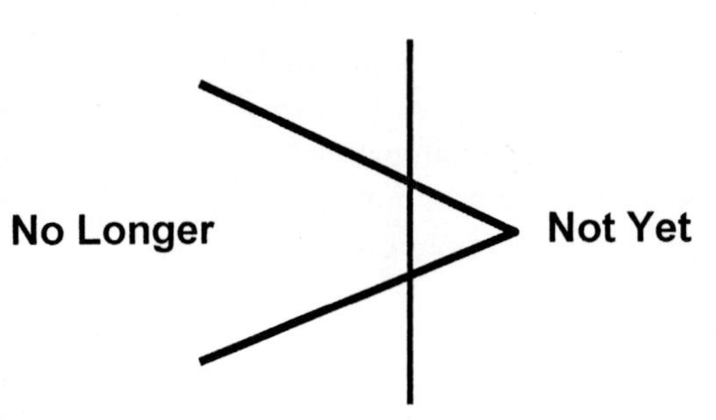

Figure 1-2: The Wedge of History

Take this wedge to represent the goingonness that we call history – that movement from the *No Longer* to the *Not Yet*. History is not some philosophy *a la* Marx and Hegel, something you learned in school years ago, which you either flow with or get ground beneath. No, history is that goingonness where human decisions are made.

To speak theologically, human self-hood was made at the same time as history. But in our day, when the theologian is using social categories to articulate the faith, he stumbled on a more fantastic awareness: wherever you have this goingonness between the No Longer and the Not Yet, there you have the *elite cadre* in civilization. That is to say, the elite cadre lives between the No Longer and the Not Yet. The elite cadre and history are inseparable.

This goingonness of history has never taken place save there was a body of people who moved out into the twilight zone, into the no-man's land onto the beachhead between the No Longer and the Not Yet. They were calling into question the structures of humanness and their inadequacies and dreaming new visions of more adequate structures that would minister unto the well-being of all. They laid down their lives to bring these structures into being for the sake of the mass of humanity.

The People of God

History has never been history without this body of people. Call it what you will. Call it the revolutionary cadre, call it the prophetic minority, call it the testimonial remnant. History has never been history without these people. When I use the category of the "People of God," I mean those people who move out before us into the unknownness of the Not Yet and lay down their lives on behalf of the mass of humanity. That is the People of God, and when you see that, then you understand that God has never been without his people. God is not now without his people, and God shall never be without his people. The historical process is not without the People of God. It never has been and it never shall be.

The dynamic of the People of God has absolutely nothing to do with those who gather when they ring the 11 o'clock bell on Sunday morning. When you use the categories "church" and "People of God," you've got to be clear what you're pointing to. If you're pointing to what I call that twilight zone, that's where people are laying down their lives for the sake of the future of civilization.

This is not radically new. If you have any recollection of the development of the liturgy and the great prayer of the congregation, you know we took that prayer away from the great congregation and now we call it the pastoral prayer. In the original structure of the great prayer of the congregation we go around the circle twice – first we pray for the various structures of humanness, the orders of society, for domestic order, educational order, economic order, political order. And when you are symbolizing it on behalf of the whole congregation, it means responsibility for every structure in civilization. This is what Bonhoeffer means by the category of obedience: that you are totally responsible for every structure of humanness. Then we go around the circle a second time in prayer and we remember those who have fallen out of the structures: for example, the widows, the orphans. We pray for the ignorant and the bigoted, for those in prison, and all the suffering. We pray for the poor and the unemployed.

The Perpetual Revolutionaries

As long as one person is suffering in this world, I intend to keep at it. That's the prayer of the People of God, the perpetual revolutionaries. As long as one baby suffers in this world we stand as a protest. We stand in revolt. We are the ones who utterly embrace this world and at the same time are the perpetual protesters. That's the People of God.

But don't you hurry out there, into the Not Yet, if you want community. Don't you move out there, for out there is the solitary life. I mean you stand there alone. The person who moves out there asks no one. She moves at night. She is a solitary. This became clear to me as I was marching in Selma. I became downright irritated with the white people alongside the line, but I became angrier at the black people sitting up there on their porches, sitting in their rocking chairs, waving at us as we marched down the street. Down inside I was screaming, "Why aren't you out here? This is your revolution." Then I remembered that the revolutionary of God is out there of his own volition, on his own, in the first instance.

This reminds me of my eschatological hero heading toward the place on the edge of the Not Yet, and he walked on ahead. If you want sweet community you stay back in the No Longer. That's their business. The People of God have a solitary life. If what you want is a real sense of entitlement, don't move out there into the Not Yet. That's their business back in the No Longer. They give you a sense of integrity. It's their business to remind you of the certainties of life and give you a sense of righteousness. They give you a sense of peace. That's the business of the bourgeois. If you move out there into the Not Yet with the eschatological hero, he's the one who calls the certitudes of humanity into question. He's the one who calls the justices of humanity into question. He's the one who calls the complacency of humanity into question. His life is lived in perpetual uncertainty, ambiguity, and anxiety.

Out there in the Not Yet, people witness in a strange way to the joy which is the joy unspeakable, incomprehensible, to the strange peace that passes human understanding. The peace that passes human comprehension is the peace that is no peace. It is the joy – do you remember the great phrase "the merry men of God"? The merry men of God are merry in every situation, even in the midst of those three hundred thousand who slept out on the sidewalks of Calcutta last night. The one out in the Not Yet takes upon herself the tragedy of the whole world and in that finds her life's joy and peace.

No Rest, No Time Off, No Rewards – Just the Cross

You want some kind of rest? Don't you move out there into the Not Yet, not if you have to have a day off a week, your wife is sick, you've got to be home more, be with the children, and you have to have a month-long vacation with pay. And if you think you have the right to retire at 65, then you stay back there. The People of God are on duty 24 hours a day, 7 days a week, 365 days a year, until they are 92 – unless they live to be 93.

To be the People of God you have no time off. This is not for pious reasons; it's because the job is never done. About the time you deal with some structures that misuse people and build some new ones, about the time you get it finished, you look back and see you missed somebody, or your new structures are abusing many. You have to go back and build another structure or radically renew old ones. Do you understand? The job is never finished. That's the task of the People of God, the ones who know their work is never done.

If you want some kind of reward, for God's sake, don't move out there. There aren't any merit badges in the Not Yet. To put it in mythological categories, God loves me just as much but not any more than he loves anyone else. This is why those in the No Longer are God's People and those in the Not Yet are the People of God. Each drops just as fast from the Empire State Building, and each dies just as fast. Back there they have all kinds of recognition. They pay salaries that can indicate you are somebody, they have positions that indicate your status. There's only one reward out there in the Not Yet – the cross.

These are the strange ones who care. I mean they care. If you want to have nice lovey-dovey relationships, then you stay back there. But those out there in the Not Yet are those who really care. If you talk to them about being a loving person, they ask to see your life being laid down for humankind. The People of God: there's nothing pious, nothing religious, nothing Christian about it. It's not some philosophy. It's cruciformity, with open eyes and a joyous heart.

Sometimes I wonder how our fathers came up with that bit of poetry, "the way it was in the beginning, is now, and ever shall be." Nothing religious, just the way it is, which means that every person who ever lived on one level or another with one degree of consciousness or another, with one poetic image or another, has made a decision as to whether or not she's going to be God's people back there in the No Longer or the People of God out there in the Not Yet. Every person who ever lived made the decision as to whether he is going to be a part of the masses upon whose behalf the others laid down their lives, or whether he was going to be a part of those who laid down their lives on behalf of the masses. Every person who ever lived – in one metaphor or another – made the decision as to whether or not he was going to be the Church, with a capital "C". There's nothing pious about that. There's nothing religious about that. And there's nothing Christian about that. Being the church is just a part of the way life is that we can decide to be, with all the passion of our being.

The Twofold Task: Witnessing Love and Justing Love

Let me talk about the task of the people who live in this no man's land. It's a twofold task, it's the task of the *word* and the *deed*, and the two are inseparable. It's what I call "witnessing love" and "justing love," and I say the two are inseparable. While the People of God are thinking about the line between the No Longer and the Not Yet, they are busy announcing the secret since the very beginning of time. It's the secret that everyone knows in his heart. It's synonymous with the self-conscious part of oneself. But one has to hear it from another to know that he knows the secret. While they're busy digging the sewer lines of civilization, the People of God are pronouncing the *word* that enables one to know what he already knows. They have a million and one languages, and they understand that there's not any content to this *word* other than the suffering of the person that he's dealing with. This brother pronounces the *word* to enable humanness – the *word* without which no human being ever shall be a human being. Our fathers were so very clear about that.

I need to point out that the emphasis comes down upon the *deed* and another time the emphasis comes down on the *word.* Now is the hour of the *word.* This is the time of the new evangelist, and I do not mean whatever is meant by the Department of Evangelism of some denomination. This is the age of the evangelist. This may give you pause as you rush into social action work, even as men are leaving the ministry to get really engaged in justing love. How stupid can we be? Now the church once again acts as the stand-alone caboose, after the engine has already pulled out of the station and gone down the track.

Let me see if I can spell this out. Yesterday in the church we were concerned with the laity. Tomorrow, only with the cleric, but not in the sense of that antiquated dichotomy between some characters known as clergy and laity. All God's people are born to be clerics, born to live on behalf of all. Out there in this twilight zone, a self-conscious person – I mean one who knows he's the church – understands that there are other people out in this twilight zone who would not be caught dead within the 11 o'clock service on Sunday morning.

You know some of those men and women in the twilight zone between the No Longer and the Not Yet of our time beckoning to us, "Come on out." I always felt like I was a little tiny mouse crawling behind the giants – the non-church giants of our time. I call them the latent church, after Tillich. They're damn well there. Let us beckon others to join those giants, whom I can name by the score, and so can you.

And yet, as I have crawled along behind some of those giants that wouldn't be caught dead being in the church, I've come to see something. I'm out in front at the same time I'm crawling behind them, and I am one of those countless nameless ones who went before, who kept this *word* in history. Do you think that the Jean Paul Sartre's could ever have been out there had they not been in a civilization that had been impregnated with this strange *word* of humanness?

We only remember in terms of mythical figures such as Luther and Calvin and Anselm. They were the ones who thrust this *word* into history. And mark you, the church always understood that its evangelism has to target those gathered in the community and those who cannot be gathered.

Since history began, the *word* has been spoken month after month, year after year. The play goes on. The *word* is about being a human being, coming to terms with your pretensions about being a human being. That's the role of the church. Our Roman Catholic friends understand devotedness to the ministry is to assume responsibility for keeping the play of civilization going, whether you feel like it or not.

The second way to keep that *word* in history is through a ridiculous inner faith, and if you don't see the ridiculousness of it, you don't have the discipline. Despite what sociology, psychology, the natural sciences, philosophy, art, history, and theology may be discovering, our role is to make it clear in history that the *word* is that Jesus Christ is Lord. That seems such ridiculous language, yet if we can make it clear it will keep releasing the Gandhi's of our time.

And the third way to keep the *word* in history is to *be* the people. *Be* the people. There are not clergy and laity anymore. Some of the people are lawyers, some doctors, some plumbers, some teachers, and some of them are pastors – they are in different disguises. Behind those disguises there's a cleric, only a cleric, the People of God.

These revolutionaries, these People of God, have a double task that is really one. Besides witnessing love, their task is to engage in what I have called "justing love." These people out here are always digging the next foot in the ditch of the civilizing process, right down in the midst of the political struggle, in the economic struggle, the educational struggle, the struggle as religion turns into the new secular religion of our time. They are always there. And they have to be there because the person of faith is always concerned. I noticed your prayers in the service we had this morning. You were concerned with the poor. You were concerned with the widows and the fatherless. You were concerned for those who were under the heel of tyranny. Now what in the hell, in the 20th century, does it mean to be concerned? Does it mean that you have a sensitive feeling? I remember when I was a little boy. Mama was always gonna die. (She's still alive.) But she was always gonna die. And she must have had several great final acts in history. The doctor would finally call us in, and they could hardly get me in that room to say goodbye to Mama. And they all thought that Joe had a real tender heart.

Well, secretly, I think even then, it wasn't that I could not live without Mama, I just couldn't stand the pain within myself of seeing my Mama suffer. Do you see the difference? If you and I are concerned about those who have fallen out of the structures of society, that means that we have to be pushing into the future. That means we have to call into question those wonderful structures of justice that left even one soul out.

And since structures of justice are always relative, the People of God are always on the move. For when the new structures of justice are formed, somebody spills out, and that means the job is never done. That's what I mean by justing love. That's what I mean by the kind of love that manifests itself in the kind of action that's always altering the civilizing structure in such a fashion that in depth and scope humankind is always reaching after well-being.

One more thing. The person out there in the Not Yet has already died. This is the source of courage. The one who owns his or her death can never be threatened by anybody anymore. Their death is already rendered up. These are the people who take the drama and act it out in the actualities of the world.

They're the ones who do the *word* and *deed* for the sake of the journey of humankind. They are the ones who stand there until their death, because they are called to be and have decided to be the church, the People of God.

This Is the Time of Sanctification

Sanctification in History

Every movement in history has been a movement of recovering justification. I do not mean simply movements in the church. I mean any movement in history. Whatever term you use – enlightenment, a recovery of humanness, a breakthrough in consciousness – it always begins with what has been stated in Christian terms by the word "justification."

Then as a movement matures it comes to "sanctification." When you use a term like that, you find it hard to shake off the idea that justification is a doctrine. Justification is a term that points to a happening that is humanness. As we grasp it, there is not such a thing as being present to humanness save through the gate of justification. There is only one door, and that is the Christ Happening. There are not two doors. Anybody who attempts to climb over the wall or come in any other door is obviously a thief; that is, s/he is a phony, a conscious or unconscious phony.

The Christ Happening is also the only gate to sanctification. Sanctification is a state of being. It is a dynamic of humanness without which humanness is not humanness. Because of the relationship between justification and sanctification, there is a kind of sequence. That is true, I believe. There is not such a thing as sanctification save on the other side of justification, but I do not like the words "in sequence," for you can reverse it. Save there is sanctification as a dynamic of humanness, there cannot be the dynamic of justification. This is your age-old problem which in our day is to be found in the term "existence precedes essence." Then you have to say that one's essence is that existence precedes essence, so that essence precedes existence. I would judge that one way of talking about the great drama of humankind is to be found in this interplay of justification and sanctification. Sanctification is that from which justification proceeds, which leads one to sanctification . . . and so on.

Bergson dealt with this dynamic in his *Two Sources of Religion and Morality*. I have used it and quoted from it many times, but only recently did I really read the book. He talks about the journey of a person or the dynamic of history in terms of the "mystical" breakthrough. (I always changed that word to "prophetic" because I was afraid of mysticism. As a matter of fact, those of you who work carefully with the great resurgence of theology in our day know that one of the main points is to say "no" to mysticism. Almost everything that Barth wrote, and Bultmann, too, was fighting against the decadent mystical understanding of life.)

Bergson speaks of the rhythm of the prophetic or mystical breakthrough. In secular language today we would call it an implosion in consciousness. And then he talks about the cooling off of the white-hot lava, a cooling off that holds history together until the next breaking point; then out comes the prophetic again. Bergson was caught in the Age of Progress, so he always saw his breaklooses going up and up. I am not so sure I agree with that point. For instance, he would use as an illustration of the breakloose the great Exodus happening as described up to the 19th chapter of the Book of Exodus. The rest of that book is an example of where that breakthrough solidifies into law, into the structures of society, which maintain the community until the next breakloose comes. You have a breakloose that says "no" to the crust of lava, the structures of existence, and then that new breakthrough necessarily has to manifest itself in the structures of society. This is revolution, radical revolution. This is why, at this moment, we are concerned with such things as morality. We have to say "no" to morality in order to be moral people. But we are building.

In his books *The Theology of Culture* and *The New Being*, Tillich worked on kairotic time. There is a kairotic moment in history, and yet if every moment is kairotic, there would not be any kairotic moment. You and I know that. For a person of the Spirit, every moment is kairotic. And yet we also know that if every moment were kairotic, there would not be kairotic moments. This, in a way, is part of the pain: it means that you and I are always only a little way from schizophrenia, and we must never forget it. Only the wild people in history know anything about the kairotic. There have to be such people. They are the odd ones, the ones that are creatively thrown out of the solidification of structures of society. The kairotic moment is the experience of living between the times. This is when you re-culture culture, and Tillich is pretty clear on this, though I never heard him spell it out the way I would have liked for him to.

In our movement, it was when we saw that *knowing* was not divorceable from *doing*, and doing was not divorceable from knowing. That disclosed to us the category of *being*. We had been in existence quite a few years, mainly on the knowing pole, just before the doing period, which started in 1964 in Fifth City and lasted just four years. Then the implosion came. It was the intensification of knowing and doing. Then came an implosion in the implosion, and the bottom was kicked out of being itself. We have been in that implosion ever since.

There is white-hot Spirit in the cooling off of the lava. That white-hot Spirit is the implosion into being, which is the intensification of knowing and doing. Categories like "chastity" would help here. Anyway, in the broad historical picture, or the broad attempt to understand philosophically the dynamics of the journey of humanness, sanctification is that solidification. That word "solidification" worries me, because I do not think that you experience it as solidification save you pull back from it. But what you do, so to speak, is to box up what cannot be boxed up.

You remember in the New Testament where it says you work out your own salvation? It is as though justification is passive. Something happens to you. Then, in principle, you spend the rest of your life working out that which happens to you. In the great debates of faith and works, that working out was interpreted as the way to salvation. No. No! The New Testament is about this salvation working itself out in every fiber of your doing and knowing and being. I think what both philosophers, in their way, and theologians, in their way, have been trying to clarify is how this working out is not the same state of being as the state of justification.

It is possible to be utterly solitary in justification. I do not mean that it ever happens outside of community, but it is utterly solitary. But sanctification is the making manifest that solitariness.

At any time you always have sentinel bodies that represent the masses of humanity. It would be interesting for us to try to get clarity on precisely where the sentinel bodies are. Back in earlier days, the college campuses were the barometers of the time in which we live. I do not think they are now. In fact, today, I am not even sure that the sentinel bodies are discernable. That, of course, is not a true statement. What it means is that we don't have eyes to behold precisely. They are manifest, all right, but they are probably not going to be what comes to your mind or my mind immediately.

The Dynamics of Sanctification

I want to turn and look head-on at the dynamic we call "sanctification." As we do so, we have first to remember that we are doing this for the post-modern world and that you therefore have a different twist. You have to remember that you are dealing on the ontological level and not the moral. As you look back, frequently it looks as if our fathers of the faith were dealing with the moral. I want to be very kind to them. If I were standing where they were standing, I am not so sure that they were only dealing in the moral. Perhaps we could take a Psalm, or Flew's book on perfection, or samples from several different writers on the holy life and see if you could work backwards to see how they penetrated through the moral to the ontological. Maybe what we are saying that by the time what the church pointed to with sanctification got down to us, it was thoroughly moralized. Anyway, sanctification has nothing whatsoever to do with our moral life, only with the ontological deeps of it.

The second thing we have to remember is that, although I am going to use the language of virtue to try to get hold of sanctification, in our day we do not think of virtues as interior habit patterns. We think of virtues as objective relations. That is quite a turn in our time. It appears that our fathers may have been dealing with subjective qualities. Whether they were or not, some of you emerging theologians have to dig that out and footnote it. But in our day we grasp sanctification as something utterly objective. Sanctification, to use language that we are clear about, has to do with the decisional dimension and the relational dimension, in which the decisional aspect of humanness has become manifest.

There is a third thing I would call on us to remember. In the past, maybe because of the worldview, it looked as if sanctification had to do with the individual. Certainly in this century, where an intensified pseudo-individualism has defined Western society, this was the case. I believe it was present in Wesley, also, but sometime I'd like to say more about that. Today, at least, sanctification has to do with society first, rather than with the individual. This is not only because society is the arena in which sanctification manifests itself, although that is fundamentally the reason. There is also the fact that a person who is not busy building the New Social Vehicle will never know anything about what sanctification is. You cannot be aware of it outside of radical engagement in building a new world.

These three things help us over a crucial problem that has to do with the so-called doctrine of assurance. That is, sanctification is a state of being that is in no way a psychological state; therefore, there can be no assurance in some feeling. I am trying to say it is not an experience; it is a state of being. This is its decisional aspect. You can sense in the Psalmist a kind of unbelievable assurance, the kind of assurance in which he is able to say all hell has broken loose. His assurance, if you will notice, is decisional assurance.

You remember that when Calvin had to deal with the problem of assurance, his words were, "There is no such thing." He said that nobody can be sure about his final salvation. Final salvation means that you do everything you do for the glory of God. If you are not sawing that board for the glory of God, even if you are, that is no guarantee that you are saved. So you need to be out there building a new society, but that is no assurance of anything. I do not even see this as debatable.

Justification and Sanctification

There is another great issue is the relation of justification and sanctification. It is not divorced from the problem of assurance. Both Calvin and Luther tend toward the direction of saying if you are justified you are sanctified. They saw that relationship as very immediate, or that justification and sanctification are two sides of the same coin. We have often used that in our day to get ourselves out of perplexity. That relationship is shown in the diagram below (see next page).

In justification we draw the triangle with the Father or God pole on the left, the Son or *word* pole on the right, and the Holy Spirit or Freedom pole at the top. Then I have drawn the sanctification triangle as a mirror image so that both spirit poles are in the center and the God and Son poles are on corresponding sides.

If we use the language of virtue to point to the happening of justification, we call the God Happening "humility." You can understand that. I remember the first time that was ever put up, one colleague was very irritated. He could not stand humility, and he was going to have nothing to do with a Christianity that had to do with humility. He outgrew that when he saw that humility did not mean

Uriah Heep. A person of faith is not humble before me; s/he is humble before God. Take the word "contingency" and put it into the sense of a virtue or basic relationship to life, and you get your secular equiv-alent. You are a creature, forever a creature, and that is humbling to know. Then, in the Son dynamic, "lucidity" is the virtue or the relationship that is present. In the Spirit part it is "freedom."

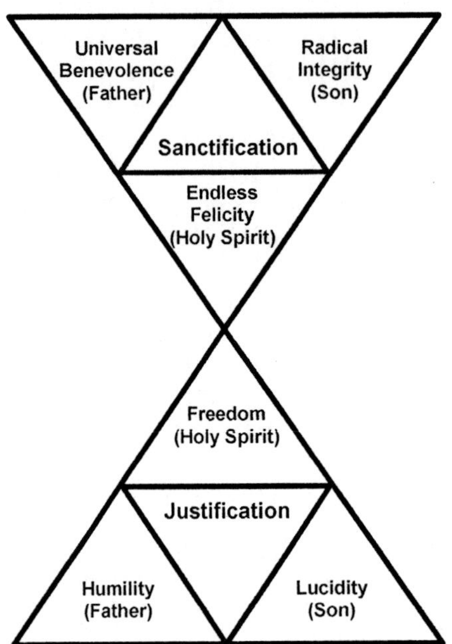

Figure 1-3: Sanctification and Justification

You can do the same thing with sanctification. The equiv-alent to humility is "universal benevolence." But that word is ruined for us today. Maybe "good will" holds it. The word "universal" helps to hold it. Then, where the Son dynamic is, I want to put "radical (and I mean by that "foundational") integrity." Here would be included the virtues associated with the stoic sense of honor. The self-control of Aristotle could fit into that. Or the category of wisdom could fit in there. Then, on the Spirit pole, I am going to put in a word like "eternal" or "endless felicity."

I would like to add that justification is the category of *knowing* when you think of it as a whole. And sanctification is the category of intensified *doing* when you think of it as a whole. Then the center, the intensification of both, is the category of *being*. It is right here where all that business about becoming the being of your being happens and no other place.

Also notice that on the left is the God dynamic and on the right the *word* dynamic. Since justification and sanctification are but two sides of the same coin, you can see a transparency within the transparency that is there for each pole and for the whole. That is, if you place the two behind each other with the poles corresponding, you can look through lucidity, which is justification, and see integrity, and vice versa.

The Dynamics of Justification

We also need to articulate the dynamics of justification. First, there is the breaking in of no-thingedness. In justification you begin with the external happening in your life, which could be the bite of a bumble bee or the death of your son, that throws you to the edge of the universe where you find something that is absolutely other than you. That is the beginning of it. It is into that vacuum that the awareness comes. It is the awareness that you have no other universe to live in. It is that simple, that mundane. Or it is the awareness that "My God, I made it! In a great big hunk of nothing, here I is!" It is very mundane.

The next dynamic, the most frightening one of all, is that that awareness in the midst of being over against finality leaves you no choice but to make a decision about the decision of your life. You have to say just one of two things: "Yea, verily!" or "No!" If you say "No," you have made a decision. You never say just "No." That's an incidental thing. What you say is, "Something else is going to be my god." It is like the woman who says, "I would do it but I can't give up my children." There is no sentiment in that. All she is saying is that she has decided that the children are going to be the center of her life. No weeping in it. That is just the way it is. That is what she's decided. She could say, "Yes," and for the sake of God, decide to give them up as the center of her life.

That decision to say, "Yea verily," is the embracement of the freedom that we are. There is the burden, but also the great joy and great fascination. That is what we mean by the Holy Spirit, only the Holy Spirit is the whole thing. The Holy Spirit took your cherished idol away; the Holy Spirit brought you to the awareness of possibility; the Holy Spirit pushed you up against the unavoidable decision. Then, when you can say, "Yea," when you embrace who you are, you be your freedom.

The Experience of Sanctification: Universal Benevolence

It is at this point and no other point that sanctification has any reality. After justification, you are standing in the center of the Spirit, but the happening of sanctification does not start there. No, you start on the Father pole. The best way I have to get hold of what happens here is that in justification the divine activity is pulling the rug out from under you, leaving you standing on nothing. That means pulling every rug out from under you, or you do not have nothing. Sanctification is not that way. God does not pull the rug out, but takes a hundred-ton crane and all at once drops it on you – CRASH! The bit of humor in that is that you are already standing over nothing. That is hard enough to do with just your own body, and now God has dropped a hundred-ton crane – obviously, the universe. Oh, God is mean, and anybody who does not see that God is an S.O.B. has not yet arrived at the center. Well, if you thought God was an S.O.B. there, now in sanctification it is squared, mainly because you have nothing to stand on. If we were on good solid ground, most of us could be a reasonable facsimile of Atlas, but where you have nothing to stand on, then it is entirely different. It is utterly irrational. If you thought justification was irrational, then sanctification is doubly so.

Sanctification is when you become aware, to put it in mundane human terms, that you were pulled out of the rear end of a cow. I mean you were not born first into your family, or into your nation, into your race, religion or into your church. You were born first into humanity. A cow had you, not your mamma. That is the hundred-ton crane. Every single fiber of your being right at this moment is trying to find ways to deny that, even by saying that this is an awfully crude picture – saying anything to get out from under that crane.

All this does not happen when you are sitting around on cloud nine. It only happens in the concretions of life. As Kierkegaard says, when you are beyond the naïve stage, you do not have to be hit by a sledgehammer to have the effect of being hit by a sledgehammer. Even your imagination can tear your world to pieces. Before, it took ten deaths in your family to do it. But when you are in sanctification, there is a subtleness, but the force of it is unbelievably squared. You know that right now in your life you are having the deepest spiritual struggle you ever had, all of you. And some of you are not going to make it. You are going to find three good reasons to give up. Not that I expect you to want that, but those are just the hard facts of life. You have to remember that you are not one bit different from everyone in the room. This is the beginning of the experience of being pulled out of the tail-end of a cow.

In our day, it may be intensified by external occurrences, where you have just a whiff of a culture other than your own. I have noticed it among people in the East who have been angry with me, a person of the West. I have noticed in them the kind of struggle that I have in me. One way to try to stave off having to become a global person is to be angry with those of another culture, saying that they do not understand your culture – an obvious fact.

It is not that sanctification, as we are beginning to talk about it, has not been going on for years. Ten years ago, twenty years ago, when you first got the slightest inkling of that hundred-ton crane, that was sanctification. Think of the hundreds you have known who, as long as you were playing the tune of justification, danced to the drummer's beat. But when they smelled sanctification, they sank for reasons you cannot even understand.

Radical Integrity

What I have described is not the pain. The pain has to do with awareness. It is awareness relative to integrity. It is as if the problem of lucidity turned into the problem of integrity. You can talk about this inside yourself. Remember how exciting it was to be lucid? And then how painful it was to discover that lucidity had a price? And guess what the price was: integrity. It has nothing to do with morality. It has to do with standing, but you do not say it aloud. You say it inside, as when you line up your teen boys and say, "Boys, you know that you got stuck with a stupid, broken, fragile father, but I want you to get one thing clear:

whenever you come back, he is going to be standing right where he is now." There is the pain beyond the pain of life itself.

This dimension of awareness cannot happen until the hundred-ton crane falls. I am trying to say that every person has his or her integrity, but it is the cause of the god s/he worships which defines that integrity. If you worship your kids, you have a kind of integrity because the cause of your kids becomes your cause that defines your integrity. But that is not what I mean by "radical integrity." In that awful moment when the hundred-ton crane has crashed on you, then integrity is laid bare, and that is the pain. It is only when I have to face the fact that all that my life is about is hundred-ton cranes crushing on me that the pain starts.

Endless Fulfillment

You are faced with the unavoidable question, the question of your happiness. As one of my colleagues said, "This happiness is no laughing matter!" You have no choice about having to choose. This is the pain of the human happiness of fulfillment. You decide to expend the freedom that you appropriated in justification. Kierkegaard, in the first six pages of his *Philosophical Fragments*, says freedom is like a penny. It is a penny until you spend it for an ice cream cone. Then you do not have a penny anymore, you have an ice cream cone. Freedom must be spent. Here is where Augustine and Pelagius had their confrontation. Unfortunately, many of us have picked up the Pelagian viewpoint, which is the rather obvious awareness that you are always making choices. You have to decide whether to go down this street or that street. Augustine saw so much deeper – Pelagius was not even able to follow him. Augustine saw that there is no such thing as a will except a committed will. It can be conscious or unconscious, but that will is committed. Freedom is spent. And then, out of that already spent will, you make your choices. This is why he emphasized the fact that new birth had to be radical. It had to alter that conscious/unconscious, committed will.

The paradox in this freedom, when freedom is committed to this radical integrity, is that freedom is like the woman's barrel of meal: it is spent but always full. It is as if when you give that freedom to the cause of nothingness, then that freedom which is spent once and for all is always there to spend. The moment you worship some idol, which is the means of reducing the weight of the hundred-ton crane, then you spend your freedom; and though you may not know it, you do not have it any more. Fulfillment is only when you take this full responsibility, which means the job is never done. Should creation last 40,000 octillion years, this job is never done. And this is what Aristotle and Plato meant by happiness. It is not having fun, in a mundane way, but it is this expenditure. Never again will the definition of happiness decide you, but rather you decide the definition of happiness. The expenditure of that freedom is like the new birth. It is a once-and-for-all which has the quality of being ever-again. This is your fulfillment. You want a fulfilled life? Then you decide that here is your integrity, and here is your happiness.

Then you say, "Look at me. I am happy. My life *is* happiness." You know you have always wanted fulfillment. I think of a colleague who is searching. When he set out to find fulfillment, he had the chance of deciding that his life was fulfillment. Your life *is* fulfillment, and only in deciding that fact do you maintain your freedom. If you think that happiness is anywhere other than your life, you no longer have any freedom. But when you spend your freedom for the cause of God, then your freedom is always full and running over. I like Phillips' translation of Amos 5:24, "Let justice roll on like a mighty river, and integrity flow like a never-failing stream!" The categories of justice and integrity are both, in Paul's terms, right-wisedness, righteousness coupled with joy and peace. But it is the joy which is unspeakable and full of glory, and the peace which passes temporal comprehension.

Loving God Is Being the Religious

For a long time we have wondered what it means to love God. In justification all of us learned the unbelievable lesson of what it means to be *loved absolutely by God*. In sanctification we are learning what it means for a person *to love God* – no piosity, no morality, no legalism, no abstract doctrine, just life lived to the hilt. I believe that our world today is no longer struggling in justification; it is struggling in sanctification. And we have the responsibility of announcing the *word* that enables people to name the happening of their life, so that they can *be* what is going on in this time in history.

I am talking about becoming a *religious*. The happening in humanness, which is the expenditure of your freedom in which you decide your life in the midst of that happening, is what happiness and fulfillment are all about. In the midst of that happening, you discover you have a vocation for the first time in your life. You are elected; you are chosen. You become aware you are set aside. You become aware you are different from other people. God never calls the clergy. Culture calls clergymen and laymen. God only calls the religious. God, or the Mystery in life, could care less whether you are a religious as a lay or cleric. The moment of resurgence in history is when society becomes aware of the mysterious election to be the religious.

Many of you laity and some of you clerics have known for a long time that there is a strange thing here. I thought, until recently, that perhaps there was a difference between a religious cleric and a lay cleric. Not so. A religious is a person who knows what I am talking about. That person has no question about being called. She or he is just called. The religious is an engaged person. Whether in law, business, medicine, or priesthood, the religious is engaged to the hilt. No more time belongs to the religious. The religious is a deeply disciplined person down inside. The religious is a radically corporate person, belonging to the whole race. No longer is there any sense of being an individual. S/he is corporate. The religious is an obedient person, obedient with a strange kind of detachment that allows one to experience the Holy Spirit as a power and a force most people would never dream of. Nobody can call a religious or not call a religious. The religious is just called, called to care about all of humanity.

Certain things have to be done for the religious – for all of us. In order to keep from being burned to a crisp, we first have to be given a *context*, in which this is related to the whole of history and not simply to our own little interior being. Secondly, we have to be given a *construct*. Try to do this alone, and we are lost souls. That construct, I believe, has to be multifarious, but it has to be a construct. Lastly, we have to be given a *climate*. By climate I mean what I am doing now. Those of you for whom this has no meaning, forget that you are here for awhile. I have been climatizing you. You have time over the next three years to work this through together. If I were you, I would read again *The Journey to the East*, or I would get a little book called *The Journey of Kierkegaard*. I believe that I would also read *Dark Night of the Soul*, and even though I might understand only one out of every ten sentences, I would stay with it until I got to the bottom of it. That is what I mean by being in the climate.

Who are you? You are like an advisory board to what may be an unbelievable global movement. You understand that without such a board there could be no global movement. To be honest, sometimes I wish you were merely advisors. But you are not. You are what I have been talking about. You wonder what it means to be a man or woman and launch out into the unknown like those who went before. You are on the verge of adventure and there are perils with adventure.

I worry about you, just a little. Now, you have yourselves a good life till we meet again.

The Barefoot Jesus

The Present Question

Today I am going to talk about the barefoot Jesus. When you talk of the shape of the church to come, you are talking much more deeply than just external structures. You are talking about the depth understanding of the People of God. That means that you and I not only sever ourselves from Christian bigotry completely, we also have to understand how that bigotry came about.

I am convinced that the church of Jesus Christ in the early Hellenic period slipped into abstraction. That shocking happening, which the church talked about as the Christ Happening, turned into an idea about the Christ Happening. The tendency of the church was to substitute a belief in that happening for the happening itself. She has struggled against such an abstraction for the 2000 years of her history but never really conquered it until this moment. That is one of the reasons why I believe the hour at hand will be seen in years to come as the church's finest hour. The victory is at hand.

In our day the church is slowly becoming aware that the meaning of Christian faith is rooted in profound empiricism and not ideas about life. I wrote an article one time called "The Christ of History." If I were going to write it again, it would be "The Jesus of History." I wouldn't really call it that, because modern theology stole that term and ruined it. I would say that up to now I have thought mostly of the Christ Happening. These days I am thinking of the Jesus Event.

I still like to play, as I did in that paper, with the Jesus-Christ, but this time let's call it the Christ-Jesus. This time put the emphasis on Jesus. This has to do with a deepening awareness of the spirit journey in myself from that happening of profound awareness, which is something of a gateway into the Other World in the midst of this world. The Jesus Event is maturation within the Other World, or learning to be at one with the Other World right in the midst of this world every day, every hour, of your existence. But the reason why I am concerned with the Jesus figure goes further than that.

The Present Task

It has to do with what we intend to implement. I have said many times that our task is to find the social vehicle for the nurture of those who care, who have become awakened and engaged.

We have said many times that each and all bodies of those who care must find a way to go through the glorious but reductionistic poetry that is ingrained in them, until they are consumed by universal humanness. This is behind the statement that our colleague made that he no longer feels like an Australian, but like a human being; or the statement I made that I no longer feel like a man, but I feel like a human being. Somebody later asked why didn't I go the rest of the way. I felt with that audience that I dare not. But with this audience I can. I no longer feel like a Christian, I feel like a human being.

Mark you, I say that I don't feel like an American. But I want you to understand that I am an American, and I am extremely proud to be an American. I hope that if our Australian colleague were up here he would admit what I know, that he is an Australian. I would hope that he would also admit that he is proud to be an Australian. What I'm talking about is on the other side of that. I am a Christian. I was born a Christian and I intend to die a Christian. I am proud to be a Christian, to participate in the glorious heritage that ministered to the whole wide world, directly or indirectly. But I don't feel like a Christian; I feel like a human being. To get this articulated, we cannot go with the rubric of Christ unless we go through the rubric of Jesus. That's why I am interested in the barefoot Jesus.

Visit to Israel

We went to Israel this year in order to study their comprehensive cooperative. There is no nation in the world that knows more about that than Israel. We had a fine time. I had never been to Israel. I have avoided going to Israel like the plague, for I never felt that I was ready to put my feet in the Holy Land, which is the source of many memories which are like realities in my own life. I was reluctant to go to the Holy Land for I was not prepared to go. But I was there. Being the pharisee that I am, I tried to see nothing that was not a part of the mission of why I was there. I do not recommend this kind of pharisaism to you. For instance, I passed within 10 kilometers of Bethlehem and never stopped.

But, fortunately, powers beyond my moralistic control sent me to a kibbutz that was at the foot of the Golan Heights. The Golan Heights is on the west side of the Sea of Galilee. Of necessity we drove through the famous Valley of Jezreel, or the Jezreel Plain. What a wonderful experience, for there, across one way and then the other, the great armies of ancient history marched. The coastal plain is flat, and down the middle of Israel is a long rough mountain chain running north and south. But there is a break in that chain up along the Sea of Galilee that cuts through. The armies of Mesopotamia would come down to Egypt and the Egyptian army would cut through that valley to get to Mesopotamia. Alexander the Great marched his armies back and forth through that valley. On the south side of it is a famous biblical town and later a mighty fortress built called Megiddo, from which the book of Revelation got the fantastic symbolism of Armageddon. On the far side of the valley, high in the mountains and hard to reach, rests what in ancient days was the little village of Nazareth where the barefoot Jesus grew up.

The reason that Nazareth was up high in the hills was that until close to the last half of this century, that valley was malaria-infested, and the only way anybody had any hope of living in that area was to get up high. Also, in a secondary sense, it was good protection from those armies that moved back and forth through Israel's plain.

The plain to the south is very frequently filled with fog and mist, and billowing clouds cover over what is supposed to be the Mount of Transfiguration. It has the strangest mountain shape of any I know in the world save Fujiyama. It looks just like a huge, man-made, evenly smooth, coal mining slag heap. And often I would judge that you see just the bare top of that mountain sticking out from the clouds. Never was I anyplace in the world where I felt the kind of strangeness that I felt there. This even includes the moors of Scotland, which would run a close second for me.

Part II: The Barefoot Jesus

I went up to Nazareth on the way over to Galilee and stopped on top of the hill. I began to reflect, and it seemed to me like the heavens opened, and there was a voice. The term that was in my mind from then on was "barefoot Jesus." I began to understand how, in the midst of this kind of terrain and environment, something like a twelve-year-old Jesus came to be. I believe that story of his sitting with the scribes and priests and confounding them was based on some kind of truth. That means that before he was twelve, something radical happened to the barefoot boy. And he remained that barefoot boy for twenty years before he did anything about what happened to him back then. Twenty years is a long time to call into being some overwhelming profound awareness.

As I stood there and thought, two things came to mind. One thing that happened to that barefoot boy was that he became aware, there on the edge of the Valley of Jezreel, of the awesome mystery of life. The clouds became the external manifestation of the awe that he experienced as he became aware of what, for him, became the absolute finality of reality. And the clouds enabled him to grasp the fact that this awe was not something that came forth out of his subjectivity, but the awe itself had compelling objectivity. I know not how it happened. But then this boy became aware of the fact that this mystery, which was final reality, was his father. I do not mean he was drawing some kind of a silly analogy that most of your Sunday school teachers talked about. I mean he became aware that he was the offspring of final being, of this strange mystery that seemed closer to him than any temporal reality that he experienced.

I am trying to say that this young boy literally came to believe that Joseph was not his father, but that which sired him was the Mystery itself. As a matter of fact, Jesus talked very little about "our Father" but very frequently about "my Father."

Then something else happened to him. I am not so clear how this happened. I think that in those twenty years he found that you know the Mystery in the eyes of another person. That seems to me by far the most important thing about him. You discover that you can look through eyes, and when you look through eyes you become aware of mystery. And out of this came the awareness that it was not only "my Father," but it was "your Father." Perhaps this became most clear to him as he beheld the hunk of humanity's eyes in human suffering, later in his ministry. I think he became particularly concerned with the eyes that have no eyes, the blind. He had the immediate experience, not some analogical abstraction, that this which sired me, sired you, and not only you, but all, and not only all, but everything.

Remember the story that happened later when somebody came to him and said, "Your mother and brothers and sisters are outside," and he looked at the crowd and said, "What do you mean? These strangers are my brothers and my sisters." I want to repeat that this wasn't drawing a conclusion from some abstraction called the fatherhood of God and the brotherhood of man. For twenty years he lived simply in relationship to these inseparable awarenesses. That is the barefoot Jesus.

John the Baptist and Jesus' Message

The next picture I have is Jesus walking out of the desert and bumping into a man named John Baptist. They became friends. Maybe John was the closest thing to a friend Jesus ever had. And John baptized him. John had a movement going and Jesus submitted himself to that movement.

Then it is in the movie "The Gospel According to St. Matthew" you see what you can forget, Jesus starting his stride. He walked down the road flinging over his shoulder, "The Other World is at hand, turn yourselves around and believe this." And he never stopped. He didn't pause to see whether anyone was impacted, and by no means whether there was some kind of follow-up. He flung it over his shoulder and moved on for the rest of his life, three very short years. Or were they very long years? And, as another aspect of the drama, as he strode along he would fling over his shoulder, "Come on, follow me." He never stopped. He could care less; if he cared he was no longer about his Father's business.

The interesting thing is that he looked back and saw two or three, five or six. I don't know how many he asked, maybe a couple of hundred. All the details are not there. Did he expect to get 100 out of a 1000, and then to lose all but 10 out of the 100, and then to discover that only 1 of the 10 had guts enough to stand? We don't know.

The Training of the Twelve

When he saw the little group behind him, he began an exercise called the training of the twelve. Take a look at that training method. He always walked, and as he walked he seemed to be always talking. He was throwing over his shoulder sayings, not teachings, but sayings. What do I mean by that? Well, he had no code to transmit, no creed to transmit. What he was doing was jarring these few into the awareness of the Other World in the midst of this world, which these people had always known about, but didn't know they knew. He was jarring them into existential, decisional awareness. That was his first job of training. It was not to prove that there is another world in the midst of this one, but to jar them into the awareness that here in this existence were the deeps of life itself.

The second aspect of his training of the twelve is more astounding to me. It's like he took those who walked along behind him and stuck their noses, literally, into the human suffering that had been around them all their lives, which they had taken for granted. I'm talking about myself, who got far too old before I became aware of the suffering, the incredible suffering of humanity. Like it wasn't enough just to pass a blind man on the way. He halted the troops and stuck their noses into that suffering. It wasn't enough to walk by a lame man; Jesus stopped and stuck their noses in it. It was not enough that they walked by the leper's cave. No, he grabbed them all by the ear and dragged them down into the midst of that leprosy until they saw, with their own eyes, with their whole being, the suffering of those who were sired by the same Father.

When John wondered, "Is he the one?" and sent his men to inquire, Jesus, with a kind of nonchalant and low-key style, just said, "I have no answer. But you go back and tell my friend John exactly what you saw: the blind see, the lame walk, and the good news being preached to the poor." No abstraction. He merely indicated the reality of the moral issue that they knew. That was the training of the twelve.

The Anointed One

The next part that got played out is what I call "the anointed one." It begins by one of the most nauseating things that I can think of. I'm talking about the absolutely ridiculous killing of John. I haven't found the right words to describe the silliness of John's death. A brutal, an insane death. The picture of course is Herod's court. He has some of his buddies in high places sitting down to lunch. Herod was not just a mean old guy. He had a daughter that was pretty and talented, and he was proud of her as you yourself are proud of your children. He sat there trying to impress his peers. He thought, "Now I will really give them something; I will show off my daughter." So he asked his daughter to dance. She was like most daughters you spend a lot of money on teaching them to play the piano and sending to dancing lessons; when you ask them to perform, they invariably say "No." So, Herod, like most of us fathers, decided to bribe her. He said that if she would dance he would give her anything she wanted. And I bet he had in mind the prettiest thoroughbred Arabian stallion or a little villa set aside in the countryside. But the last thing he had in mind was that she would demand the head of John the Baptist.

I cannot tell you about the vicious old lady who must have been extremely bright, far more intelligent than her husband, Herod. She saw in John the Baptist, this innocent, non-political, non-revolutionary figure who was just going up and down talking about religion, she saw in him a depth her husband never dreamed of. She saw her own demise. So she whispered in the ear of her daughter. I hardly know how to account for the fact that her daughter was so enslaved by her mother, but there was something going on. And then the shock on Herod's face. There were his peers. With great reluctance he gave the sign and John's head fell.

The next scene of the movie shows Jesus. He heard. And he shed just one tear, just one. At about that time, a man came by and said, "As soon as I bury my father, I am going to come and join you." With a kind of anger that you would not believe, Jesus threw back at him, "Let the dead bury the dead." And he marched on. From that time on until the day he died, he was an angry man.

Immediately he took this little band up into the hillside for the scene of the great transfiguration. He gets up there, walks away from them a little bit and turns around and asks, "What do people say about me? Who do they say that I am?" They gave no supernatural reply; they said, "Well, they think you are another Elijah. Others think you are one of the other great prophets. And some others think you are really the power behind John the Baptist's ministry."

Then came the question. He turned to them and asked, "Who do you say I am?" I imagine there was a bit of stuttering. Then they said, "Well, you are the anointed one." If you will forgive this, Jesus replied not out loud but to himself, "Why isn't one of you the anointed one?" But he knew, when they killed John, where the contradiction was. He also knew that if he dared touch that contradiction he would end up exactly where John did. And he also knew that if that breech were not attacked, there wasn't any hope for the poor and the lame and the blind.

Anointed to do what? You are the one anointed to splash your being against that which deters the possibility of profound humanness for everyone, and particularly the poorest of the poor. There is nothing mystical about the anointment. Then, if you remember, "He set his face like flint toward Jerusalem," which was the citadel of the powers and the principalities standing in the way of profound humanness. From that day on he was a doubly angry man. From that moment on I mean he really took on the Scribes and the Pharisees and the Sadducees.

The prime act of his life was standing on the temple grounds and delivering his fantastic speech of "Woe To You." His attack was not on the religious establishment as over against the secular establishment. Such a dichotomy did not exist in his day. And he wasn't against the establishment for the sake of being against the establishment. He was against the establishment because it did not do what it was called to do. Not only would they not enter the Other World, but their woe lay in the fact that they spent their lives preventing others from entering the Other World.

Jesus took upon himself the symbolism of the anointed one from his tradition. He was very clear that the reason he rode an ass into Jerusalem was to coagulate the symbols unto himself, to amass the symbolic power that had to be amassed to effectively throw his life finally against the established powers. From that day on, he was like a broken record. He was interested in only two things.

The first is illustrated by the story of the fig tree. The fig tree was a powerful symbol. If you remember, he walked up to the tree and said, "You did not produce any fruit." And when you are called to be the People of God and produce no fruit, you wither away and God raises up new vines in the most unsuspecting places. You who should have known about the Other World did not enter into it. But more than that, you stood in the way of the poor experiencing what it means to be human beings. Who are you, who are the affluent of the world in this room, who are you identifying with in this strange story?

The second, and he was almost insane about this, was being humble. He used the children here. Occasionally, when someone would boast, he would bring in the little children and say, "Save you are like one of these, you don't know anything about the Other World."

The anointed one. Anointed for what? To lay down his life at the point of the moral issue of his moment in time. The interesting thing about the anointed one was that Jesus never once said that he was the anointed one. In fact, you and you alone can say that you are the received one, that you are the one loved of God. But you cannot ever say that you are the anointed one. It is for a power far greater than you to say that.

It was all over in Jerusalem when he delivered his final great address, the great "Woe" speech, and the soldiers appeared. Then came that strange scene before the High Priest. "Are you the Christ?" he asks. And Jesus snaps back, "It is you that says it." It's like he said, "You said it, I didn't." The movie really ends here. He's done.

Forcing the Kingdom: Anointment

And now you can understand how the church, in pointing out what life finally is all about over against ultimate reality, said it is *anointment.* Schweitzer, in about 1906, wrote *The Quest for the Historical Jesus*. In that book his key phrase is that Jesus tried to "force the kingdom." We wouldn't use the word "kingdom." We would use "the Other World." He tried to force the Other World into disclosing itself in his time in history. He tried to "force the kingdom" by throwing his own being against the stone wall.

The bottom-line: at every moment in history the kingdom has to be forced by the anointed one. I have been trying for a long time to get my mind around four paradigms of profound humanness: *The Hunter Warrior*, *The Saint*, *The Wise One*, and *The General.* Someone drew a diagram with these names we've used and put the Jesus figure in the middle. For a long time I wondered what to name that center figure. Now I know: *The Anointed One.*

If you attempt to take the great historical religions of the world, I think you can organize them under the category of "the enlightened one" or "the illuminated one," as in Buddhism or Hinduism. And then Taoism is a little harder, but it might be "the victorious one" or "the effective one." Now, when you intensify awareness and engagement, you have the third category of being, the profound core of human-being-ness, which is *the anointment*, to lay down your life on behalf of the mistreated of the time in which you live.

That is what the Christ Jesus is all about. In the overall framework of the play, it all begins with the virgin birth. The church was trying to say that the way of Jesus is the way it is, period! The drama ends with the resurrection. Here the church was trying to say that his resurrected life began with a boy who intensified his life until his death, that all may participate in this resurrection. The question is Did Jesus force the Other World?

The Residue

What he did broke loose something that catapulted into being one of the most powerful spiritual thrusts history has ever seen, the Christian movement. Christianity is not the only spiritual thrust in history. Time and time again the kingdom has been and still must be forced if people are to be human. But here I am. And turn around and look at yourselves. There you are. We are the residue of the life and death of the barefoot Jesus. And, mark you well, the hour is now come again when the kingdom is being forced, and the thing we have learned from the man of Galilee is that the kingdom is not forced with somebody's life. It's forced rather with somebody's death.

You remember, like Jesus, Paul was struck down with an indescribable awareness. Immediately after that Paul disappeared for three whole years or longer, up to fifteen years. Nobody knew where he was or whether he was still alive. He, too, was all by himself, where whatever he was after happened to him. For three years he stepped back from this story of Jesus I have just told you and he looked at it and tried to stick his fist through the meaning of it. Finally it dawned on him, and he came back and built the church. He suddenly showed up again. And he had the *word.*

What he told them was this: "I've got it, I've got it, I've got it. In this happening God was reconciling the world unto himself. In the midst of all this, the Mystery decided to show itself to all mankind so that there might be, once again, human beings." I too can offer that statement of Paul's. It was such a profoundly true statement, and it was the vulnerable point in Christendom which allowed abstractionists to take over, so that we were asked to subscribe to an idea that God was in Christ reconciling us unto himself, rather than *looking through* what Paul said about what happened to a barefoot Jesus.

Could it be, could it be that there could be in our day, for the sake of all mankind, a corporate Jesus? It's a question of anointment.

You go around the clock once. The question no longer is, "What is the meaning of going around that clock once?" The question you have to face now, and you have to face it in absolute solitude, is what in the world are you going to do with that one life that goes around the clock once, not twice.

The second decision you have to make, and you have no choice, is to decide where the moral issue is in history. Let's say it's not where we've been saying it is. That's fine. *You* have to decide what it is. Once you decide you have only one life to live, then you must decide where *the* moral issue is. For you are going to use your one life where the crucial import of your time in history is. There is nothing moral about the moral issue. The moral issue is an ontological reality. No longer do things such as salaries, badges, and degrees have meaning for you. It is where the issue of history lies, in your own lifetime.

The third decision you have to make is whether or not you are the anointed one. Jesus and his disciples were getting awfully clear that somebody had to knock their skulls against the establishment which was smothering the suffering people of the time. Jesus asked who is the anointed one who will knock his skull against the fortress that was the establishment. Those disciples said, "You are the anointed one."

When you're dealing with your own life in the moral issue, it's a vocational decision. There's a chemist, there's a doctor, and there's a lawyer. When you're dealing with what I am talking about, those things seem quite incidental. The real vocation of life is what you decide that you are anointed to do in history. Then you do it. You alone can decide it.

The final decision you have to make is about your death. You have to decide whether or not you are a dead person. If you have decided that you are a dead person, the moral issue can't throw you. If you have not decided you are a dead person, the moral issue will chew you up and spit you out. You have to decide to embrace your death. You have to decide that you have one life, and that it is to be stuffed into the moral issue, and that you are anointed by the powers that be. I'm just dealing with the hard-headed realities of being of service to the poorest of the poor in this world.

Endlessness

Memorial talk at the celebration of death of John Donaldson Mathews, Joe's son

Grace be unto you and peace from God our Father and the Lord Jesus Christ. Amen.

I have been under something like the doom of death. Little did I suppose that it would come to fruition in the death of my son John. As a memorial to him I want to talk about the memorial I promised God I would give: that in some way or another I would be responsible to see that we found a way to articulate to ourselves what "endlessness" means. Or, to use the traditional category, what "immortality" would mean in the post-modern world.

I am not sure I am going to be ready for several months to get inside and spin it outward the way it ought to be, but I thought perhaps I might now, for the sake of clarity for myself, just deal abstractly and intellectually with it to try to get the target located. I sense that all of us know more about this from the inside than we know that we know.

Living in the post-modern world as a one-story universe – and you have to put your foot down hard here or you will get lost – we know and acknowledge in gratitude to God that when you die, you die dead. There are no "ifs," "ands," or "buts": you are dead. You do not even raise that kind of question. That is part of having lost any upper story of the universe. Death is death.

But the next thing you have to begin to work with is the transparency within the one world that you have left. It is within the transparency that you are going to find the reality for which you are searching when you use a category like "immortality." In beginning to try to look through humanness, it is pretty obvious to us – and to anyone – that what happens is that the Mystery comes, or, in terms of your interior being, the awe. You are located, as you begin to try to think about this, over against the Mystery, which you are aware of only in and through frightening dread and scintillating compulsion at the same time.

Once situated there, as I look back, the first "big think" that comes is something we have talked about many times. A person never finally lives life until he or she lives death. That is to say, John is now one step beyond me. I have yet to experience the unbelievable, wonder-filled dread and fascination, which is the experience of death; and until a person has, that person is not fully human. If you bracket everything else and think only of this, when you look through the transparency, John is now more human than his aged father. I think this is probably the first awareness that comes.

The next one is the awareness that life is as mysterious as death. It is pretty clear that anybody who says he knows anything about the dark domain of death, except that it is death, is self-deceived. Death comes at you as just sheer mystery.

If you are looking through to the center of things, there is just sheer mystery. But you have to do a double take to grasp the fact that life is just as mysterious as death. If somebody would ask me to say what life is, I would be as hard put as to say what death is, except for one thing, which I will get to in a moment. I do not know what life is. It is exactly as mysterious as death. It is exactly as wonder-filled, both with dread and fascination, as death is.

The exception is that if somebody asked me what life is all about, I could easily rattle it off. Life is mystery, life is freedom, life is love, and life is fulfillment. The interesting thing is that if somebody would ask me to say what death is all about, I could do it. Death is all about mystery, and freedom, and love, and fulfillment. That is what you mean when you say, as Saint Francis did long ago, Brother Life, or is it Sister Life? I do not know which, Brother Death, or is it Sister Death? That is, you are in exactly the same hands, in the hands of the same final reality, in life as in death.

When you get pretty clear about that, then I think you are ready for the transparency to become transparent. I do not quite know how to say this yet, and I have to start rather slowly. As you live in the Land of Mystery (this was true long before we had the categories), and the River of Consciousness, and on top of or down underneath – I do not know which – the Mountain of Care, and since you have waltzed on the Sea of Tranquillity, you have become increasingly aware that you are your being. When this becomes intensified (I do not know whether it is sudden, although the last jar of it I think is sudden), you become aware that you are simply the rolled-up ball of all the awe you have been. This is what you are.

Here you bracket the metaphysical questions and do not even raise the question of immortality, whether grossly or subtly, in relationship to one's attempt to define oneself. The ancient pharaohs were going to maintain the human drive of immortality by building pyramids that nothing could wipe away. Or it could be the more subtle and more crude personalistic philosophy of foreverness as the continuation of personal existence. You can even remember hearing people say, "If there is not a continuation of myself in death, I will have none of it."

You are dealing with states of being. You are dealing with the phenomenal in life that brackets the metaphysical, which brackets a rational explanation of the numinal. (I am on a bit of a tangent now.) When you see that, then you become aware that when a word like "immortality" or "endlessness" broke into history, it broke into history as a phenomenological state, as a state of being. People become *aware* of endlessness. That is what you are trying to breakthrough on when you say that you experience yourself as being.

But you can only understand that if you put it negatively. No longer are you aware of yourself as living. No longer are you aware of yourself as dying. You are aware only of your being. You people from India will have some understanding of this. That is to say, in the Other World I am no more alive and I am no more dead. Categories of living and dying do not apply to the Other World. There are only categories of being.

I was very irritated with the verse of the song "Come and Go With Me To That Land" which said, "There is dying in that land." There is not any dying there! But what I was not bright enough to see was that the song was theologically incorrect even beyond that verse. Another verse said, "There is living in that land." Well, there is not any living there! In the Other World there is only being. Therefore the rubrics of life and death have no significance. Only the rubrics of being have any significance. There is only being there.

This is what St. John means when he talks about eternal life. Eternal life is not something that is going to happen after you die; it is not something that is going to happen before you die. It is the eternal moment that is beyond the rubrics of both the living and dying. In the Other World, there is only being.

It is only when you get that far that you can even begin to understand what Kazantzakis means when he talks about "Saviors of God." Oh, that is offensive to anybody who is sensitive. It is extremely offensive to me. Did you ever think you are a savior of God? In the experience, when you grasp that you are beyond life and death, in this terror-filled awareness, you know that the Mystery, which is being-in-itself, has no opportunity to be except through your being.

Finally, you understand that God is present in this world. The Aboriginal people in Australia and the African people long ago understood this, although they had no word for it. God – and if this sounds next to sacrilegious to you, that is the way it should sound – or Being, is dependent upon my being. And although you never lose the sense of your own distinct being, you know there is no being without your being. And, since everything but being-in-itself, the Mystery, is contingent and temporal, that means that my being is everlasting. If I may put it into poetry, God and I in this state come to terms with one another. It is as though I were to say, "God, I will be your being, in my living and dying. I will be your being." And God says, "All right, all right, and I will let you participate in my endlessness." Do you hear that?

This is why Sartre's "No Exit" is quite different from the play that I am writing here today. There are mirrors there, but in this play when you look in the mirror, you see the face of the Son of Man. That means you and I and John up there in heaven are all going to look somewhat alike.

Section II

The Religious Life

Commentary by John Epps

Talks:

Meditation (1970)

Prayer (1970)

Poverty (1970)

Transparent Being (1970)

The Recovery of the Other World (1972)

The Long March (1974)

Hope (1974)

SECTION II: THE RELIGIOUS LIFE

Commentary

By John Epps

The religious life for Joe Mathews was nothing other than the human life profoundly lived. It did not consist of a special arena in which virtuous people spend their time while the rest of us wallow in the evils of secularity. In fact, some of his most scathing remarks were directed at those who thought of religion as essentially different from life as it is usually lived. "Piosity" was his epithet: for Joe it referred to a ridiculous fawning over shallow and very human sentimentality. It had nothing to do either with authentic religion or with life.

Religious practices, of which Joe was a lifelong devotee, were simply ways to highlight and dramatize dynamics in the very human, secular, everyday life we all lead. His talks on religious practices, then, explore and expose those profoundly human features of experience. The function of religious practices is to bring them to consciousness, to make us aware of important features of ordinary life that we tend either to overlook or to deny.

For example, worship. One of Joe's earlier writings was entitled "Common Worship in the Life of the Church" (not included here). In it he emphasizes that worship is a drama that we enact, a drama that highlights the shape of authentic life. Its three acts of confession, praise, and dedication dramatize three values of profound humanness: humility, gratitude, and compassion.

This may sound "ho-hum" to students of theology, but Joe took this basic insight further. Worship doesn't do anything for the worshipper, and if you go to worship "to get something out of it," then you're looking in the wrong place. You go to worship to enact the drama, not to collect a prize. And the reason it's important to reenact the drama? To keep that story about life alive and well and active in history and in our lives. There are many competing stories about life – that it's about acquisition or about patriotism or about victimism or about revenge – and each has its dramas and symbols that hold it in being. So we who adhere to the story of life as crucifixion/resurrection need to perpetuate that story so that it retains its life-giving power.

For many years a major portion of work of the Ecumenical Institute was in developing the "New Religious Mode." It was clear that most traditional religious practices had become so immersed in piosity that they had lost any connection to living profoundly in the real world. Joe's aim was to restore that connection. A landmark event was a research assembly in July of 1970. Joe and others on the staff presented nine lectures summarizing the research results.

The nine covered meditation, contemplation, prayer, poverty, chastity, obedience, knowing, being, and doing. Four of the lectures that were delivered by Joe are included here; in each one he was concerned to disclose the element of profound humanness of those dynamics:

"Meditation" builds on the fundamental sociality that characterizes humans, and consists of carrying on an intentional dialogue with your internal council of advisors.

"Prayer" consists of the decisions before the decision in which you focus your intentionality on the future you plan to create.

"Poverty" is the basic detachment people have from any of the things that tend to limit their freedom.

"Transparent Being" is an intensified journey of consciousness.

These four are about the dynamics more than the exercises. There are exercises that are designed to help us develop these basic human capacities, but the reality of meditation, for example, is not the exercise but the interior dialogue. Much more is said about these dynamics in the talks themselves. These comments are only to whet the appetite.

Two years later, 1972, marked another significant moment in Joe's grasp of the religious life. After years of intense work in the intellectual realm, trying to increase consciousness of authentic religious dynamics and of the social dynamics in local communities, and intense work in the practical realm working on community development in an urban slum of Chicago, something momentous happened. The Other World became manifest.

It was as though in the intensity of intellectual and practical work, another dimension of life showed through. But it was very much in the midst of this world, and not in some imaginary Shangri-La.

A brief word of background: in the past, the church expressed all its wisdom about profound living in the two-story cosmology of the day. When the scientific worldview collapsed the two-story worldview, it seemed also to collapse that wisdom. The result has been a conservative supernaturalism on the one hand and a liberal secularism on the other. The former verges on superstition, the latter on trivialization.

The talk "The Recovery of the Other World" explores life's depth. The Other World in the midst of this world refers to a state of being that is in touch with the mysterious dimension of life. It is a common phenomenon that is the wellspring of innovation, commitment, creativity, and meaning. But the experience of the Other World is quite complex, and before Joe was done, some 64 distinct states of being had been identified. This work, he believed, provided the basis for a new language for talking about profound human living. The Other World in this world allowed people once again to own their deepest experiences and not consider them, by default, as psychological malfunctions. Clearly its potential is enormous.

But the New Religious Mode and the Other World do not exhaust profound journey of living. Most of us have the impression that once we really reach our potential and become profound, authentic human beings, then we have reached a desirable state in which everything is okay. Nothing could be further from the truth. Neither history nor experience validates that assumption, which is based on illusions or wish dreams.

The religious life as profound human living is a journey with three distinct stages: the dark night of the soul, the long march of care, and hope beyond hope. Each of the three is described as it is experienced. The *dark night* involves humiliation, resentment, weakness, and suffering. It is not something you "go through." It is forever. So also with the *long march*, the experience of root-lessness, ineffectiveness, weariness, and unfulfillment. If you ever get over it, then you've simply given up on unlimited care. But then *hope* sometimes appeareth. This is not the experience of hoping to get into a more pleasant condition, but is simply hope without a particular object, hope in the Mystery. The experience here was described as ghostliness, ceaselessness, nothingness, and salvific presence.

"The Long March" talk includes the *dark night*, followed by the talk on "Hope."

These seven talks provide some fresh images of timeless realities and beckon us to join Joe in the adventures of profound living.

Meditation

Introduction

Without disciplined corporateness the reconstruction of the local congregation cannot occur. You are passé individualists if you think for a moment that you could do this as an individual, or that you could do it in your congregation alone. You're going to do that only as a disciplined body of people across this globe, marching together in step.

But far more true, you'll not come off with the sociological reconstruction of the local congregation if you and I do not experience something akin to a new birth. The spirit within us will be released in ways that heretofore have not happened.

There is nothing very unusual about what I have just said. Whenever there has been a radical revolution in the civilizing process, it has been built upon a new breakloose of the Spirit. There are many, many revolutions in history that have not been radical. When radical revolutions have happened, they have been built upon a new breakloose of Spirit or finding a fresh way to articulate what it means to pray, what it means to contemplate, what it means to meditate, what it means to be one of poverty, what it means to be an obedient one, what it means to be a chaste one, what it means to *know* transparently in the deeps, what it means to *do* transparently in the deeps, what it means – how shall I put it – to *be* your being transparently.

When you look back through the stream of history, this is easily discernible. Every social carriage that has been radically reconstructed has been preceded by a breakloose of the Spirit springs of life. Think of the great social vehicle of Hinduism. It's not a religion; it's a great social vehicle. Think of how that oozed its way into every consciousness of that part of the world and manifested itself in every social structure. That was preceded by a brand new invention of humanness that bubbled up from the interior. And so it has been, time and again, in history.

In these hours together we are trying to get at the bottomless bottom of the new religious mode. The black revolution is waiting, the youth revolution is waiting, the feminine revolution is waiting, and the revolt of the non-Western world against the Western world is waiting for this task to be done. And it shall be done! If you and I cannot do it, that will not upset the Lord. And if we choose not to do it, the Lord will not be upset but will just raise up a stone or a stick or a mountain and accomplish it. The times demand it! The one thing that's very interesting is the Lord always does exactly what the time demands.

The complexity in the charts that describe the "solitary office," as we call it, is overwhelming. I find it extremely difficult to hold in my mind. When the charts are put on the wall, this is the way I believe they should be put up.

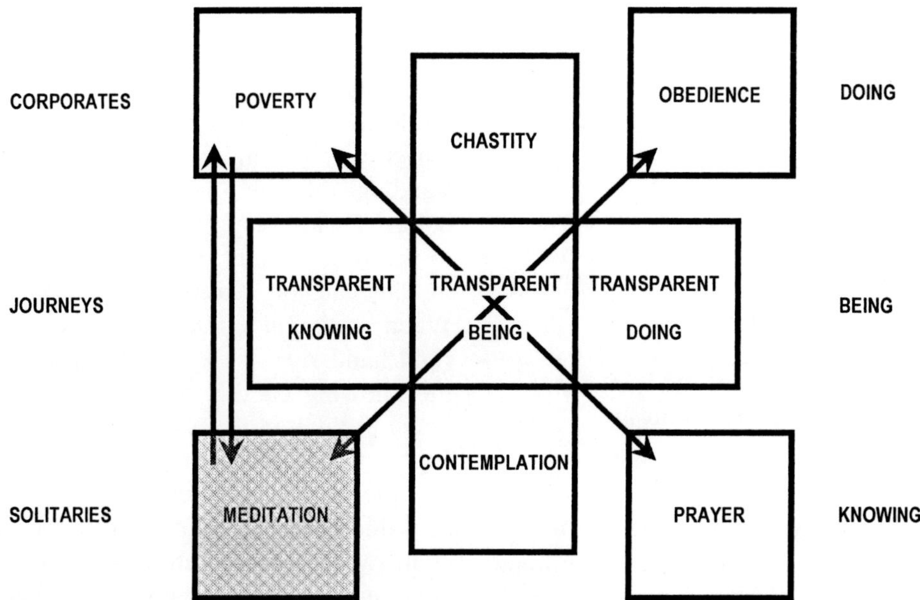

Figure 2 – 1: The New Religious Mode

Here are the charts: this is poverty, chastity, and obedience. This is meditation, contemplation, and prayer. And this is transparent knowing, transparent being (you have to say it a little bit differently here because you don't mean what most people mean when they use the words know, be, and do; for us they are under the rubric of the intensification of knowing), and this is transparent doing. The interrelationship of these is tremendously important. You have to draw arrows as are shown in the diagram. This is a dynamic construct and not a static one. If you are to know what you mean by prayer (see above), you have to see its relationship to contemplation and meditation and also its relationship to obedience and to doing.

Those of you who are familiar with some of the graphics of our group know that we began with the knowing pole, which shoved us into the doing pole. Then the bottom broke loose, and that drove us into the being pole of life. But being does not exist. Someone said to me the other day that a halo over any spirit person was a brass zero. I like that very much. That is, a spirit person doesn't exist. S/he is sheer presence, if you please. Our being does not exist; there is nothing there. It becomes pretty clear that being is an intensification of knowing, or being is knowing become transparent. And being is the intensification of doing, or it's when doing becomes utterly transparent. Having been shoved into the being pole, we began to try to grasp what the intensification of knowing is. And in our opinion, this illustration shows what the intensification of knowing is.

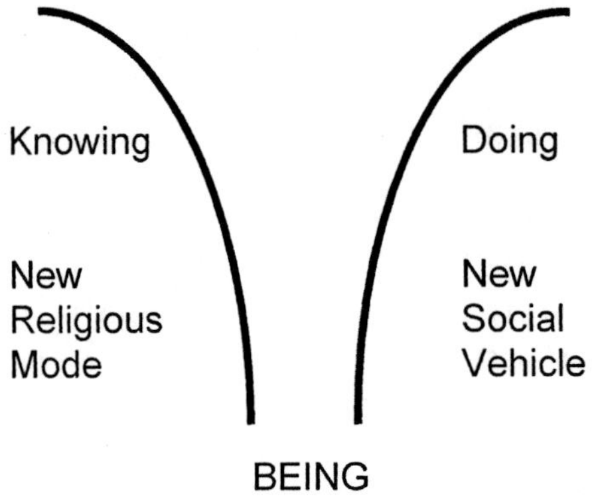

Figure 2 – 2: Transparent Being

As we begin to move with rigorous seriousness into the sociological or socio-spiritual reconstruction of the local church, we have to move in our own reflection to the understanding of the intensification of doing. Then, hopefully, we'll be able to grasp something of what is meant by the category "transparent being." When you begin to intensify the whole right hand side of the chart, prayer is the knowing on this side. When you begin to think in terms of the way life actually comes, you do not think according to the relations of the horizontal arrows. You think according to the relations of the vertical arrows in the diagram. When you're dealing with the abstractions, which you have to do, you think according to the relations of the horizontal arrows. When you are dealing with practical manifestation, you think with the relations in the vertical arrows. And at this moment I'm concerned with the practical manifestation.

Now, I have to stop and talk a little bit to myself. I'm uneasy because, before I do what I'm going to do now, all of you need what I call "lecture number one," in which we look at just the basic meaning of meditation. What I want to do today is to take that basic meaning and blow the bottom out of it. And so I'm uneasy. I've got to try to do both, give the basic meaning and push it to the depths.

The second word that I have to say to myself because of my overwhelming insecurity is that what I'm going to do this morning has never been done before. I'd like to be in a small group like our collegium in the morning before I start out over 70,000 fathoms of water. But I thought that because this is a research assembly and we've come here to really research, you could put up with me and my stuttering, which manifests that I am nervous, and I'll try to put up with your response to it all. So I think that I'm prepared to start lecturing now.

In our day, and this is a wondrous day, people have rediscovered themselves in ways that sometimes they just don't realize. And I mean people, not some asinine religious character like myself. I mean just people on the street, secular people. We have discovered sociality in our day as if we never knew it before. We have discovered that a person is in society like a fish is in water – that there is no such thing as an individual, no such thing as an individual, and no such thing as society. Both of these are abstractions. There are only individuals in society and society in individuals. Those of you who want to be gigantic individualists are going to have to learn all over again that only in the midst of corporateness are you an individual, and by corporateness I mean the intentional manifestation of sociality.

The second thing we've discovered is that we are freedom. This is overwhelming. It's not that a person *has* freedom. That is a degenerate 17th and 18th century psychologistic understanding of people. Today we have discovered that a person *is* freedom: you and I are raw creativity. Or, to use a phrase from the lecture on prayer, we have discovered that a person is *act*, that a person is *do*, that a person is *thrust*, as Luther would like to put it.

The third thing that we have discovered is that there is a mystery in life. Not the kind of mystery that goes away tomorrow when we learn more; but there is mystery that never goes away. And persons are the consciousness of consciousness only when we self-consciously embrace our relationship to that Mystery that never goes away. (If I were talking on that subject, I'd like to illustrate it for you in the scientific disciplines, in the hippie movement, and in the youth revolts.)

Those are the three things that people have discovered about humanness. Meditation has to do with the new discovery that a person is sociality. Contemplation has to do with the discovery that a person is mystery; we are our relationship to mystery in the final sense. And prayer is our grasp of ourselves as freedom. I am going to deal with sociality, so I'll not deal with all of these at the moment.

People have discovered, I would say, that they do not exist except in a social nexus. When the church uses this word "meditation," it is pointing not to our sociality *per se,* which is the first step, but to our self-conscious embracing of our sociality. That is, not only are you in society whether you like it or not, but society is in you. I remember reading a sermon by Dwight L. Moody. I don't know where he got it, but he said that God got Lot out of Sodom, but he never got Sodom out of Lot. Meditation is the self-conscious embracing of our sociality.

The word is used really in two different ways. The first way that you use "meditation" is to talk about a state of being. And that state of being is the self-conscious appropriation of our sociality. The second way you use it is as an exercise of contemplation that enables us to meditate in terms of a state of being.

When you do your solitary exercise and are dealing with meditation, that's nothing. That's a huge joke. And if you can't laugh at it, you don't understand what you're doing. It's like going to church or participating in a liturgy. If that isn't the most asinine thing, to go aside and spend thirty minutes going through that great big old play when you know good and well that life is out there! And so what that becomes is a means; the play in worship becomes a living reality in every life situation you're in. That's what the exercise of meditation is.

I'm not much interested in that point at the moment. I am interested in meditation as a phenomenological reality, as an inward state. That's where I want to begin. But before I do that in some detail, I have to relate to its counterpart in the diagram, poverty. In meditation and poverty we're dealing with intensified knowing; the chart of knowing comes in there too. Then I have to say a word about its relationship to prayer and to contemplation. That will be enough for me to do.

Meditation as a state of being in itself is brooding. But brooding never takes place alone. Brooding takes place only when you are conversing with another. And this indicates that meditation is dealing with the community before community, the internalized community. When you use the word "sociality," you are not talking about the fact that you are among people you can wave at. You are talking about the fact that people are in you. That's what the term "sociality" means. And meditation deals with this. That's why I like to say that prayer is the act before the act. Likewise, meditation is the community prior to the community.

Meditation as a state of being is a dynamic, like all states of being are. There is something going on, brooding. This is a relationship with others. Brooding is like making stuff. Yet it's a funny kind of stuff: it's almost pre-stuff. It is almost taking the void and bringing order before order into that void: I call that "pre-stuff," but it's imaginal stuff. It's the stuff out of which you forge your operating images.

This means, then, in relationship to contemplation, meditation mediates the Mystery. Maybe it would help you if I just say something really fast: meditation is that which creates God. If you let Tillich come to your mind, you'll remember that he talked about the God beyond God. The God that you and I relate to practically is the God this side of God. Idolatry is when you don't know that. You can bite here and not get any mystery, and you can reach there and not get any mystery. I think that the reason people do not know what it means to walk and talk with God in our day is that they no longer know about the state of being of meditation, which mediates the burning presence of mystery. That's its function, if you please; it literally creates God. Only I mean meditation prepares the stuff out of which you forge your images. Yet you have to remember that the Mystery itself occasions the meditative process that mediates the mystery. For only when life puts you up against sheer mystery is the state of meditation even possible. It's a polar dynamic as I grasp it.

As an aspect of prayer – and this is most exciting to me – sometimes I call this stuff an interior montage that is in all of us. Anyway, that is the stuff out of which prayers are made. To put that in a more secular way: no artist ever created the miracle of an art piece – that's prayer, if you please – without first engaging in the state of being of meditation. I'm trying to point out that you're dealing with humanness right up to your armpits. You're dealing with what you've been engaged in all your life, whether you were self-conscious or not. This is the stuff that creates the act before the act, which is that which alters the course of history. And history was never altered in any way except through prayer. That's what you mean by the deed before the deed, if you please.

But then what is the relationship of meditation to prayer? It has to do with this fine-spun stuff of pre-images. An image is always practical. The difference between an image and a concept or a construct is that the image is always practical. It has to do with defining myself in the concretions of life. And it's only the pull of action, or the demand for creative expression, that triggers meditation or allows it to happen. This is to say that nobody ever knew of the state of meditation who was divorcing himself from the practical demands of life.

Don't get this mixed up with the religious in history. For although there are many phonies, just like there are non-religious who are phonies, the religious are most highly practical individuals. This is to say, monasticism itself was only for the sake of the mission of changing the world, and I mean secular society. I wish that some of the Catholic orders could recover that in our time.

I have to relate meditation fundamentally to poverty. Poverty is detachment – I don't want to talk about that – but poverty is a state of being. It has nothing to do with how much money you have or don't have, or what you spend or do not spend – nothing whatsoever to do with how little you eat, or how nice your clothes are or whether you live in a hole in the wall infested with rats. That's not poverty. Poverty is the detachment from the things in life that wish to reduce you to your relationship with them. As long as you have to have children, as long as you have to have your wife, as long as you have to have your country, as long as you have to have your split-level house, you don't know what detachment is, and you have not experienced poverty.

If a person cannot come here to Chicago and live in this place, then he has to come. If he can, then it's not necessary. Unless one is detached in that fashion, this process cannot happen. The last thing you want to do or can do is to brood on the Mystery. The last thing that can happen to you is an address of the Mystery that desires to become self-conscious. And it is fundamentally out of this stuff that transparent knowing takes place. Maybe that's enough for the broad context, though you can see perhaps two or three lectures just in that area.

Four Rubrics of Meditation

I want to deal with meditation under four basic rubrics. I want to talk about meditation as first of all inherent community, second as pristine dialogue, then as ultimate covenant – fanatical discipline – and lastly as incessant warfare. I don't think that that's very good poetry, but it has to be poetry because that's the only way you can talk about it.

1. Inherent Community

We're trying to look at this state of being first this way, and then that way, and then another way, and then still another way, trying to say out loud what we think we see. First of all, meditation is *inherent community*. Before you ever become aware that there is such a thing as community, you already have a community inside yourself. And, ah, what a community it is for those of us who walk in the way of the Lord. There is Jeremiah, Amos, Mark, Paul, Augustine, Anselm, Thomas, Luther, Calvin, Rauschenbusch, and my great grandmother, and your great grandmother, and then all of those hosts who walked along the way with the giants whose names shall never be remembered on earth. We'll know them only when we all get to heaven. And what a day of rejoicing that will be when you meet my great grandmother, I meet yours. Now that's assuming a lot.

This is the community that is inside me. The ones that are inside me such as Amos, for instance, are far more real to me than most of the flesh and blood people I encounter. I used to make fun of that sentimental image, "He walks with me and He talks with me," but I don't make so much fun of it anymore, because Amos and I belong to the same tribe. Like they do in Africa, we link pinkies and we go down the road walking together and talking together. Sometimes he is mean as anything talking to me, and sometimes he is fantastically encouraging to me. And both of us have a little secret. He knows that I could not be who I am today if he were not with me. And perhaps a more important secret is that he knows that he could not be what he is without me. Do you grasp that? The things we have done to and for one another are wonders to behold. I tell you that Luther is a part of me night and day – that's one thing about this community, they never go home and they are with you night and day.

I just named one group and really there are all kinds of people in your being. The other day I was sitting on the floor and was a little worried. I heard a voice inside me say, "Hi," and I recognized the voice immediately. It belonged to a little neighborhood lad who is wandering around here these days. I said "Hi" back to him, and I said it as nicely as I could because I am scared to death of that little boy. I go out of my way never to touch him. But as we went on in our conversation, I said, "I think that the time has come to call the police on you." And he came back immediately, "Kids will beat you up, break more windows, steal more typewriters, and whatever else." And, you know, he's friendly as anything. He just said that's just the way it is.

Have you ever noticed that in this community inside there's never anyone who is really angry? They don't have to be. They just say it the way it is. Then they leave you with it. This kind of talk inside you is high shorthand, and sometimes the words are scarcely there. It's almost like a flash of an image back and forth. You are aware of that, aren't you, or am I a little crazy?

Have you ever noticed that even the most demonic people are there? Hitler is inside me, and I can't get rid of him. But he is never demonic. He just tells me that if you do what he did, what happens is what happened. And he's not mean at that. What he says, I think, is angelic wisdom.

And so with the neighborhood lad. That was angelic wisdom: "Call the police, and that and that and that will happen." And I said back to him, "I think

I'll postpone calling the police a little while." I sort of became a new human being during the conversation.

Outside that communion of saints I do not know who I am. Mark you, they're all saints. Hitler is as much loved of God as I am, and don't you ever forget that. And the black neighborhood lad, I think, is a little more loved of God than I am at this moment in history. But I do not know who I am outside of that great communion of saints. Isn't it funny how that phrase "communion of saints" became nonsense because it was not rooted in humanness itself? Everybody and his brother is looking for *koinonia*, looking for community, wanting to be accepted. When you dare to meditate, and I mean that as a state of being and not as an exercise, when you dare to be present to this host within yourself, you never have to seek the affection of one other soul in the world.

It's been a long time since there have been individual giants. Some fellow we took out to dinner not long ago was intrigued as anything with what we are doing, but he felt he had to say a few words against corporateness. And so we let him talk. What he said was, "Corporateness takes away your individuality." And there I was, sitting across the table. I am an individual, and I am the most corporate character that you could ever find. The individual giant is a corporate man, and he begins his corporateness in community before community. He walks and talks with those within.

The Roman Catholics have forgotten much of their wisdom on saints. The concept of your saint as one who watches over you, your guardian angel, is an example. I wouldn't want to exist in this precarious world without one. And I haven't got just one. I have thousands upon thousands of guardian angels.

You'd be amazed at how quickly Luther will move when I get my foot off the beaten path. When he calls me into question, it's really something. Some people thought I was just standing there nude. But no! I have an army that's on my side. But don't think they agree with me? They are the first ones to call me into question. They have beaten me to a bloody pulp many times. That's all right. We fight and then grab fingers and go on again. This is community. And when a person no longer has to go out and find some two-bit character like himself to be pleased with him, then he can spend his time trying to create community wherever he goes. But as long as you have to have community, you can never enable community for someone else. That's what I mean by inherent community.

In meditation, this fellowship is not finally with Paul or with Amos. It's with God. Yet there's no fellowship with God outside of the communion of saints. It's meditation as a state of being that enables you to be concretely related to the Mystery that never goes away.

What I am trying to do, however poorly, is to analyze human sociality in its deeps by using the phenomenological method. I'm trying, as a 20th century man who has a very particular way of using language, to indicate the not-me-ness, the just-there-ness that I mean to point to with the verbal sign "meditation." And if anybody intends to stand where I am standing, looking in the direction that I'm looking, at the object that I have my sights on, he or she will say, "Yeah." Now she might add that she has always called that "wonkus" rather than "meditation." But you see, that doesn't bother me, for I'm not interested in words for the sake of words but in signs and symbols that indicate the thereness that I am engaged in describing as a human being.

2. Pristine Dialogue

Meditation is inherent community. Secondly, meditation is pristine dialogue. Thirdly, it is ultimate covenant. Lastly, meditation is relentless warfare. Or – and I really prefer this – it's a bloody battlefield.

I say meditation is pristine dialogue, primeval dialogue, primordial dialogue. It's the dialogue down under all the dialogues that go on inside us. If you remember, I'm insisting that unless we meditate, we are not human beings. First of all, a person meditates whether s/he knows it or not. Dialogue goes on every moment within our consciousness. But when I use the word "meditate," I mean self-conscious intentionality has happened relative to our dialogue. That's what I mean when I say that the word "meditation" points to a state of being. Meditation as a spiritual exercise is something different. I'm not talking about that right now.

Everyone has the dialogue going on. It's very interesting to me that meditation, as it was brought to its fruition in the Middle Ages, fundamentally meant musing, reflecting. That's the way you and I are conditioned to use it. But in the 20th century, we have become aware of the fact that musing is impossible unless there is an "other." You only muse in relationship to something that is un-synonymous with yourself. As a matter of fact, the whole reflective process is grounded in that.

Secondly, when you think of musing, you think of an issue about which you muse. Recently I read a paper that I'd read a long time ago, Fred Gealy's "Encounter and Dialogue." The process of the dialogue he describes is something like this: life reaches up and hits you in the face. That's the encounter. Dialogue is that which takes place in relationship, so that the encounter gives you the issue about which you reflect. I want to come back to this and say that you go through the issue, but that dialogue always takes place with an "other."

Where do these persons within our being come from? You remember that Adam Smith, who wrote *The Wealth of Nations,* was also one of the ten or twelve greatest ethicists that the Western world has produced. Some of you remember the category he used of the *generalized other.* Think in terms of the 20th century definition of conscience. By "conscience" we mean an interior dialogue between ourselves and the generalized other before which we seek approbation and avoid, if we can, disapprobation.

The *generalized other* that is inside you and that you talk with is a montage of the society that you are a part of, represented through concrete individuals. In principle, we have a representational figure within ourselves who represents the whole cultural milieu that with whom we talk. In that sense, all of us who grew up in Ada, Ohio, or in the United States of America, for instance, are pretty much alike. If you grew up in India, it's quite different.

In addition to that, you have your own covey of persons who have directly impacted you, whose names you can spot. Freud got hold of one of these in the super ego, which represented your father. Now I'm not reducing Freud here. That *father* was the *generalized other.* But my own particular father is within me also, talking to me constantly. And your father is in you, too, but I don't have your father in me and you can be thankful that you don't have my father in you. So you have innumerable people within you.

This also includes objects. Trees talk to me! Buber is saying that the tree becomes a *Thou* which can mediate the *eternal Thou* in the universe, which for me is the Mystery. You know dogs that talk to you, and as much as I despise kittens, I find that some of them have talked to me. That's embarrassing. Lots of these things are embarrassing, because you have people you wouldn't be caught dead with living inside you. And I mean they are yakking in there. You can't shut them up. I think that the more you dislike them, the more they insist on being heard.

We have tried to list our saints for two years – those voices in us – and it is like pulling teeth. I'll not go into the psychological reasons, but when you have been asleep for fifty-eight years and you wake up, that is a long time to be asleep! This is why those of you below age twenty ought to break out right now in the "Hallelujah Chorus," if you are even remotely awake; because when you get to be my age, oh what a human being you could be, simply because you knew the voices that were speaking to you and you knew the ones you had to say "no" to, and the ones to say "yes" to.

The person of spirit, the one who meditates, brings self-consciousness to this community that dwells within and becomes a person in that very act. To be an authentic human being is fundamentally to decide what community you are going to live your life in dialogue with. This means that you begin to recover the names of those voices within you, understanding that everyone lives out of some interior community. You silly individualists are ashamed when you repeat an idea that somebody else gave to you. Why, how stupid! All you are saying is that you haven't even begun to be intentional about your community inside, because you've never had an idea that did not come out of a dialogue with others.

If anybody in the room ever knew Richard Niebuhr, I want you to hear me carefully: I am Richard Niebuhr. I am so proud that he is my friend and that he dwells within me and that about nine-tenths of everything I know he taught me. I would want to stand on the rooftop and say that with pride. Do you think I'm ashamed to take Paul's great ideas? They're mine, for Paul is within me, and I am proud to be his friend. And I think he is proud to be my friend – once in a while. This is intentionality.

Now for the church. To be within the church is to decide that the saints of the church are your saints. When we wake up in the church, the question that we are going to ask somebody that joins the church is, "Do you, with your whole being, intend to embrace the saints of this community as the dialogue you fundamentally listen to?"

But then I have to spread this, for the church of Jesus Christ is nothing. It is a symbol of all humanity. It stands for every human being that ever lived and every human being that ever will live. Do you understand that many of the hosts within my being have not yet been born? You say they don't talk? I wish you could get inside of me. It seems to me that these days they are raising a ruckus more than the ones from the past.

Then you always have a cultic hero. In the case of the church, that is not a strong enough term. Everybody has a cultic hero who represents the host of the intentional community within. This is why the eschatological hero is the representative of all mankind. Nikos Kazantzakis almost got to this in his book *Saviors of God* when he spoke of the cry of the ape. That cry of the ape is within my being. Jesus Christ is the representational figure that represents every bit of humanness from the beginning and every bit to the end. That is why we call him *the Man.* This means that all of life is dialogical.

The selection of the intentional community is that which gives content to my being. I am deeply persuaded that my freedom is my being, but the content within that is defined by the dialogue which takes place between me and the selected community of all the other voices within me. And, remember, it is this dialogue which finally gives form to God. Do you understand that God is the great Unconditioned? He will not submit himself to anybody's image. Yet he is only present in the images in which you or I, out of the rudimentary dialogue, see him. The depth dialogue is that which creates God, which brings God near, which makes God a lively thereness in one's life.

This is pristine dialogue. Don't you see, it is meditation that finally bends history? Meditation is the stuff out of which prayers are formed, and prayers are the deeds before the deed which make history go this way rather than that way.

3. Ultimate Covenant

Now I want to go over meditation another way, this time under the poetry of covenant. Obviously life is covenant. When you talk about meditation you are talking about the covenant in the deeps.

Israel is probably the greatest thing that ever happened in history relative to understanding that life is covenantal. I suppose you might sum up all of Israel's wisdom on this with these terms, which I got from Richard Niebuhr. There are three important things: one is that a person has to have an object of devotion to glorify, and without that, he is not a person at all. This is another way of saying that all people live by faith, and if it is not by faith in relationship to God

Almighty, then it is another god. This defines humanness. Secondly, a person has to have a cause to serve. No one can be a person without a cause to serve. And thirdly, a person has to have a community to be loyal to. That is the covenantal basis that existed in Israel. I'm talking about that community to which one is loyal

This is a dynamic covenant. It is always on the move and never stands still. I think that it is best seen in marriage. I do not think that Christian marriage is based on love in any form whatsoever. If you don't believe that, go read the marriage service in which the wisdom of the church is stated. You are not asked whether or not you love each other. You are asked whether you will promise each other. That is a moral covenant.

These saints within my being, you know, I have made a covenant with them. I suppose the quality of covenant is best seen in that old gospel hymn, "Trust and obey, for there's no other way." This is a rigorous matter of obeying. It is almost as if when I disobey Luther, he leaves. It is almost as if when I disobey Amos, he packs up and goes. That is not exactly true. I am going to come back and take that back later. But the one thing they require is obedience.

You and I are not going to obey one we do not trust. And trust is not something that is finally born by activities unsynonymous with our own. You see, I just don't show up trusting you one day. That is utterly impossible, because I know things about everybody in this room that they wouldn't dare tell their mothers. That is another way of talking about original sin. That is, every time you stumble on your colleague, he is crummy, and every time he stumbles on you, he finds crumminess. There is no trust that is immediate, unless you are naïve. For one thing, what we know about ourselves, and therefore about our neighbor, is that we are absolutely untrustworthy. The trust is in the decision.

Within trust is obedience, and that is the guts of it. This is why in the Christian marriage ceremony, when we took the word "obey" out, we didn't know what we were doing. We were trying to overcome the anti-feminine attitude of the Middle Ages, but then we destroyed the whole service in the way we went about it. Not only should they have asked the woman, "Will you love, honor, and obey your husband?" but they also should ask the man, "Will you love, honor, and obey your wife?" In case you have marriage problems, if you do not obey your wife, you haven't got any marriage. And if she does not obey you, then you haven't got a marriage. That is trust. And in my house, when my wife says hop, I hop – both of you had better hop if you want any reasonable facsimile of a marriage. That is not moralism, that is ontology. That is the way life is.

When you talk about the church, you have a fantastic picture. When somebody asks where the church is, do you know where I point? I point to my head (or maybe my heart). There is Luther and there is Aquinas – it's sort of a council. I have Amos up front in the council inside me. Gautama is there, and a host of others. Of course, these are priors out of my own life. I happen to know more about Luther than I do about Origen. I don't like John Wesley as well as I like some others, so I put John back a ways. But he sure is there and yaks all the time.

This council sits there, and this is the church. That is to say, the body – that is a sociological term for me. The body of Christ is within. Or, the Kingdom of God, a sociological category, is within. And when cynics say that the church is finished, I wish we could invent a machine that would just show who's inside us all. It is the only live thing in the universe as far as I am concerned. And the gates of Hell shall not prevail against it.

This church, which is the invisible church, is always set in the visible church, old cigar boxes with steeples on them. But this church inside cannot exist without the crummy cigar boxes with steeples on them. Calvin long since said in substance (when you get to know my friends as well as I know them, they let you paraphrase them very liberally) that though the church is never synonymous with any operating image, it is always within some operating image. And the reason why those structures have to be there is that this kind of council cannot happen unless they're there.

It doesn't make any difference how crummy the visible church is. You should have had my Sunday school teacher. I've often called her with affection, "Mrs. Bigbottom." She was one of the warpedest characters you ever saw, but she communicated to an eight-year-old boy that God loved him. I didn't have the foggiest idea of what that meant at the time, but some twenty, thirty years later, when I was trying to get out of a foxhole on a beach in Saipan, suddenly what that stupid fat lady put in my head started to burn, and I was afire with the awareness that no matter how crummy I was, or this world was, God loved me, and he loved the world he put me in.

The only church you have to love is the one that is. To bring that into your being means that you accept responsibility personally for all its sins, for all its crimes, for all its decadence, as well as for all its wonders and all its glory. All this is another way of saying, "I am the church."

You have to have the external or the visible church. It's as if you have many, many people to feed, and if you don't feed them, they don't keep lively. You see, the external church in all of its crumminess is symbolism, the factory where symbolism is produced. My saints within eat only symbols. This is what you mean by the means of grace within our time. Why, why do you read the scripture? As part of spiritual exercises to feed the saints, if you please, to keep them lively. Why do you go to Eucharist? To feed the saints.

Some character in our midst not long ago, when we were thinking about a marriage ceremony for several couples at once, said, "No! Marriage is an individual thing." When I got to my office I hit the ceiling. Nobody ever was married in the church singly. The first vows you make are to the church. When you go to that altar, you have a host of witnesses inside you that you talk with about this marriage. They are there bowing the knee before radical symbols of life along with you.

The reason you have spiritual exercises and the reason you engage in the exercise of meditation is to feed the saints, to keep them lively, to keep them quick, to keep them dancing within you. Oh, those of you who are tired and weighed down by life, I say unto thee, life is a dance. But the dance of it is the liveliness of the intentional community with whom you dialogue night and day. That dialogue stimulates the dance of life.

4. Incessant Warfare

The fourth point is that meditation is bloody warfare. The war is between the demons and the saints. The demons slip in, but the interesting thing about demons is that they never slip in as demons. They come disguised as angels. One of the best ways for them to get through is to come in as a part of that *generalized other.*

This is to say that the dialogue you carry on with that great communion of saints is never about morality. The saints don't know how to talk about morality. The only language they know is that of ontology. They never ask me, "Did you do this immoral thing or the other?" Can you imagine a pious Methodist growing up in Ada, Ohio, in a church which had reduced all of the great saints into little petty bourgeois moralists? This means that the demons had become so numerous and powerful that they had destroyed the communion of saints within me and stolen their garments. They were sitting there as some little pious, moral Luther, some little pious, fat Thomas Aquinas, and some little old shriveled up moralist called Paul. Oh, you want to know what the sickness of the church and the sickness of humanity is today? It is that we have mixed the gospel up with the moralism of bourgeois man out of the Victorian Age of the last century.

In the battle within, the saints make war on the demons to destroy them. Let me mention a few angels: "I cannot get up and march with the troops of Jesus Christ, because I have my little children I have to take care of." That would slip a demon in, wouldn't it? We are so sentimental about our children. We use them as one of the first escapes from having to stand before the Sanhedrin of saints within us. Or the demons come in with a petty moral concept of being loyal to the nation. One of the great things of the youth culture today is that they have risen up with the saints to destroy the demons disguised as moral angels. This is what I mean by an "angel."

This is another way of saying that demons always disguise themselves as the *generalized other* – the common opinion that morality is more about avoiding saloons than doing something about the inhuman treatment of the black people of this world. That last is ontology, for it has to do finally with your relationship to the mystery in life. I tell you, this is a bloody battlefield.

Somebody wrote me a letter just the other day and took me to pieces because of what she called my neglect of my children. We had a battlefield, the saints and the demons within my being. You see, what she was out to crush was anything but her petty, bourgeois moralism. Shall I mention some more of these? This is why St. Augustine called the virtues of the generalized other "splendid vices." But, I mean, they are vices!

The Christian faith very early understood that its primal categories were not good and evil. The primal categories are sin and faith. Sin has to do with being inauthentic. This is why the saints never require anything of me but authenticity. You young ones hearken to that and know who your friends really are.

There is only one question you are going to be asked when you get to heaven – if you'll allow me to use that poetry. There's only one failure in life and that's the failure to get to heaven – only one. The only question they're going to ask you is, "Did you live an authentic life?" This is why even at the last moment, along with the thieves on the cross, you can become an authentic person. But, sister, when you close your eyes for the last time, it's the judgment of God, you're frozen in an inauthentic life, as Sartre says.

This is present in the Lord's Prayer. "Lord, lead me not into temptation." That word really, I think, is "trials." "Don't lead me into the bloody battlefields within." Then he goes on to say, "But if you do lead me into temptation, then deliver me from the inauthentic." That is what it is concerned with. "Don't let me surrender," is another way of saying it. This is meditation.

Recently I pointed out that for the person of faith there is only one enemy. All of the demons who pull you this way and that are out to see that you are in good health and get to live to be ninety-two and that you have a lot of grandchildren and a split-level house plus $20,000. Aren't these splendid vices? You have but one foe – many enemies, maybe, but one foe – and that is Satan.

In one way this makes it easy. As a person of spirit, you know where you have to direct your attention. The only trouble is, Satan seems so big, and he (or she or it) has a great big tail, and he carries that three-foot pitchfork. He is a fearsome thing to have to fight. There is just one way to do it. I just did it for you. You name the demon. The moment you are able to name the demon, it is unmasked. I don't know whether it is like a Martian or something, but when you unmask him, he disappears. And the way you name the demon is to call it what it is, and the best you can call it is a *splendid vice.* Mark you, children are simply wonderful, but if they are the meaning of your life, then a demon disguised as an angel will, if he hasn't already, destroy you as a self. The only way you can destroy that demon is to name it what it is. I have nasty names, but I'll stick to Augustine's *splendid vices.*

The demon is unmasked, which is to say the meaning of life is in God alone, and not in any created thing. But when you're out to slay the eternal foe, then this war is never won. Didn't you used to hope that it would at least get easier? I'm sure it must get easier after fifty-eight years, but up to fifty-eight I'll swear it's gotten harder. It's never done, this wrestling to be a self. Isn't it terrible the way we treat the old people, as if the battle is over? No! No! My Papa was retired for thirty-five years. Can you imagine that? And we stick them aside somewhere as if they don't need any help in the great battle of Armageddon within their being.

There is a second battle and it's worse than the first. In the second battle you become aware, in the mist of fighting the demons, of God standing off to the side with his hands on his hips just looking. Extremely irritating. But when you're busy with the devil, you don't have much time to worry about the Mystery just standing aside. But the second irony is that it's his war to begin with. When you've slain the devil then you reach out for the prize, the Mystery. But it starts to flee. God starts to run. So you had better be swift of foot, and if you are, you'll get him by the nape of the neck. You and I know why he is fleeing. It's because we want to know his name – that is, we want to give God form, and we want to give God an image, without which we cannot relate to the Mystery. The Mystery cannot be named. God cannot be named.

In the wrestling match of Jacob, Moffatt translates the angel as "the nameless one." I like that. That is what you mean by the Mystery. God is beyond the human power to comprehend. Every attempt to draw God's image is inadequate. This is to say that God is freedom. But I got God by the nape of the neck. God has to wrestle, and I mean we have it out! By this time, since I have slain Satan, God is over against a protagonist, and we wrestle all night.

Granted, it is a lonely experience, as Jacob found out. It is an experience in pitch darkness. It is dread-filled to the point of death. But one secret you know: this one, the Mystery, gave you life and one day will destroy you, will give you your death. Ah, what a one to be wrestling with. God gets a hip lock on me, but I hang on and round and round we go.

In the story of Jacob you remember that the way God is able to capitulate is that God turns Jacob's question back on him. He says, "All right, man, what is *your* name?" And Jacob didn't want to say it because his name was *Deceiver.* You know, he had deceived his brother and his uncle. He was the deceiver. Finally, the dawn was coming, and Jacob gave in and said, "All right, all right, my name is Jacob. I am this horrible creature that I am." And God said, "No more. Your name is Israel, and that means one who was in mortal combat with God." (Wouldn't you like that name? Well, that is my name. This is why we are children of Abraham. That is my name.) Then old stupid Jacob says back to the nameless One, "Well, what is your name?" And the nameless One said, "Do you need to ask that?" No, because God named God when God called me Israel.

And at that moment God and I get up and we are friends. But never forget, God is first among equals in this situation. God not only has me "*in* his hands but also *on* his hands." That is what it means to be a friend of God, and there are times, I am sure, when God regretted ever making me a friend.

How does the story end? On that day when God puts the knife in me, as the knife goes in I smile, and God winks. Being-in-Itself winks. My victory is that I forced Being-in-Itself to wink at my life.

And I am through with this talk on meditation.

Prayer

I'm scared to death as usual when I have to speak about what I have to speak about – even more so today.

My mind recently went back to Anaximander, who, if I am right, was the radical pre-Socratic philosopher who held to a monistic understanding of the primary substance in the universe. I've known for some time and have confessed it that a new kind of Platonism is welling up within me, transposed hopefully into the post-modern world. I've been very clear for years about radical monotheism; but that's something different from monism. Now I'm finding a bee buzzing around in my mind that tends to make me a post-modern monist. This is indicated by suggesting that there's only one reality in the world, and that's spirituality. I've got to call everything else unreality. There is only one substance (that word has not been easy for me for thirty years, but I can use it now), but it's spiritual substance. Everything else is non-substance. This I suppose is what Kazantzakis is trying to get hold of when he says that our task is to transpose matter into Spirit. Matter, as he uses it there, is unreality made into reality.

I wish like anything that we didn't have to do all those things that we have to do, so that all of us could go aside and study. Where I want to study is in the practical aspect of the development of the People of God in history. Forgetting their great intellectual struggle and wisdom, I want to know how they took that and shaped what I'm trying to call spiritual substance, in the sense of practical sociological forms in history. I wish I could go back to Leo I, get to know him, for he's the one that carved out that gigantic machinery we call Roman Catholicism. I wish I knew more about Benedict. I wish I knew more about Huss. I wish I knew more about Wesley, although I know more about him than most of you. I wish I knew more about Calvin and what he did sociologically in Geneva, practically, where he took stuff and created spiritual substance out of it.

We are taking the stuff of the decadent church and using that to create the new spiritual substance sociologically in our time. Spiritually I've never left the local congregation. Indeed, I feel like I've been hammered, blow by blow for twenty years, deeper into the local congregation. But I've left it in terms of the detachment that was necessary to see it as an utterly objective vehicle that can be used to give sociological form to the spiritual substance that has to be created. Therefore, there's no romanticism. If you've got some sentimentality left in you about the local parish, you'd better not go back there. This has got to be a hardheaded, revolutionary spiritual posture, this creating spiritual substance. Renewing the local congregation is creating spiritual reality.

The irony in all of this is that you only do stuff; you only fool with stuff. A spirit person's a funny thing. We want to go away and be Spirit. But that's always denied us. We've got to be dealing with just plain old stuff. We fool with stuff in order that others may participate in the spiritual reality that's being built. That's the key and the fright underneath all the fears that we have.

Prayer Is Radical

I want to talk about prayer. I want to talk about prayer as radical happening. I want to talk about prayer as radical tactic. I want to talk about prayer as radical combat. The New Religious Mode (see chart, pg. 117) is nonsense if anyone can be human outside of it. I used to think prayer was something you could do or not do and still be human. If it is, then we ought to say, "The Lord is with you," leave the room and the whole damn outfit forever.

For awhile I was thinking, "How in the world could I be motivated to go and bring off a local congregation?" That's the wrong way to put it. I've got to be the New Religious Mode, and the tactics for the local church will take care of themselves. Tactics have to be transposed through my unrepeatable being, through your unrepeatable being, into the New Religious Mode. I tell you, what's ahead is no job for boys and girls. It's a job for spiritual men and women, spiritual giants. If you are not, don't go out and try to be giants. The hell with that! You're not trying to grow yourself up in the sense that you can pick yourself up by your own bootstraps. It's something far deeper than that. The New Religious Mode is the reality that you have to bring into being.

These three – prayer, doing, and obedience – are utterly inseparable. You can't put them sequentially. They have to be there all at once. Save I know what radical obedience is, then I cannot pray. Those of you who open your mouths during worship and let prayers flow out as if you were spitting, I call you into question. A prayer – I don't mean what flows out of our mouths – only comes out of radical obedience. It's in the midst of obedience and prayer that one begins to sense what eschatological doing does to the journey.

Radical Happening

Prayer, first of all, is happening. Nothing ever happened in this world, only prayer. Prayer is happening. Nothing ever happened in this world, only prayer. This is why when we were first trying to ground this category in humanness, we said it was action. It's the action down underneath the action, a happening transposing action into deed. What I mean by happening here is the action underneath the action that transposes action into deed.

We've also said that prayer is freedom. I laugh as I think back through some twenty-five years of people fooling with the word "freedom." They want to be free. They want to vote on this or that. They want to have a chance to express themselves. They want to have a chance in a course to dialogue with the teacher. This is freedom? No, freedom is only prayer. When you talk about freedom, you're talking about the nothingness at the center of your being, and out of that nothingness comes something. Freedom is a happening. It is the happening before the act that transforms the act into the deed.

Prayer is literally creating out of nothing. When I was in seminary we used to have silly debates about whether or not man instead of God could create out of nothing. I insist that what in our day they've meant when they discovered afresh that man does not *have* freedom, he *is* freedom, is precisely that – that only when you bring to be that which never was before are you freedom. And to bring to be what never was is prayer, nothing else. This is why we've been very clear through the years that the most painful task was that of prayer. Prayer is creativity. To turn this around, creativity is prayer.

Turn it around. Freedom *is* prayer. Can you for a moment just blast everything that your Sunday school teachers or anybody else ever said that prayer was and begin to get a new peek? A happening is prayer. When was the last time you happened to happen? Well, think of it. Then you prayed.

Prayer is that goingonness in which the Mystery becomes tangible as mystery. One of the greatest postures that Carl Michaelson ever took in history is that "revelation is God revealing his unrevealedness." I like that. This isn't anything abstract. Prayer is the manifestation of the Mystery as mystery. This is why when you want to define in a little box what prayer is, you never can do it, because prayer is filled full of mystery. Do you understand that? Without that mystery, it is not prayer. Prayer is the irrational of the irrational – what did you think we meant when we called it freedom? What did you think we meant when we called it sheer creativity?

It's a funny thing. Nobody ever prayed until at that moment he or she was overcome by the Mystery. When you were overcome by the suffering of the people in Africa and you prayed, you did not pray. Mark you, that's a fine upstanding human feeling, but I'm talking about prayer.

I like to repeat what that submarine commander in World War I said, the one who became a cleric, Niemoller. He was the first German theologian we let back into this country after the war. His one word was that the church is never substantial, it's a dynamic. The church never exists; it becomes. Snap your fingers and we're the church. Snap them again and there isn't any church any more. That's the dynamic in history.

You could come at this a million different ways. Nobody has got the guts to create anything, save he stands on the shoulders of colleagues from the beginning of humanness itself. If Gautama walks not with thee, if Richard Niebuhr is not more real to you than your own brother, if Amos has not long since stood one step ahead, you never created anything, and you never prayed.

There's no such thing as prayer without contemplation. There's no such thing as prayer without meditation. I hope you don't think I mean sitting around brooding, or sitting around contemplating. That has its place, but here you're dealing with the ontological reality and not the exercise.

Radical Tactics

Prayer is a happening, the only happening. Prayer is tactics.

I had a little fun with the second tallest man in our Order. I heard him praying in the Daily Office about the region here in Chicago. What I've been waiting for when I go in his office is a chart, about the size of the wall, to be up in there of a battle plan of how they're going to do something about the region. I won't know for sure if he's really praying in the Daily Office if the plan's not there. If "there" is only in his mind, then I am absolutely sure he's not praying, for prayer is tactics. Prayer is the most difficult human goingonness that you know anything about, and prayer is tactics.

I like to joke about the failure mentality in our group. One thing a revolutionary, a spirit person, will not allow to exist in his or her being in a failure mentality. Sure, we fail. But a failure mentality is to anticipate failure, even to work out statistics that only 10 percent of our courses this quarter did not come off, and 15 percent the quarter before, and 28 percent. . . . That is the failure mentality.

I tell you, a spirit person is so damned shrewd. I've ofttimes mentioned Thomas Aquinas, who said, sure, the church must permit revolutions against the government. But he gave several criteria, and one was that before you start a revolution, you've got to be as certain as you can that you're going to win. He was a spirit man. He knew what it meant to be a revolutionary.

The revolutionary takes a jab, and if she sees that it's wrong, she withdraws. She pulls back before it has a chance to fail. The one who always makes the decisions six months before so that everybody can be ready and participate is not a revolutionary. You hold those decisions just as long as you possibly can before you pull out your weapon. It might even be that you won't have to shoot the man. You find another way to win.

Prayer is tactics. The person who doesn't have his or her tactics does not pray. This is why we said the other day that a revolutionary always dies in his tactics, never in his in goals or objectives. She never dies in inclusive plans, but dies in her tactics. That's why when a prayer is verbalized, when it's a prayer, it's always a prayer relative to tactics and not to ends.

Radical Combat

Lastly, prayer is combat, radical combat. It is combat with God. It is life and death struggle with Being-in-Itself. This is not saying anything different from what we said at the beginning: prayer is happening, or prayer is freedom, or prayer is creativity. The prayer within a person's being is the place and the only place where that person intentionally touches raw being. No place else.

As Jacob wrestled with the Nameless One, he was alone and he was terrified. There was just one thing that the Nameless One was after and that was for Jacob to say out loud the way it was.

When you see that, there comes a scary complex of dynamics. When you take on Being, you always lose. Being has always won every contest. God has not lost one wrestling match. This is where the people of the Islamic world are extremely clear. They believe that a person is free, but that freedom is in the absolute sovereignty of God's will. God has never lost. Being has never lost. I suppose that there have been billions and billions of souls who have struggled with Being. As far as I know, every one of them, minus none, is rotting in the grave, and Being marches on. God always wins.

You've got to say that to yourself at least ten times: God always wins. If you don't see that, you don't see the stupidity and the overwhelming dread that consumes a person that dares to match up against Being. Who is stupid enough to shove his life against Being knowing that Being always wins?

The beginning of Psalm 2 is that God is in derision as he looks at the kings of the world. He's laughing. One of the horrors of it is that you know he lets you win sometimes. He lets you win sometimes. If you were playing some silly, asinine game, you wouldn't think anything of it. But if you were pushing your one life over against Being, and you win, the dread is not less than when you failed; it's multiplied by one thousand. You think, "What's that bastard up to, laughing at me when he lets me win, when I know very good and well that he never allowed anybody to win?"

And then comes the flip side of that. In the wisdom of China, if you save somebody's life, you have to take care of him the rest of your life; that's rooted in humanness. When God lets you win, whenever he lets you win, you've got a monkey on your back that you didn't really want. And we all knew this was coming: you're obligated to what you prayed for. He lets you win, and oh my God, you wish you hadn't prayed for what you got.

Oh, it's more complicated than that. You take the four phenomenological levels. The first is just the idea. Nobody who does not know what I just got through saying, no matter what poetry they use, never prayed. It's just the idea. And to put it in terms of what I've been talking about, it's just the idea that you pit yourself against Being and Being has never lost, never lost. Just that idea is the beginning of prayer.

Then it gets concretized. I always look upon this as sort of like sticking your big toe in the water. To put it in terms of combat, on this level you deliver a pull-punch, "Lord, those Biafrans over there, they've had the hell beat out of them, and everything. Bless them." It's concretized. That's sort of like the pull-punch from God. God plays with you very frequently. He lets you pull that punch, and just steps back. There are other times when he kicks the pants off you just for playing with him the least bit.

The next level we call personal. I never liked that. It's predictive prayer. This is where you just stand there. You don't ask this or that; you tell God the way it is. This is where you always come with a four-point program. This is where the tactics come in, like, "Damn you, God! This is what we're going to do.

Do you understand?" This is where, as Fred Gealy used to say, when you're a great teacher you always go into the class as God, knowing full well that you're not God. That is, you go in to run this universe, knowing good and well that God runs it. This is Lot, who wasn't as weak a man as we like to think. This is where you bargain with the Lord. Isn't it interesting how sometimes the Lord backs down? God backs down. Don't you wish you knew when God was going to back down?

Then comes the time, and I like to think of Moses here, on the final level. What a moment this is when you say, "God, you're going to have to kill me if it's not this way." Remember when Moses came down off the mountain and they were fooling around with the golden calf? I tell you, he told the Lord, he said, "You wipe me out, but don't you dare destroy these people." And the Lord ran.

Fred Gealy also is the one who says that the spiritual life is nothing but a dialogue, a dialogue with God. You say, "Over my dead body will Being continue the way it is." That's what you mean when you say that a revolutionary only dies in her tactics. God never slaughtered anybody who stood up to him, except in her tactics.

This means that every prayer always leaves Being different. Don't you tell the Lord this. In fact, we ought to whisper about it, for even when the Lord wins, I win. Being is never the same when I force Being to say "no." That's a little secret you never breathe.

Those of you who teach RS-I, remember what may be the greatest sentence you ever teach in the Niebuhr paper, where it says that Jesus forced a different response out of God when God beat the pants off him. That's why only a revolutionary can sing, "O death, where is thy victory? O grave, where is thy sting?" This is a smart aleck statement. Do you understand that? "Ho, ho, ho, death, where is thy victory? Ha, ha, ha, grave, where is thy sting?" But you don't tell the Lord about this. Or maybe this is what Abraham meant when he suggested, "God and I are friends." But he's God, mark you, and he never lost one contest.

So I sometimes think that the peace which passes all human understanding and the joy which is unspeakable and full of glory is this little secret, that in the midst of being beat to death there on the street, you can smile back into the face of Being. That's not a stoical attitude. That's an attitude of faith, for this secret was never known to the stoics, only to the people of faith.

Confession, Gratitude, Petition, and Intercession

One more little thing, and then I'll stop: confession, gratitude, petition, and intercession. You know, speaking dynamically, that we have it divided in half. The first two are more passive and the second two more active. Confession is more passive and gratitude is more active. Petition is more passive and intercession more active. One has to do with the dynamic of the *word* and the other has to do with the dynamic of the task or the mission. It's pretty clear that when you're giving an intercessory prayer, you're doing all of these. Petition is the key to what I'm talking about today.

I'd like to talk about all of them, but just a word here. Nobody ever made an intercessory prayer that was not on the other side of a petitionary prayer. Our strength comes out of weakness, always. The prayer to change Being only comes out of the awareness that only God wins. The other side of that, pushed to its radical edge, is my radical contingency, and that is my radical inadequacy.

A prayer, therefore, was never about anything except that which was impossible, and that is to change the structure of Being itself. When you pray for whatever you pray for, it's over against the impossible. The other side of that coin is the awareness of your own inadequacy.

This grounds us in the *word*. Only the one who is in Jesus Christ has ever prayed or ever will pray. That's why there's a body in history who has brought that to self-consciousness and who ends every prayer in his name – nothing reductionistic, nothing magic, nothing supernatural – just his name. In no other name has any prayer ever been offered or ever will be offered. That's why, and for no other reason, we look forward to that day which shall come just as surely – no, even more surely – than the sun will rise tomorrow. Before that name every knee shall bow and become human.

I would want to insist that save you and I have become people of prayer, in a way that I am quite willing to confess that I have not yet become, we are not ready to be consultants for the local church. Save we understand corporately that prayer is a spiritual task, and that the doing of it is bringing about spiritual reality, then we're going to do far more harm than good, and should never set forth.

Then I would call upon us – and I hate to put it this way, I'm afraid to put it this way – we've got to experiment in prayer. I'd like to see what would happen if Fifth City got prayed over. I'd like to see what would happen if this nation got prayed over. I'd like to see this summer be the time in which we create the means whereby this nitty-gritty, mechanical, thing-a-ma-jig, tactical model of the local church was bound together inseparably with spiritual reality. I don't like the way I put that. I'd like to see the movement blend the warp and woof of Spirit into one great tapestry this summer in preparation for our re-entry into the local congregation for the sake of the world.

Poverty

I feel very close to the church at Philippi these days.

> Every advantage that I had gained I considered lost for Christ's sake. Yes, and I look upon everything as loss compared with the overwhelming gain of knowing Christ Jesus my Lord. For his sake I did in actual fact suffer the loss of everything, but I considered it useless rubbish compared with being able to win Christ. For now my place is in him, and I am not dependent upon any of the self-achieved righteousness of the Law. God has given me that genuine righteousness which comes from faith in Christ. How changed are my ambitions! Now I long to know Christ and the power shown by his resurrection: now I long to share his sufferings, even to die as he died [*Is that the death urge transfigured? It doesn't say here.*], so that I may perhaps attain, as he did, the resurrection from the dead. Yet, I do not consider myself to have arrived spiritually, nor do I consider myself already perfect. But I keep going on, grasping ever more firmly that purpose for which Christ grasped me. I do not consider myself to have fully grasped it even now. But I do concentrate on this: I leave the past behind and with hands outstretched to whatever lies ahead, I go straight for the goal, my reward, the honor of being called by God in Christ. (Philippians 3:7-14. J.B.P. translation)

We are going to talk about poverty. I wish St. John of the Cross were here and we could turn a button and he would be a 20th century man. We would listen to him gladly. Or I would be even more than willing to hear St. Teresa. What a woman!

We turn a corner today. We move from what we've called the *solitaries* to what we call the *corporates*. But I am aware when you move from one to the other you're going around a corner somehow.

That is a prophecy. As far as I'm concerned, all we're doing this summer is preparing for next summer. The imperative upon the People of God is to build the picture of the new society that is even now being born. Putting our own house, the church, in order is but the necessary means to get that done.

I want you to think of the interior box in this illustration as the *new social vehicle*, and the outside one as the *new religious mode*, though where there is no religious mode, there is no social vehicle, and where there is no social vehicle, there is no religious mode. The two interpenetrate one another.

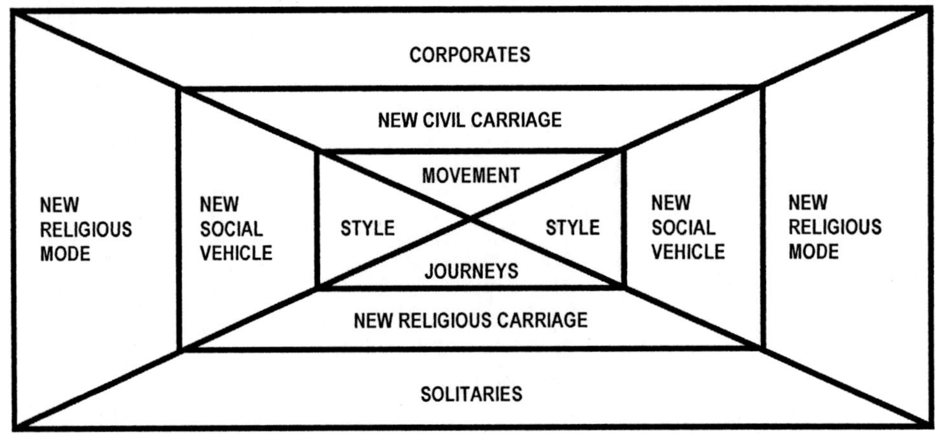

Figure 2 – 3: The New Civil Carriage and the New Religious Carriage

What we call the "solitaries" are at the bottom of the chart in the *new religious mode* square, and what we call the "corporates" are at the top of the new religious mode square. Within our model the social aspect of this is always at the top, and the individual aspect of this is at the bottom, so that the top of the new religious mode square has to do with corporate individuality, and the bottom has to do with solitary individuality. Therefore, both of these have to do with what Kierkegaard calls "the solitary individual." I want to come back to that.

In the interior square you are dealing with the new social vehicle (and I prefer that it be sitting in the midst of the new religious mode, rather than the other way around). This is the new civil carriage and the new religious carriage. The new civil carriage has to do with the sociological reformulation of civil society, and the new religious carriage has to do with sociological reformulation of the religious community. We are well on our way, I suspect, in creating the new religious carriage, although the end nobody will ever see. Both of these have to do with society. There never was a new civil carriage until the religious mode was formed, and we'd better hearken well to that.

The second thing that we have to do before we can start is to go back once again to the diagram of the new religious mode charts.

Actually it's a tic-tac-toe with the ends filled in, isn't it? Here are prayer, meditation, and contemplation; here transparent knowing, transparent doing, and transparent being; here chastity, obedience, and here we are today, poverty.

A poetic way of talking about the self, the individual, is the consciousness of consciousness, or perhaps the consciousness of consciousness of consciousness. The last category would be equivalent to Kierkegaard's definition of the self as the relationship that relates itself to itself. And when that relationship becomes the relationship that relates itself to itself, it grounds itself transparently in the power that constitutes it. That is what I mean by a third consciousness. Anyway, consciousness of consciousness, for me, is knowing, and it's acting or doing, and it's presence or being. That is what I mean by consciousness of consciousness.

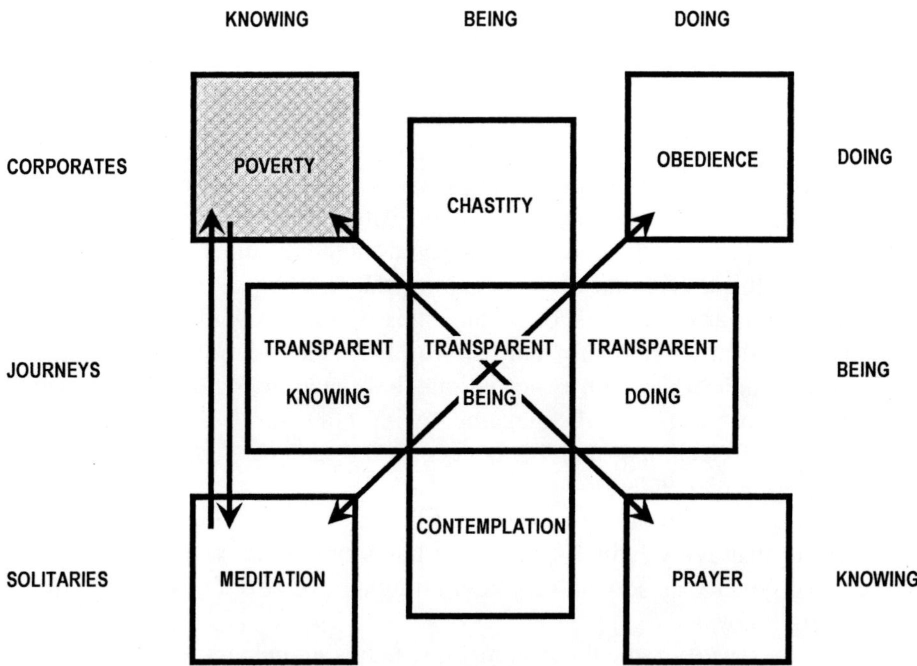

Figure 2 – 4: The New Religious Mode Dynamics

That gives you the most abstract category in grounding the religious mode in humanness itself. This is the way in which you check yourself every moment to be sure that this is in the context of the secular worldview, and not sneaking in the back or side door. All this has to talk about humanness as you and I experience humanness.

In talking about meditation the other day, I left out a sizable hunk of what I was going to say. You probably noticed when I jumped pretty quickly through the section on the conscience. Let me say this much. The way you can spot a person of faith – a clue – is whether you dare to live out of your own interior resources. Or you keep your own conscience. Nobody keeps it for you. But, you see, we've got a secret that the naïve person hearing that doesn't know anything about. That person is not an individual here. It is a collective we. It is as if Luther, Amos, Jeremiah, and I keep my conscience.

What a fellowship! The external activity of the divine happens and questions my life, and I have to run to the council and to discuss it. After we discuss it, I have to make a decision. It must be a loyal one, although it may very well be in loyal opposition to Mr. Luther, if you please. But it's *we* who keep that conscience. It's not *I* who lives out of my own interior resources. It's *we*, through the gracious activity of God, which peoples my being with the great spirit characters of the world.

Out of that meditation comes the possibility for radical poverty. I don't know how to get this said with adequate poetry. The one thing that council demands is action. They are not even going to sit at the table with you if you're piddling around with some intellectual, theoretical problem. Poverty issues out of meditation that is required before meditation is possible.

So, let's talk about poverty. The basic category I'm going to use is the word "detachment." I don't like the word "disengagement." I like detachment. Poverty is detachment, and obedience is engagement. Anybody who is engaged without detachment is pseudo-engaged, not engaged authentically. Unless you are detached from this world and the concerns of this world, you cannot stuff your total being into any given spot within this world. And *vice versa*. This detachment is not a withdrawal *from* the world. It is a withdrawal *in* the world. Any kind of withdrawal which is not intimately related to engagement, or is not for the one purpose of fanatical engagement within the world, is not what I mean by detachment. Detachment and engagement are interdependent as poverty and obedience are interdependent.

When I use the verbal sign "poverty," I mean to be talking about a human state of being that every human being does know or can know about. I can also use the word poverty as something like a religious exercise, but I'm not talking about that right now.

I mean by poverty radical detachment, which is an inward posture related to an external sign. When you are dealing with the state of the solitaries, you are talking about something more passive. The state of the corporates is more active. The state of the solitaries is more subjective. I don't mean that the way some of you will hear it. Both of these states of being are the most objective things in the world. To help you, the state of the corporates is more objective in the sense of being perceivable from without, or having signs that are perceivable from without. The key difference between these, minus one thing, is that the corporates as states of being have to do with postures toward the world or society. The solitaries have to do with relations to the mystery. I use the stylistic category "posture" intentionally. The solitaries are more the givens; the corporates are more the intendeds. You cannot actually divide any of these from one another. There is an intermixture at every point.

I want to put up the basic categories by which I intend to talk about the state of being that I call poverty. First of all, poverty is intentional detachment. That is what I have been trying to point to here to get started. Secondly, poverty is conquered contingency, but I don't like that term. Thirdly, poverty is fantastic benevolence, fantastic in the sense of "unrestrained imagination." In the 17th and 18th centuries, "benevolence" was a tremendous word. It has been out of favor now for a good fifty years. It was there in the Victorian age. I want to recover it again. In one translation of Luke, "peace on earth and goodwill to men" reads "and benevolence to men." And finally, by poverty I mean sacramental portent.

I'd like to use the word "sign," but I want a rough and mighty word for the fourth category.

Recollect what I said a moment ago, that by poverty I mean an inward posture (intentional detachment) and an outward sign (sacramental portent). The middle two categories put the content into that. I'm going to use some ancient words here. Conquered contingency is humility, divine humility, if you like, and the other is benevolence, or love, if you please.

You are not going to get on top of this if you are not keenly aware that the great monastic movements in history were not leaving the world. They were missional in their intent. They saw society going one way to its destruction and they decided it had to go another way. They threw their lives into the breach of history to create a style of life that would bend the course of history. They were missional. I would like to rehearse for you the Dominicans, the Benedictines, and the Jesuits in terms of their fantastic secular causes that brought them into being.

It was in the midst of this that the great classical language of the orders came into being. It was there that their vows were formed, the vow of poverty, the vow of chastity, and the vow of obedience. Each one of these was pointing to a stumbling block that would keep the mission from succeeding. This was not some kind of an ascetic superimposition upon life.

If you are not well aware of the fact that the economic aspect of existence is one of the most gigantic stumbling blocks to corporate mission, then you haven't even lived in the 20th century, let alone the 8th.

Second, obedience. Every two-bit character who hasn't decided to be human wants to do his own little thing. He wants to become bishop, he wants, he wants, he wants. "Nobody is going to tell me what to do!" Unless that problem is solved, there is no corporate mission.

Third, chastity. Do not think for a moment that this is to be understood primarily in terms of the psychology of the Greeks. This again is missional. Those of you who haven't been married very long have to see that the family always gets in the way of corporateness. Not sometimes. It always gets in the way! I need not rehearse in sentimental language about the woman or man who has to have so much attention from the spouse. "The mission doesn't matter. Look at me. Here I am." As a matter of fact, we've written tons of psychology books to support that kind of wretched un-selfhood. Shall I mention the children? Chastity was dealing fundamentally with the problem of the family as it related to God's purpose in history. What a solution they had to it! Oh, they didn't get rid of all the problems, did they? You have a family with you even if you don't have a family. In the 20th century the answer to celibacy is the missional family. That is the new celibacy. That is the meaning of chastity whereby one thing can be willed.

The people we are talking about are always the fanatics in history. They are always the odd ones. They are often seen as the psychotics, even, because as everybody knows, to be normal is to be just what the *generalized other* always tells you.

These people are the perpetual revolutionaries in history. And by these people I've gone way beyond the religious orders. Any revolutionary, secular or otherwise, always – not sometimes – always lives by these three vows: obedience, chastity, and poverty. Are you clear about that? Shall I pull out the little red book of Mao and read his discipline? If you didn't know he wrote it, you could have thought that Thomas Aquinas wrote it. Shall we pull out the rules of some of the other revolutionaries – Che, for instance – and look at them in terms of poverty, chastity, and obedience?

But I haven't hit the bottom yet. A revolutionary who is authentic is a presentation of a style which is a manifestation of humanness at the radical bottom. Therefore, you and I have to grasp that if one does not participate in poverty, he or she is not participating in authentic humanness. The same statement is true of chastity, and the same statement is true of obedience.

Intentional Detachment

Now, let's get to the four categories that point to poverty. I say that detachment is foundationally human. Adler, the renegade Freudian, based his whole psychology upon one image: everyone has a hole in his/her center. In the center of a person's spirit or being there is a hole, a bottomless hole. A person spends his whole life pouring sand into that hole to fill it up. The basic propensity of a person is for status or power, according to Adler, but he or she cannot get enough of it. I mean, it is bottomless. That's what I mean when I say that a person *is* detachment, detachment from things of this world.

Because that hole is in the center and cannot be filled up, everyone is consumed with dread. Those of you who know Søren Kierkegaard's *Concept of Dread* will remember that he works this out. Because of who one is – that is, because one is contingency – he or she experiences dread. This dread is turned into the drive after security by attempting to grasp security by taking things of this world and bestowing upon them the power to fulfill the meaning of one's life.

Do I need to say that over again? Out of this dread comes the drive for security, which means that we attach ourselves to things of this world – our nation, mama, children, fortune, and right down the list, naming all of the gods. In doing that, one surrenders the detachment that finally defines one's being. You find yourself along with the mass of humanity seeking after one hunk of security and then another hunk of security, knowing and not knowing that security can never be realized. So in the midst of fallenness, one still experiences one's detachment, though it is a fallen detachment.

Poverty is this kind of intentional detachment. I've brought in the word "intentional." What I mean by the word "detachment" is a return to the pristine detachment that defines what it means to be a human being. This is what consciousness means. The return to detachment is the decision, the intention to be what one actually is. This means it is an experience in the twilight of the gods, or the death of the gods. It is breaking the bondage that one is in, when for security's sake one is related to one of the goods of this world.

All of that is another way of talking about radical monotheism. The person who is detached lives exposed before God. Just exposed. One's basic loyalty is there, the basic obedience is there. Remember the section on "Freedom" from Bonhoeffer's *Ethics.* What he is saying is this: the person of faith is utterly obedient, obedient to God; and God has only one rule for mankind: *be free.* God says, "That is what I made you. *Be* what I made you." That is practical, radical monotheism, that in every situation you live before the final reality.

One last word here has to do with my friend Gautama, the Buddha. I tell you, I love that man. You remember how in his understanding of life a human being had to overcome all desires. Overcoming desires is detachment. He was very clear about one thing, that if all of a sudden you could overcome all of the innate propensities, you would go to Nirvana immediately.

But I want to speak back to dear Gautama. It's not overcoming these desires that's the problem. The problem is dealing with the dread at the fundamental core of being that is always turning itself into a drive after security. That is the problem.

Manifest Contingency

The second category of poverty is manifest contingency. The one who is detached is aware of her contingency in a highly lucid fashion, understands her frailty, is aware that she was born naked and she is going to die naked. I don't mean just intellectually aware. I mean she is aware with her whole being.

The awareness of contingency here is simply absurd. Did you ever notice how absurd a dead person is? It is even more absurd when you are able to picture yourself as that cadaver. I mean it is repulsive! But the one who has experienced detachment pre-remembers death – as one remembers or recollects the past. Before you at all times is the horrifying experience of your own death. That is what I mean by manifest contingency. We manifest in detachment our contingency. Other people are in the midst of always fleeing from that scene I just described – the fatefulness of their own death. But the one who is detached, on the other hand, is always living before it as a true reminder.

When you talk about the cruciform principle, some people say, "You don't really mean really dying, do you?" I tell you, I go all to pieces inside when I hear that. How stupid can you get? Barth said, "I'm talking about a six-foot hole in the ground." I mean this is utterly literal. One lives literally before death. Only then can you say as Socrates said, "No harm can befall a righteous man." I'll put that in the gospel: "No harm can befall a dead man." You cannot scare a person who is holding his own cadaver within his hands. He may be trembling down inside; but after the steamroller has gone over him, he is still standing there, trembling as he may. This is what I mean by divine humility, in which you embrace the total givenness of life. We have got to become humble in a new way.

Radical Benevolence

This is also radical benevolence. The detached person is the only one who has comprehensive concern. Do you understand that? The one who is driven by her security is always concerned for her family, her nation, or whatever else her idols define. The detached one is comprehensively concerned. This is an impartial concern. The only one who can be impartial is the one who is detached, who has given up the things of the world, if you please. It is an endless concern. I mean it is there every day. What I am pointing to is that if you are not continually concerned, you have not discovered what detachment is. It is unlimited concern, laying down one's life on behalf of others.

It is this detachment which is the basis of all society. The social structures of humanness – family, fraternity, nation, church – were based on this detachment. I might point out here the times when God acts in history and says, "No." You remember Amos. He wasn't after those cows of Bashan wallowing in their riches because riches were wrong. Amos always attacked the religious dimension – their relationship to God – because that is the foundation of any social structure.

If you look for a moment at the revolutionary, you can see what I'm talking about. The revolutionary is the one who is loose from the given situation that he or she is in. The detached person is a perpetual revolutionary, the one that keeps society fluid, for only when society is fluid is it society. Watch that revolutionary who is always under the discipline of poverty.

Sacramental Portent

The last point is sacramental portent. One of the things that makes me unclear in this area is the external sign. The external sign is to the corporates what transparency is to meditation, contemplation, and prayer. Transparency is that which (and my poetry is very bad here) travels you to the Mystery, face to face.

I forgot the greatest quotation in the Jacob story I told the other day when I talked about meditation. At the end, all it says is this: "He saw God face to face and did not die!" Interesting, isn't it? That is the moment of transparency.

What I mean by this sacramental portent, or this external sign, is that which gets you to the world. It is that which gets poverty to the world. Poverty is a posture towards life. It is the posture of detachment. The sign is that which quickens it. I mean, I have to create a literal sign in history before this is anything else than an intellectual insight. That is what I mean by traveling the distance.

Let me illustrate that. About two weeks ago there was some trouble in the neighborhood here. When I heard about it, God made it clear that it had happened because of me. Do you understand what I mean? That wasn't anybody else's problem. It was my problem. I had done it, and it had happened to me. When you obey God in terms of forging a posture, that posture does not become alive until you make a sign. Now I get up about thirty minutes earlier than usual, and every day I'm on that street if at all possible. That is my sign in traveling the distance.

How else shall I say this reality comes to me? One of my boys came home one time with long hair. I don't worry about people criticizing me here and there, but when I misuse one of my boys, watch out. I had him cut his hair after I lied to him – I didn't know I was lying – well, I'm not sure of that (You have to keep your theology clean, don't you?) – I told him it was for the sake of a cause. What a fool! He did it. But he should have told me off, but he didn't. If he had told me off, I wouldn't have violated him. Do you understand? So I let *my* hair grow long. That was my traveling the distance.

I like to say if you live in the white suburbs, and if you are not willing to live in the crumminess of the ghetto, then you have *got* to live in the crumminess of the ghetto. But if you are willing, you don't have to. And then some people are just stupid, and they've got to. There are other people, as Kierkegaard says, who can do it in their imagination. Then there are people in between. Those are the ones who have to put all their furniture in a big van and drive it down to the ghetto, leave it all night, and then go back and put it all back in their house in the suburbs. This is the only way they can possibly know, so that this position becomes quickened and alive in their life.

So you have to become poor. That is literal. I want to underscore that. If you have got to have anything, if you have *got* to have your husband, if you have *got* to have your sanity, if you have *got* to have your children, if you have *got* to have your automobile. I've seen guys in our Order keep ice boxes around here two or three years locked up, because they couldn't get loose enough to say they didn't need them. I find people who keep their cars when they come here. They can't get loose from them. I have nothing against their keeping their cars, if they find another way to communicate to themselves that they own nothing.

On the flip side of that, then you don't have to become poor at all, because the disposition of poverty has nothing to do with how many goods you have, or how many you don't have. It doesn't have to do at all with how much money you have or don't have – on the other side of not having to have any of it. Then it gets transferred into the rubric of mission.

How does a person capture one of these signs? One man that comes here on the weekends has a rather luscious house in the suburbs. One day, sitting around at a party of some kind at his house, I looked over at him and said to the other people sitting around us, "One thing I know of this man and that is if tomorrow I needed this gorgeous house, he would give it to me." You should have seen the look on that man's face. I said, "Wouldn't you? Wouldn't you?" Very reluctantly, in a low voice, he said, "Yes."

Whatever the sign is, it has to be there. Without the sign, what I mean by detachment is not there at all. The person who is not detached has never authentically engaged in life. As Luther put it, he is always subtly serving himself. Only the detached person can labor to death without trying to save his own soul by his own labors. I'm talking about real poverty, folks.

Religious orders come in here, too. God bless them all. Sometimes you need a sign of your sign. If the man with the large house turns the deed over, let's say that would be a sign that he doesn't have to have it. But maybe he needs another sign. St. Francis tied a rope around himself, and every time he saw that rope, that reminded him of his sign that he was a detached man. Thereby he called upon himself to be universally benevolent.

The religious orders, oh my, the sign of poverty that they created. But that's been so misused. The worst thing about it is that today they don't even understand it anymore. Catholic priests are asking for a raise in salary. I was kidding a Sister the other day about the nuns taking off their habits. You see, every time – not every other time – every time anyone beheld a nun, they were held up to the sacrificial portent of detachment. It didn't make any difference whether they hated the nun or whether they respected and loved her. I mean, every time they passed a black habit, though they may never have known it, this happened to them. The sign of their clothing pointed beyond. I said to the Sister, "After all the blood has been spilt to get and keep the symbol of your habit in history, the Sisters come up and yank it off as if it were nothing, and have all kinds of excuses about the modern world." The religious orders in history have been a sign of the possibility and the glory of detachment. They have been an indication that a person is detachment and has to be a slave to none.

But you don't have to go to the orders. Why, that man's house, his not having to have it, his having come to terms with this, that's a sacred sign that points beyond. This is like a sacrament itself. Indeed, it is a sacrament, an outward and visible sign of inward and spiritual grace. It is a call to humanness.

My last word is that you are not about to come off with anything remotely related to the revitalization of the local congregation if you have not taken upon yourself the discipline of poverty. One of the greatest social inventions that history has ever seen was the invention of the tithe. There was nothing pious about it. It was just the machinery worked out whereby if ten people gave up one-tenth of their income, they could have a guru sustained in their midst. By the time I came along the tithe didn't seem to have any relation to authentic reality. In the beginning, however, the tithe was a sign that the person was detached from the world.

But whether it be that or another, a sign must be. And when that sign be's, then it is a sacrament to everyone everywhere, pointing to the wondrous and glorious and painful deeps of being human, and to that Mystery which is beyond all of our petty gods.

Transparent Being

Grace be unto you and peace, from God our Father and the Lord Jesus Christ. Amen.

The lecture I'm going to give this morning I've been working on for twenty-five years. I asked my brother about that the other night and he stated it as fifty years. Sometimes I feel that I've done nothing but prepare for what I want to say this morning.

Let me read a bit of scripture from the Gospel of John.

"You must not let yourselves be distressed – you must hold on to your faith in God and your faith in me. There are many rooms in my Father's House. If there were not, should I have told you that I'm going away to prepare a place for you? It is true that I'm going away to prepare a place for you, but it is just as true that I am coming again to welcome you into my own home, so that you may be where I am. You know where I am going and you know the way I am going to take."

"Lord!" Thomas broke out, "We don't know where you're going, and how can we know the way that you'll take?"

"I myself am the way," replied Jesus, "and the truth and the life. No one approaches the Father except through me. If you had known who I am, you would have known the Father. From now on, you do know him, and you have seen him."

Then Philip said, "Show us the Father, Lord, and then we will be satisfied."

"Have I been such a long time with you," replied Jesus, "without your really knowing me, Philip? The man who has seen me has seen the Father. How can you say, 'Show us the Father?' Do you not believe that I am in the Father and that the Father is in me? The very words I say to you are not even my own. It is the Father who lives in me that carries out his work through me. Do you believe me when I say that I am in the Father and that the Father is in me? But if you cannot, then believe me because of what you see me do. [What he had to say there was really something. It's disgraceful.] I assure you that the man who believes in me will do the same things that I have done, yes, [and this is a great thing he said] and he will do even greater things than these, for I am going away to the Father. [And then, bless him, he said] Whatever you ask the Father in my name he will do – that the Son may bring glory to the Father. And if you ask anything of me in my name, I will grant it."

I have now cut out three of the lectures for this morning, but I can still identify five left, and I'm sure that there are more. Two years ago when I came back from our first teaching experience overseas, something deep had happened to me. I went into seclusion.

Oh, I was around, but the veil was drawn. That lasted almost a year. Then, three of my colleagues got hold of me and beat the daylights out of me. They said they had stood it long enough, that I had to let the water over the dam. I was angry with them, deeply angry with them, for I wanted no one to touch me.

When they forced me, I went to the board and drew this figure (see Figure 2 – 2, p. 118). We had dwelt on the knowing side in deeps that shuddered the fibers of our souls, and we had participated in the doing side with the same kind of frightening intensity. Then we had seen the relationship between these two, and just when we had the universe wrapped up, it blew from the bottom. And we were in no-thing. This knowing and doing were no longer meaningful to me. The bottom had blown, and in that blowing we had a vision of being, of what it meant not only to *know* your know and to *do* your do but finally to *be* your be.

Then we saw that being was simply the radical intensification of knowing and doing, or the radical intensification of intensified knowing and intensified doing. So we began to articulate the intensification of knowing in the *new religious mode*, and began to articulate the double intensity that comes in doing in the *new social vehicle*. And then – and this is *all* I've got to say this morning – the moment that the new religious mode began to get clear, and the new social vehicle began to get clear, it took only a flash for the bottom to blow again (where maybe it took decades for the first blow to come). Yes, it blew again and the bottom of bottomlessness itself blew. And that is what is in the center of the charts. You have to call that the intensification of the intensification of intensified knowing and doing. It is the *nothing* upon which you and I are grounded. We call this *transparent being.*

Before I start, I have to groan out of myself in abstraction what I mean by knowing and doing three times intensified. For me, just as the act before the act is the key to understanding prayer, so the being underneath any *be* that I can recognize in myself – and that is underneath any manifestation of presence that you can recognize in me – is what I mean by transparent being.

As transparency is to the solitaries, and as the sign is to the corporates, so sheer poetry is to the journeys, and the poetry underneath all poetry, or the story behind all stories, is what I mean by transparent being. It is sheer Spirit. It is sheer discontinuity. Underneath our freedom, underneath our sociality, underneath our detachment, underneath our engagement – all of which are the manifestations of the consciousness of consciousness of consciousness – is the sheer Spirit that can be stated only in the rawest form of poetry

Now the charts are not quite right yet, but they look something like this. I think I'll put the categories in circles for a moment. Here is transparent being, transparent doing, transparent knowing, and this is chastity, contemplation, poverty, then obedience, prayer, and meditation.

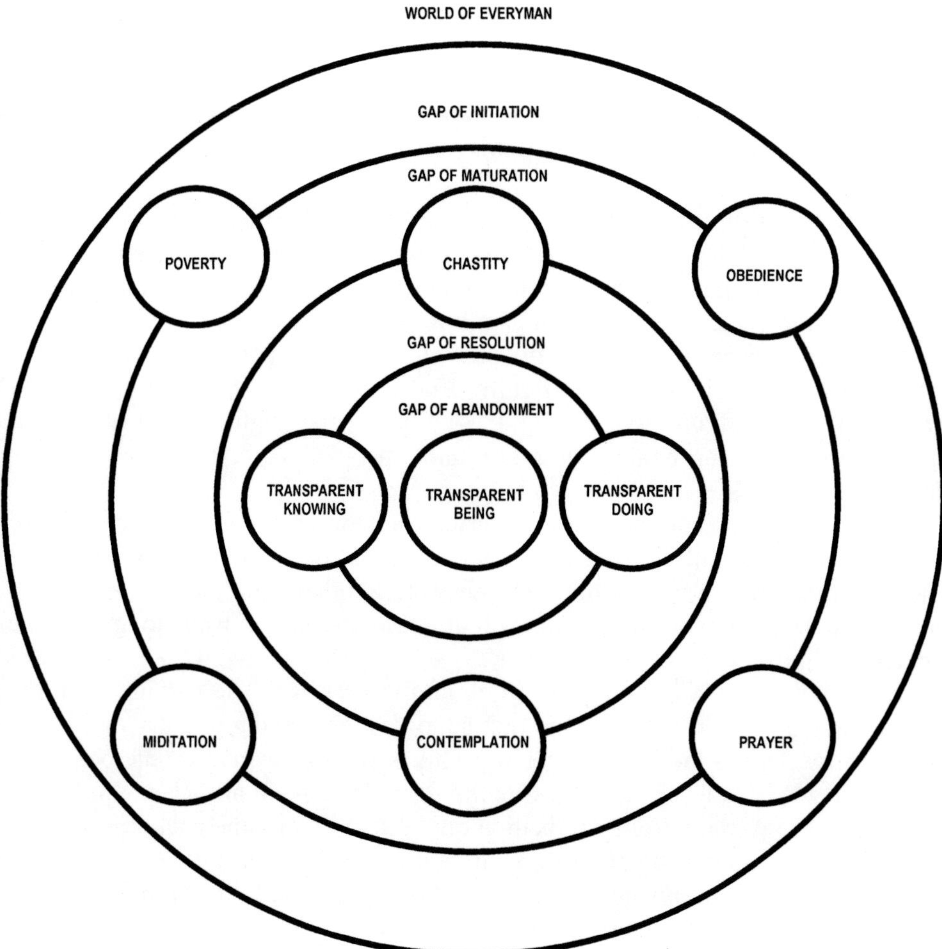

Figure 2 – 5: Transparent Being and the New Religious Mode

Oh, the way these are oriented is something when you begin to think under the rubric of journey, for that's what we're dealing with: the *journey to the center* of the self, the journey to the center of humanity, the journey to the center of the universe, the journey to the center of God. That's the journey that brings us to where I want to talk.

I've left out relationships because they're built in. Here are the four categories which I will use to discuss this, and I don't like them. The first is extreme discontinuity (for a long time I have really called this incarnational union). Under extreme discontinuity, transparent being is interior universe, dark passage, awe-full theophany, and eternal return. The second major category is unrepeatable demonstration. The third one is impossible reduplication, and the last one is imputed being.

What you have here is the universe within. You have to let your mind loose at this moment as you never did in your life. When you think to the edge of the last galaxy of the universe, when you take that same distance and superimpose it upon your image of your interior consciousness of consciousness of consciousness, then you begin to get the feel of this inward universe.

Extreme Discontinuity

There are something like four galaxies within and each galaxy has its own universe. But the galaxies are not the important thing. The important thing is what I call the gaps. The outermost gap is important because all of this is sitting in the world of everyman. This is the one who is fixed rigidly on the surface by attachment to petty idols. I mean rigidly. And if something doesn't happen, s/he was born rigid and s/he will die rigid. S/he hasn't the slightest idea of what it means to be a human being. These are "most people," as e. e. cummings calls them.

You have gaps here and the gaps are the important thing. These circles are way stations, if you please, but when you talk about discontinuity, the journey is the gap in which you pass from one galaxy to another. The passage is what is important. I don't want to explain all of these because I want to get to the centermost gap.

But maybe I can just say a word about the first gap. The passing from the surface world of everyman into the first galaxy is the passing of entry or the *gap of initiation.* This is the first awakening. This is what happens to some people in RS-I. It is why you teach RS-I. You're not out to give them any idea. You're out to catalyze the passage from the fixation on the surface into the galaxies that lead you to selfhood, that lead you to humanness itself.

All of these moments of discontinuity are times of wrenching. The wrenching sometimes comes out as a fist in the face of the teacher. I've seen it take ten years before one got out of that wrenching.

The next wrench, the *gap of maturation,* I'm not much interested in for this lecture. That's where you decide to be God's person. The wrenching here is much deeper than in the first gap.

The third one, the *gap of resolution,* is where you move on the journey of descent. It's a particularly painful one, and I don't know how many years I was in the throes of that. But I have a little story to tell you. I think that for twenty years of my conscious life I never allowed anyone to touch me beyond this level. Never. I don't know just why – maybe I was protecting myself or maybe I didn't have guts enough to tell what I knew down inside of me. Maybe I was afraid that I would misuse it or other people would misuse it. I don't know.

I remember one time a colleague came into my office. He said he had a problem. After you got through the superficialities of it, you knew that this wasn't a problem. It had to do with realms about which the person knew nothing whatsoever. That fact rocked the bottom of my being. I took him aside and went out on the back steps of the far end of the building. I said, "Sit down. I never said this to anyone before, but I'm going to say it to you." Then I took him by the hand, if you please, and led him, out of the book of Hebrews, "through the veil." This is a moment of great suffering. I have an idea that there are times when he hates my guts and that he wishes that he could have remained where he had been and know nothing about what now he knows and can no longer escape.

I'm really interested in the innermost *gap of abandonment*. It's the race to the center. That's what I want to talk about. What I'm talking about now has nothing whatsoever to do with the *word* in Jesus Christ. Then I want to say it has nothing to do with anything except the *word* in Jesus Christ.

The first stage of the journey begins with the hearing of the *word* "You are received, the world is good, the past is approved, and the future is radically open." Then, when you get to the center, the name written on that center was on the thigh of the One in white on the white horse, leading ten thousand times ten thousand. That name is *W-o-r-d*. Now you keep that in mind so you don't get lost. You begin with the *word*, and you meet the beginning in the end. It's only after the encounter with the *word* that you see that the great companion on the Way, without which there would have been no way, was the *word*.

Unrepeatable Demonstration

This last descent our fathers before us have called the "dark night of the soul," the time in which one experiences her/his contingency with a force that not only wrenches but racks one's interior being. Language has not been invented extreme enough for the mystics in any culture to articulate what they meant by the gap that they called the "dark night of the soul." Nothing but poetry, the rawest poetry, could even begin to communicate. They have hundreds and thousands of poetic words to talk about this. I think that they boiled them down into three basic images.

One is the image of the desert; the other one is the image of apostasy, or of dread, or better yet, of hell; and the third one is the image of blindness or darkness. Now let's see if we can get our minds around this.

The first image is that of aridity, or the *arid desert*. And the fantastic pain, spiritual pain, in this experience is the double paradox that's present in it. You and I know about arid moments in our lives. We've had them again and again, when meaning in this or that or the other collapses. It doesn't happen that way in this. What I'm talking about happens only when the rains are falling and all is abundant, it happens when you are not only full of meaning but there is a plethora of meaning in your being. Therefore the emptiness that comes is not experienced as a fading away or a seeping out, which is the way we experience aridity on the more superficial levels. You experience meaning as having been wantonly snatched from you. Filled with meaning, it disappears. The mystics all have been very clear about this. There's no meaning left. You become, as it were, a meaningless particle of dust, spinning in space itself. You put more poetry on that because I must hurry on.

The second image is *fearful dread.* It comes at the moment when you can point to great do's that you've been involved in, at the moment when you are more clear about a relationship to the Mystery and that you're grounded in God, at the moment when your theology seems to be just dancing for you. It's in that moment that the experience of indescribable dread attacks you. It's not as if there was a collapse. You are left racked with self-doubt in the midst of fantastic confidence. You are left in the midst of no longer being able to sense God's presence at the moment when you have clarity that you'd never had before about the presence of God. You grasp yourself as hurled into apostasy. You doubt God. But you not only doubt God, you see him, at the moment when he's the Father of all, as the demonic force behind all demonic forces. The atheist to you now seems like a saint. You could go to the board and talk about universes within, and you could talk about prayer with a power that you never dreamed. Then in the midst of that fullness, it all becomes a pile of manure. Even this fullness becomes a nothing. I tell you, there's a sense of being naked that you'd never thought was possible

The last image is *blindness.* It's not only hell, being cut off from God, but blindness. This comes at a moment when the vision, the cause, is more real than it's ever been in your life. And it isn't as if you get tired and the vision grows dim. It's as if, in the full life of the vision, pitch darkness drops over it all. It's almost as if you stand there gazing at the blazing sun in the midst of pitch darkness. Vision is gone. This is the racking our fathers called the "dark night of the soul."

Now, I'm ready to talk about *the center.* In the midst of that arid desert, in the midst of that burning hell, cut off from the Father, in the midst of that blindness, you levitate. We were joking recently. I believe that the moment that we could be utterly dependent upon the forces in the universe we would levitate. But none of us, you know, speak much anymore about the times we've levitated. I suggested to some that we all have levitated. But we don't speak about this, not out of humility, but because in our day we've lost the poetry,

Well, you levitate, for you were standing here, see, and you didn't move, you didn't walk, but suddenly you woke up and the darkness is intensified. I mean it is pitch black darkness at the center. And as you stand there in that blazing light which is sheer darkness, you see what you cannot see, a figure, the *center of the center*. And you say, "Aha! Is it a stone? Now that I am at the center of consciousness of consciousness, what's there? Is it a stone?" And it seems as if you are drawn closer, and you peer at it. It's no stone. Oh, the Aborigines in Australia would like to be here this morning. You say, "Is it a tree, the Tree of Life, maybe?" You're drawn closer, and you peer into the darkness, "It's no tree!" And you're drawn another step, and you say, "It's *nothingness*!" That's what ought to be at the center. And you say, "No! It's not nothingness!" And you come a step closer and behold, "It's a human!" It could have been naught else. Once you behold it, it is a human, I mean a common, ordinary, dirty, smelly man. It could be naught else.

This is what the mystics have talked about in every culture when they have talked about the union of reality with the center of the interior universe. It's a man. Is it Gautama? Yes. Is it Moses? Yes. Is it John Smith? Yes. Is it Sally McGillicudy? Yes. Is it Henry what-ever-his-name-is? Oh, you bet it is! And so you're drawn another step closer. And you peer, and behold, it is *the man*. I mean Jesus. I don't mean Christ. I mean Jesus.

You remember when they came to Gethsemane to get him? Jesus said, "Who are you looking for?" And they said, "Jesus of Nazareth." Now they go around this twice in that story. The first time I am sure that Jesus, who could out-act any actor, said, "I am the man." And they all fell down as if struck by lightning. Do you hear what I say? And when they got up, Jesus started over again. "Who are you looking for?" And they said, "Jesus of Nazareth." He says, "I'm the man," You get that story? At the heart is Jesus. Not Christ but Jesus. Oh, I don't care whether you want to use other poetry. At the center of the universe is the figure that represents *everyman, every person,* or consciousness of consciousness of consciousness in all of its fullness.

You won't believe what I'm going to tell you now. You see, down in the center of that figure of Jesus, a little light glows, in the midst of the pitch darkness that is bright light. And you notice exactly at the same time a kind of circle of light surrounds him, and the light grows stronger, and brighter, and hotter. You step back, for there's the key: the Mystery shines through a common, ordinary man. Then as you stand there, you hear for the first time in your life – no! no! you behold it with your own eyes – what Jesus meant when he said, "I am in the Father (I am in the light of the Mystery) and the Father is in Me."

But you're not through yet. For you notice a strange glowing in yourself, and you step back up to the figure, and do you know whose face you see within the face of Jesus? Your own unrepeatable, crummy, broken, perverted face.

No, that's not quite right. It's the face of that crummy, perverted one who has passed through the dark night of the soul, in which he is stripped of everything except his or her contingency. The same old crummy me, but collapsed into a heap of shaking palsy. The mystics called the dark night of the soul the "time of purging." But you say that only on the other side, for you know that you cannot behold the meaning of consciousness of consciousness as long as you have any way to hide from it: even spiritual exercises, even spiritual poetry, even awarenesses that are rare.

It's our face. And then for the first time in your life you understand. And because you say, "Now, I have beheld it with my own eyes," you understand the second part of what Jesus said: "Father, as I am in you, and you are in me, so I will be in them, and they will be in me."

What does it mean to have the eschatological hero in your being? There's nothing mystical about this, nothing ethereal about this. You are dealing with concretions that are so concrete that any authentic hippie would know it immediately. I always thought it was Peter that did this. He said in the midst of transfiguration (no magic in transfiguration), "Let's build three tabernacles." But Peter's not the one who said that. I said it. I wanted to stay, and there in the midst of that wonder of wonders, I offered a prayer that I might never go back. Obviously, my prayer wasn't answered. Oh, that's wrong. It was answered, for God always answers prayer. He just said, "No," and I got sent back. He did do that for me. Now, I like the word "companion," for when he sent me back, he sent me to be a companion for humankind, and nothing else.

That reminds me of the great story about Gautama, the Buddha. He experienced what you and I have been talking about and he was taken to Nirvana. At the gates of Nirvana he said, "No! As long as there is one ounce of human suffering upon the earth, even though I am worthy of Nirvana, I will not accept it." He returned to walk among people, and he walks to this day, serving suffering humanity, being a *companion of humanity*.

This sending back means that you get born all over again. You are born of a virgin. That means that you have your commission, and that you have no right except those papers. But being born of a virgin is like what Luther meant when he said, "That babe in the manger was actually a man on the cross." Your commission is so rigorous that there is no possible way for you to avoid your death on the cross.

Transparent being is a state of being that everybody experiences. It's not for the few mystics. I don't even like that word. It's not for the rare ones, though we're going to have the rare ones. There will be the rare ones who can make what I've said this morning sound like utter prose. They are professionals in the sense that they must be signs to the rest of us. But I am talking about a state that is in everyone all the time, yet I am saying more. I am saying as I tried to say of meditation that when we use the term "transparent being," we are talking about a state of being to which radical consciousness is brought. That's a state within a state and it's an amazing thing.

The state happens to us because this is who we are, long before we have any images or poetry to say to ourselves that it happened. When you come back, when you come to be the companion, you carry the scars the rest of your life. Night and day there is a bit of desert of aridity in you. The rest of your life, day after day, there's a touch of apostasy within the deeps of your being. Day after day, for the rest of your life, there's a touch of darkness that never goes away. These are the signs.

And then there come moments when there's a shudder. There come moments when there's just the bit of a glow. Any life situation begins to bleed its inner meaning, and you remember the journey that you were on and know that you're still on that journey, and know that as long as consciousness is consciousness, there is an *eternal return*. In the beginning was the *word*, and in the ending was the *word*, and all along the way you walk with Jesus in whom the Father is and who is in the Mystery. Amen.

II.

These lectures every other day are an effort, and if I were self-depreciating, I'd say a very feeble effort, to ground the new religious mode charts in humanness. I should think that by a year from now, or two years, you people would have accomplished that. This is but a start. This job is far more important than renewing that local congregation. I didn't put that right. This *is* the renewal of the local congregation. It's going to take you forty years. Those charts are terrible. They're just terrible. But it's a start. I think you young ones are going to be the ones who have to do it, and the younger you are perhaps the better. You don't have to unlearn so much as those of us who are older. And you are immediate to this arena, whereas some of us have to struggle like crazy even to come within spitting distance of it. Relative to the new religious mode charts, I don't know what I am doing in this lecture. But I suspect that I'm tangentially dealing with the relationship of the gospel to what we've been talking about.

The most important thing for us to remember about this area, I believe, is that it has nothing in the first instance to do with the gospel of Jesus Christ. It has nothing in the first instance to do with Christian theology. What I attempted to do in the first part of this talk was to describe the blown out bottom of humanness, or extremely intensified consciousness. When you deal in this area, I repeat again, you have at your disposal only raw poetry – it cannot be done any other way – just raw poetry.

I got an unsigned note in the mail which said, "Mysticism is idolatry." I didn't think that would have been too much to sign your name to. I suspected my wife for a while. I happen to believe that, also, that is if you get mysticism mixed up with the gospel. Very obviously you make use of mysticism, the poetry of mysticism. The reason why you make use of mysticism is because the mystics have experimented in these deeps. Or to put it another way, anyone who experiments in these deeps gets that tag.

It's very interesting that in every culture there are those who have set themselves apart to explore in this area. I haven't time to rehearse it, but in the concept of Muntu, out of the black man's invention of humanness, is the dimension that I was talking about in the first part of this talk. This is obviously present in the Tao out of China. One of the very interesting things about this, which took centuries to be accomplished, is that the ontological and the practical aspect of the Way were held together. I want to talk about the practical part of it.

But you have to go to India to find the experts of the experts. My brother pointed out to me the other day something that I did not know. The term "upanishad" literally meant the disciple putting his ear up to the lips of the guru. That's interesting, isn't it? Then the guru pronounced into that ear the secret of life. Those of you who are familiar with that culture know good and well what those words were. They were "Tat tuam asi." Get your ear up there to that guru's lip, or you'll miss the effect of this. You ask, "Guru, what's the secret of life?" And he says, "That thou art." And it's all over. You have the secret: "That thou art."

I have deep quarrels with the mystics on their own ground. The first and major one is that they have attempted to make the journey into a specific experience instead of seeing the dark night and the illumination as what the deeps of human existence are about all the time. You have pretty good evidence that they're wrong about this, for when I, with my poetry, was describing this in the first part of this talk, everyone of you minus none was sitting there saying, "Yes, listen to that. I know all about it." You might have preferred another kind of poetry in order to articulate it, but you knew all about it. When I was describing the illumination, you were saying, "Yeah, yeah."

I think that one of the great experiences that we've had in our Order is when we studied Teresa of Avila's *Interior Castle* and struggled several months with her to get from Mansion One to Mansion Seven. The shocking thing was that when we got to the end of it, everyone in our group knew what she was talking about. Do you hear that? It's describing what life is, what human existence is, what consciousness is, or what heightened consciousness is.

My second quarrel with the mystics on their own ground is that they infer that the aristocracy only can know of this and participate in it, rather than seeing that this is a description of an "un-state" of being for every person. To the end of time there are going to be certain individuals set aside who use themselves on behalf of all to explore these deeps with a kind of scientific thoroughness that most would not care to give themselves to.

I want us to go down into the "beyond the bottom" once again. Remember it's pitch dark in the midst of overwhelming light. You also have to get some image, like utter *stillness*. This comes again and again in the great classical discussions. To get hold of that I think you have to start out on the surface galaxy. You see, I'm standing on the earth. It's moving like anything, but I don't experience motion with it. So when you get the first glimpse into the galaxy beyond, that galaxy seems as if it's going ten times the speed of light. This is why RS-I becomes intensely frightening the moment a little chink comes in the armor. This is why they have to crucify the messenger, and the sooner they do it the more easily they can try to replace that chink. I warn you of something you already know, that if you start out to do this job, you are not going to make friends. You are going to make enemies. Let's be sure we make them for eschatological reasons.

If you participate in that gap and land on this first inner galaxy (poverty, obedience, meditation and prayer), it doesn't seem to be moving at all. But the moment you get a glimpse into the next galaxy, it seems like it's going a hundred times the speed of light. But that center is going so fast that there are no metaphors capable of describing its speed. Then when you levitate there in the midst of darkness, you experience utter stillness in the midst of fantastic speed.

I don't want to take time to talk about the peace that passes all human understanding. You talk to yourself a little bit about that

The other thing you're aware of is utter *silence* in the midst of unbelievable noise. You know I had to have a little medical work done on myself recently. Afterward, I went away to a suburb outside of Chicago. For three weeks I lived in a house all by myself. The first week I was there I knew that something dreadful was wrong. I couldn't figure it out. After about seven days, I became aware that what was wrong was that it was quiet. Then I knew the horrible noise that you live in here in the midst of the ghetto, twenty-four hours a day. What I think that noise at the center is coming from is, first of all, the screams, the cries of all humanity that ever lived, live now, and ever shall live. It's the scream of the ape. Then mixed with that is the rawest noise of off-key angels who are rejoicing over one human being experiencing the center of consciousness itself. But in the midst of all that noise is utter silence.

I have had little patience with people who have been around me who want to experiment with silence, for I am not persuaded that they knew the ontological meaning of silence. You don't play with these kinds of symbols, or they'll burn you alive. You have to deal with the fundamental meaning of them. This has to do, I believe, with the center of consciousness.

In the midst of that blackness and painful stillness and painful silence comes your commission. I have suggested that you'll want to stay and not return. The fascination fights the dread, and if fascination didn't win over dread, you and I wouldn't be here. Can you in your imagination think of that first burst of consciousness into history? I always feel it as unconsciousness oozing up through the ooze of life, and suddenly consciousness dawns. The head pops up. That is the invention of humanness. But the first experience is overwhelming dread, and that's why I suspect consciousness broke into being. Many apes broke into the kind of consciousness I'm talking about and were so frightened by the dread of it they disappeared again. How many times did this happen before what we call "human" finally stood? But along with that dread was fantastic fascination. It's almost as if the fascination is about the dread itself. And that beckoned some to stand.

Here you and I are. In the midst of that experience comes our commission. We are sent. Not wanting to go, we are sent. I've sometimes described this experience as the primordial colloquy before the foundation of the world, when I received my orders. The *commission*, when you open it, is ever the same. You are sent back to do nothing but *love*. But when you reduce the Christian faith into temporal love of one another, you haven't even begun to hear "God so loved the world that he sent his only begotten Son."

I get irritated with people who think the Christian faith is reconciliation. And by that they mean that if certain people don't like each other, you reconcile them. No, that's the way you destroy humanity. And the gospel has been reduced in it. You bet we are reconcilers, but we reconcile the world to God, if you please. When one is reconciled to God, there isn't any trouble between that person and another. The New Testament is shockingly clear at this point. You are sent back with one mission: to love.

Try to get inside Jesus' skin. He was sent to be God's love. He wasn't sent to say God's love. He wasn't sent to do God's love. He was sent *as* God's love. His job was to be a zombie, if you please – just walking around being divine love. That was his commission. It's pretty clear what happens to divine love. It always gets a stake through its heart. Always. That is a part of the commission. It wasn't that he was to be divine love even if it killed him. Divine love always gets killed.

If you're able to appreciate that just a little bit, then you're able to understand what the commission at the center is for everyone who dares to visit it. If you don't want this commission, don't get very close to that whirlpool. When it sucks you in, you finally hit the bottom. You'd better not go to any RS-I course if you don't want to end up down there with this commission. For the commission was exactly the commission that was given to Jesus, exactly the commission that you are to return as God's love.

That's your one *vocation*, being God's love in the world. The responsibility that you experience is that you have utter vocation, that you have absolute vocation. You'd secretly laugh, I hope, at anybody who asks you if you were a lawyer or a doctor or some asinine priest or a clergyman. Why, that doesn't even come in the same ballpark as your vocation. Your vocation is to be divine love. This is *the* indicative of your life, which makes clear at every point what the imperative is upon you.

You can put this in a mundane way. I heard somebody say this morning that everybody in this room has to be great. I want to put it stronger than that. Everybody in this room has to be a great deal more than great if they are returnees from the center of being itself. One way you experience this is that you can no longer sit around and wait for somebody else to be the Benedict in our time, or for somebody else to be the Aquinas in our lime, or for somebody else to be the Gautama in our time. Do you know what you have to do? You have to decide that you are it. You cannot wait any longer.

Every situation that you find yourself in, until the day nobody finds you anymore, calls for a Gautama. I want to push this further. You cannot sit around and wait for a Jesus. You must become a Jesus. When you see this, you know that the indicative is very clear. You already have your commission. You already have been assigned to be Jesus in history. That's what you were sent back for and for no other reason.

I wonder if I'm making this clear. If you dare to experience the raw heightening of consciousness, this is your fate from then on. But when you receive the commission at the bottom of your being, you have to make a *decision* about that. Those of you who know New Testament theology know that there has been a dispute through the ages as to whether Jesus was the Christ before he came or whether he became the Christ, for instance, at his baptism. That's not talking about abstract metaphysics. It's trying to talk about humanness. Jesus arrived from the bowels of being, and when you arrive from the bowels of being, you are sent with this commission. Then you have to make a life or death decision about that. Let's say that it was at his baptism and the time in the wilderness that he made the decision to be the one he was sent to be.

Impossible Reduplication

I wonder if we are not talking about the roughest decision that anybody has to make. One of the most amazing implications of this to me is that here is the primary hidden principle in any understanding of contextual ethics. My field is ethics and my mind goes there frequently. There are no norms in any situation. You have to create the norms out of which you forge your concrete act, or decision, if you please. But the hidden principle there is an unlimited affirmation of life. Do you understand that? This is to say that love, I mean divine love, is the foundation of all contextual ethics. You were sent to do nothing but love this world in an unlimited sense, and all of it from the beginning to the end.

How do you talk more concretely about this kind of love? I suppose that it is just going around opening up every future that you meet. That's *divine love.* I suppose that it is just going around and pronouncing absolution on every past that you meet. I suppose that it is just going around filling every present full of the meaning that every present has. I suppose that's what love is.

The human soul has a propensity, a desire for the divine love that is so deep and so broad that it's incomprehensible. I approach boasting just a touch here. I was given a situation in which I had a chance to love the Aboriginal people in Australia. I think one of the great joys of my life is that I wrote a bit of poetry, which is terrible poetry, but it said to them the meaning of their past, including the brutality of the white man, which is a part of their past. It gave new meaning for them. Then it painted a new possibility of the future relative to the black people across the face of the world. And it laid out the meaning of the present in terms of the demands that are here. That's what I mean by divine love. That's all Jesus did. He opened the future, made new the past, and filled the present full of meaning. That's our vocation.

The tragedy of this is absolute failure. One thing that has always annoyed me since I was a young man is when the Methodists wanted to take all metaphors out of the hymnal that seemed to depreciate man, for example, "such a worm as I." How stupid! For that is exactly how the one who has visited the center experiences self, as "such a worm as I," as a perpetual failure, as a born failure. But mark you well, that's eschatological failure and not temporal. A revolutionary never fails. The reason why is that he or she accepts the unavoidable failure at the center. Any saint experiences sinfulness the depths of which the "un-saint" could never dream. I like to say that the further up the mountain of lucidity you get, the further you can see the valley of sin in your own life. You are doomed to failure.

This is part of the struggle that Kazantzakis talks about. This struggle has nothing to do with a belly-full of butterflies you get in trying to get through a summer program. That's not the struggle they're talking about. The struggle is to win what you set out to do in the awareness of the eschatological failure at the center of your being. That's the struggle that he is talking about.

I like to think of the new religious mode charts as an electric grid with lights going on. In the image that the church built of Jesus, all those lights were burning, interrelated at full power. In some people and myself those lights blink. And there are a great number of them that aren't functioning. That's what I mean by the failure.

This, I think, is the key to what our forebears in the faith have called spiritual suffering. It's the grave humiliation of knowing that you were sent to be divine love, but you discover yourself an unavoidable failure in carrying out the commission. This is the spiritual suffering, it seems to me, at the heart of humankind.

I want to say just a word about the imitation of Christ. Some of you may remember the book *In His Steps* that came out at the turn of the century: "What would Jesus do?" Or some of you may remember *The Magnificent Obsession*: "Don't let your left hand know what your right is doing." I tell you, what we did to poor Jesus in the last part of the last century and the first part of this century is make him into something less than an effeminate boy. Somebody told me that in a Buddhist temple around here there was Gautama's picture and Sallman's "Head of Christ." You can almost see why they picked that, can't you? We have made him into a superficial, pious, bourgeois man.

Sure, you imitate Jesus, but you be sure you get clear what you are imitating. He is the unrepeatable sign of the center. I don't want to take time to do it in detail, but if you want to get hold of the Jesus you imitate, then I suggest you take the new religious mode charts and see how they illuminate him. And if Thomas à Kempis were here, he'd say, "Yea, yea, verily." You just start there.

Jesus was a man of prayer. That means that he was his own man. I like the illustration of Lazarus. You remember Jesus was going to get him out of the tomb. A lot of people came by to see him get Lazarus out, and he says, "Lazarus, come out." And Lazarus didn't come out. So he says, "Lazarus, come out!" And Lazarus still didn't come out. Then he says, "Please, Lazarus, come out." And the people got discouraged, and along about midnight they left. Then Jesus got serious. He says, "Now look, Lord. Either you bring Lazarus out of that tomb or you're going to have to slay me." Well, I mean the Lord got busy and Lazarus came out of there. Jesus was his own man. He prayed,

This man meditated. He grasped himself as the federal agent of all of Israel. He was sociality. They called him the second Adam. A detached man, a man you couldn't buy. An engaged man. You remember when the Greeks came to him just before it was all over and said, "If you hang around here, they're going to crucify you. Come on up to Greece and you'll beat the rap." And Jesus replied, "For this cause I came into the world." Shall I go on with contemplation and chastity? He was the manifestation of sheer being. That's why the church called him *the man.* This is where meditation comes, it seems to me

I would like to have time to take the four Gospels and get a portion of the gospel that just fit in each one of the 144 boxes of the new religious mode charts. It would be like creating a special lectionary for the purpose of getting a fresh montage of the one who is the unrepeatable sign in history. When you say "sign in history," it's like poverty, both in the sense of an interior posture and an objective sign. This Jesus Christ was the one who traveled the distance of history. That's what the church meant when it held him up as the great exemplar.

Imputed Being

I have one more thing I want to talk about here, that is, what I call *imputed being.* I have great trouble with this. You remember the theology of imputed righteousness? We Methodists and we Roman Catholics have never taken that very seriously. We like to talk about actual righteousness. Briefly, the great poetry is this: Jesus took all my sins and put them on himself and handed me back all his righteousness. These people saw something in humanness. And when I call it imputed being, I mean something like this: Being takes within itself my un-being and makes Being out of it, and bestows upon my un-being sheer Being. This is fundamentally where the *word* comes into focus. If you look at your own life you can see that. Here you *be* in the midst of all of your un-being. It's as if Being takes your crummy un-being and makes Being out of it; just bestows the possibility of Being upon you.

The exemplar stands at the very heart of what I am talking about here. It was within that fluke within history, if you want to call it that, that this kind of awareness came with fantastic clarity. Put another way, it means that the *word* is that without which you and I would not dare to make the inward journey. The *word* is that without which we would not dare to take the next step. The *word* is that which enables us to take the next step. When you say, "All that is, is good," "all that I am is accepted," "all that ever will be is significant," and "all that ever was is approved," you are talking about the heart of Being, which we experience as imputed Being – that all of our un-being is imputed with Being. All Being is bestowed upon our un-being at any moment. That's how, it seems to me, the Christ Happening is key relative to the categories of the new religious mode.

The Recovery of the Other World

The most astonishing thing that has resulted from the body of awakened people who more than half a century ago made the great resolve to renew the church in this century was this: they stumbled upon the Other World that is in the midst of this world. I never dreamed even ten years ago that such a thing could happen in my lifetime.

I want to try, child as I am, to talk about the Other World in the midst of this world. It has been a hidden world for centuries, a lost world. I am reminded of a motion picture called *The Lost World.* The lostness of the Other World in the midst of this world seems to be a much greater lostness. To have it disclose itself afresh forces one, regardless of the years, to experience oneself all over again as a stumbling child first learning to walk.

Church people or religious people did not discover this Other World. Ordinary people discovered it in the 20th century. It was discovered a long time before it was recognized as the Other World in the midst of this world and before it was acknowledged as the Other World.

There is nothing supernatural about the Other World. It is as ordinary as any mundane activity that you and I engage in. It has to do with the explosion of consciousness that has taken place in our day, in and through which the radicality of humanness became clear as never before in history. Therefore, I would anticipate that what happens from the disclosure of this Other World to people in our century may be more colossal than those other great moments in history, when this same Other World made its presence powerfully known. But you must be clear, when you talk about the Other World, that you are dealing with the ordinary secular world and the secular consciousness of people.

The Ontology of the Other World

One way to comprehend the broad picture is to grasp that the Other World involves an understanding of the ontological dimension of life beyond the moral. But when I say "understanding," that is not quite right. To experience the being that is the Other World is to understand that Other World. That is the way that world is. It may help those of you who know Nietzsche to think of his *Beyond Good and Evil*. This is the realm of the Other World. It is the realm of wild self-consciousness beyond the superimposition of one's rational capacities upon it. That is a rather difficult statement to make because even to talk about the Other World is to get your rational faculties engaged in it. But one of the remarkable things about reason is that it points beyond itself. The Other World is the world beyond reason that reason itself points to.

As reason attempts to understand and talk about it, what is being said is only indicative of that Other World. The Other World is radical being or raw self-consciousness, and to make any interpretation of it is to take one step backwards into this world which is the world of reason that reason invents.

Another way to talk about this philosophically is to say that in our time we have succeeded in a rather admirable way in destroying the two-story universe. We understand that we live and die in one world, and when we are dead we are really dead. That means the two-story image has been smashed. We have gotten rid of metaphysics. That needs qualification, because one never lives without metaphysics. The trouble is with the term "metaphysics." It was related to the second-story universe, or to the understanding that reason finally was the king of the universe.

In our day we are building a *new metaphysics*. You grasp yourself as living on one plane, but you have experienced the *transparency* of that plane itself. I like to think of it as holding a match underneath a paper and first seeing little streaks come out. Then it turns brown, and then it breaks through and pops into flame. That goes through my mind when I think of transparency. Or perhaps it is more like sticking your fist through life itself.

Maybe I can illustrate it this way: you and I have lived in a time in which the uniqueness of the person was emphasized, and this had to be so. This is what happens, I suspect, whenever a culture fails in making clear to people what it is to be human. Then you have a new birth of existentialistic reflection. I am not talking about abstract philosophy. An illustration of this principle is that the black people in our day, in order to be human beings, had to embrace blackness to the hilt. It so happens that in doing so they enabled some white folk, for the first time in their lives, to embrace their whiteness. But when they embraced their uniqueness to the hilt, black or white, they experienced transparency. It is as though their fist went through their uniqueness. Right now we are discovering all over again what it means to be human beyond our uniqueness, not by going around our uniqueness but by going through our uniqueness. That is the experience of transparency or sticking your fist through life.

In this one world of one plane, the transparency of that plane is the new metaphysics. But what I suspect history is going to call this, in one way or another, is phenomenology, or phenomenological thinking. The metaphysical question of *the real* as an abstraction apart from my consciousness is bracketed. Rather, it is your experience of the Other World. A state of being, a state of awareness, or a state of consciousness is the most objective reality that you have ever experienced. I want to warn you not to let the epistemology you were trained in, in which subject and object are divided, get in your way.

Let me come at this through theology. Tillich is a good example here. Those of you who know his *Systematic Theology* know that he begins with the ontological situation and then moves to the interpretation of Christ, which is the existential for Tillich. Tillich himself made the case that when you talk about the essence of humanity being the kind of essence that creates its own essence, the first use of the word "essence" in that sentence is dealing with the ontological. There is more to that than it sounds, for you could not even make the decision that determines your selfhood if you did not already have a montage in your being through which to look at reality. That is the ontological for Tillich.

Therefore, those of us who have come down hard on the existential pole, on freedom and decision, were always taking for granted an understanding of humanness in the midst of which that decision was made. The discovery of the Other World in terms of this transparency is the forging of a new montage. In this case, because the revolution is global, it is going to be a global montage that finally defines humanness that is the Other World. The movie "The Gospel According to St. Matthew" showed a man who lived his existence from beginning to end in the Other World and in the midst of that made decisions that defined the concretions of his life.

State of Being

I want to speak more about what I mean by a *state of being*. A state of being is comprised of an image, an accompanying affection, and a pre-decisional resolve.

I don't know how many of you have read Golding's *Inheritors*, but it was about primitive man breaking into consciousness. One of the figures that he used over and over was the primitive man coming into a new situation. He experienced it as though chaos had suddenly taken over. That is, the images in his mind were not capable of giving meaning to the over-against-ness that was impinging upon him. He would have to invent a new image that would give this external situation meaning. In the book he is pictured as pushing on his head to produce a new image. I like that. I have seen people, who were not so primitive, push on their heads to get that new image. I call what was going on in him a *big think.* Grasping the Other World involves a *think* – I do not want to say an image, I do not want to say an idea, I do not want to say a construct, I do not want to say a concept. It is down underneath all those. When you are dealing with a state of being, you are after the *think.*

The second thing in a state of being I call a *great feel.* I have a colleague who calls the *think* impressionistic and the *feel* expressionistic, and that is not too bad. For me, the impressionist painters were starting with what could be seen. Then they pushed it until it bent into the Other World. The expressionists went through it.

If you call that *think* a primordial think, then you have to call the *feel* a primordial feel. That *think* and that *feel* cannot be separated.

When you boil them down, the *great think* is fundamentally composed of mystery – not the kind of mystery that may be solved tomorrow, but the mystery that never goes away. This is what they mean when they talk about *no-thingness.* "Nothingness" – the *big think* of nothingness, absolute nothingness. That is the Mystery in which the *big think* becomes the final overagainstness of your total existence, not because you say so, but because you have the *big think* to prove it so. It is the primordial *big think*. It has many faces and many forms.

The *big feel* that always accompanies the *big think* is awe. Awe too has many faces. Awe, as Otto pointed out so clearly in his book *The Idea of the Holy* is always dread and fascination at the same time. When you deal with that *big think*, you are breaking through reason, dealing always with that which is beyond reason. And in the awareness of your overagainstness to that mystery, you are shattered with terror. I like to think that humankind came into existence through awe. Many stabs at consciousness of consciousness probably produced humanity because those early humans were rocked by terror, by the sheer mystery which consciousness about consciousness is. You want to use the word "God" here? You do not need to use the word "God," but when you talk about God, the God who is beyond God, you are not talking about the moral delineation of some metaphysical principles. You are talking about the One who sends cyclones and the gentle rain to grow the wheat, who rocks the ocean with mighty storms, and simmers them into a mirror of stillness. You are talking about the One who pulls you from a woman's womb and later buries you in the earth from which you come. You are talking about the One who makes you sixty years old, and you do not have any choice about it.

And yet, with this terror is fascination. That is harder to describe than terror. It is a compulsion over which you grasp you have no control whatsoever, and it pulls you on in the midst of and through the terror. These two are there at one and the same time. I remember not so long ago I thought I was caught; I thought people were onto me. Before I knew it, I ended up over a toilet vomiting, with my hands on each side. But in the midst of that terror I perceived a fascination. At such a time you do not say this is the leading of Providence. When you are finally able to get back on your feet, you know it was the hand of the One, through the grace of our Lord Jesus Christ, who you have come to call your God and your Father. He does not look like your God and your Father when he beats you up, but he is. I am proud to have lived in the 20th century, in which this has become clearer than it ever was in all of history. But its roots are back there from the foundation and the dawn of consciousness itself. Oh, in our time, how this Other World has broken in upon us!

Perhaps you have thought in the area of psychology. In a recent book Joseph Campbell deals with schizophrenia. I am not sure he says it, but if he did not he ought to, that the difference between a spirit person in the Other World and the schizophrenic is that the spirit person is swimming and the schizophrenic is drowning. Here I make a prophecy. Before twenty years are up, you are going to see the psychiatric profession turned upon its ear. It has to meet the times in which it lives, for the times which bore it are gone and new times have come.

Or what about mythology? You have been taught to believe that mythology is a fairy story that we humans have outgrown. No, not by any means. Mythology is the frame whereby people hold this experience of the Other World. The mythologies of the past are gone. They no longer communicate well to us. Probably the biggest contradiction in our time is the absence of an adequate mythology whereby one has a road map over and through the topography of the Other World. Perhaps, if you seriously intend to renew society, one of the major jobs is to create the mythology which feeds into what we have named the *Social Process*, and within that, "Inclusive Myth," that will flow out through the whole society.

The Poetic Topography of the Other World

In our time the world has slowly become conscious of the Other World in four areas. One we have called *The Land of Mystery.* In our lifetime we have rediscovered this mystery. As a matter of fact, the natural sciences have discovered it; the psychological sciences have discovered it; the mathematical sciences have discovered it. And I need not reiterate that the whole existentialist thrust in the 20th century unveiled for people their overagainstness of that which is no thing, or nothing. This is the first breakthrough of a fantastic arena in the Other World.

The second breakthrough has been in the area of freedom. We call it *The River of Consciousness.* This refers to Jean Paul Sartre's poetry of the *en soi* and the *pour soi* or Kierkegaard's understanding of the self as a relationship which relates itself to itself, and when it goes about its proper business of being a relationship which relates itself to itself, it grounds itself transparently in the power that constituted it. But these are only two of the hundreds of people who have broken through in this area.

The third way in which we have broken into the Other World is with the concept of engagement. The next two areas have been broken loose more by social upheavals than by intellectual schools, although the intellectual schools have dealt with them. I think of the youth culture in our time. This was a sociological manifestation of a search for a dimension of existence that this present world was not capable of providing. One of the crucial insights they saw and held before the world was authentic engagement in life. They are the ones who, however inadequately, began to recover the word "love." In the midst of their lostness – and no one could blame them for it – they began to grasp what it meant to be concerned with that which was unsynonymous with oneself. Their revolt against vocations, and their revolt against money for the sake of money were indicative of this awareness of another realm, which they pointed to with love, if you please, *agape.* How do we give ourselves to the journey of humankind and not just live on behalf of ourselves? This area we call *The Mountain of Care.* The Other World, which is the realm of the awe-full mystery and of radical consciousness, is also the world of taking upon your back responsibility for the historical and global journey of humanness.

Before I go on to the last of the four arenas, I pause a moment to remind you that ~~the Other World is beyond the realm of good and evil~~. ~~It is in the ontological~~ and not in the moral dimension. Whatever you say about the Other World is always in the indicative and never in the imperative. The Other World knows nothing whatsoever about imperatives, which are in this world and a crucial part of this world. Without imperatives you would not have this world. However, in the Other World there is only the indicative. When you talk about the Mountain of Care or picking up the burden of all mankind, you are not talking about something that says you ought to do it. The indicative is that the one who lives in the Other World just shows up with the world on his or her shoulders. When you live before the Mystery, the world is yours, period.

The last arena we call *The Sea of Tranquility.* I rather like that. It dawned on me that to the astronauts, when walking around on the moon, the earth is "up there." I always knew "heaven" was "up there." But when you are on the moon, "up there" points exactly to this life here, where the Other World is. I want to go there one of these days and see, just to be sure, that the Other World is right here. *The Sea of Tranquility* is the recovery of that weird peace right where there is no peace. There is no sentiment here, for the Other World is right in the midst of this world.

I never dreamed that this awareness would break loose in my lifetime. We who worked for the renewal of the church had to fight every second any nonsense about peace or joy in this world. You would never have had the renewed church if you had not slain that sentimental misunderstanding of authentic peace and joy. I never dreamed that in my lifetime it would be possible, however, to use those words authentically. I have understandings inside myself in this arena that I never dreamed could be.

Actually, in the Other World there is only one state of being, not four. For where consciousness is, there is the mystery, there is the world on your back, and there is the peace that passes reason's capacity to grasp it as peace. There is no sentiment here. This world, in which the Other World is, is a tragic world. Unamuno is quite right when he talks about the tragedy of the world. Existence itself is tragic. If the whole journey of humanity is not your specific vocation, you would never have the slightest idea what you mean when you talk about the "joy unspeakable" and "full of glory." They are woven together. When you dare to live your life before the Mystery, there is peace and joy. If you have authentic peace and joy, you can be sure you are living your life before the Mystery.

You could have drawn the road map a million other ways with different poetry. We have delineated four areas which we think broke loose in our century, and then we divided each one of those into four treks, which makes a total of sixteen treks. We then divided those treks into four states of being each. That means on the Other World charts,[8] 64 states of being are delineated. But remember they are all one.

I would like to read an illustration of some poetry in the language of a state of being. What I will do is weave together four states of being into one state in a paragraph that represents a trek. You understand there is nothing new at all in what we are doing. What is actually going on is a translation from one language to another. When you deal with the Other World, you are translating from the language of the intellectual dimension of life into the language of the state-of-being dimension of life. It is a poetic language:

> One day a person is driven by whatsoever vicissitudes of life into the consciousness that he himself must die. It is like being in a state of shock. A strange force intrudes. Suddenly he is submerged in awe; he feels it hovering all about him; he feels its penetration into the deepest corners of his innermost being. In quiet terror, and with an inexplicable fascination, he knows the fragility of his total existence. He feels his contingency, and beholds the passingness of all things. It is like a mortal wound from which he knows he will never recover. As the absurdity and the irrationality of it all seeps deep within, a burning, objectless anger rises and rages until utility itself turns into a heavy numbness and everything becomes disoriented; all is nothingness; there is no place any more to stand, just terrifying mystery. And hanging helplessly, swirling in emptiness, engulfed in awe, it dawns at long last, like the rising of a black sun, that exactly here is the finally real before which he is fated and invited to live and die his life. This is the great encounter with the awe-full mystery.

The Basic Significance of the Other World

In conclusion, in dealing with the Other World that is right in the midst of this world, you are dealing with what it means to be a human being. Thirty years ago our whole world was hanging on by its fingernails on a cliff. It was going to pieces raising the question, "What is life all about?" Now we have come out of the trough and are moving on the crest of the wave. Once again in history people have found the answer. This does not mean that there will not be many crests in the future. But in our time, it is here. Now, when someone asks you what life is all about, you have something to bear witness to.

I have said one thing. The Other World may be the most crucial key there is for actually turning on the processes that will snowball the arrival of a new web of relationships that define society. Very likely, also, within the poetry of the Other World charts is the secret of the new mythology that will enable humankind to find the way to swim, if you please, in the rivers of radical consciousness and become human. It has been a long time since people, with any sense of genuineness, could speak of what fulfillment meant, of what happiness meant.

---

[8] Ibid., *The Courage To Lead*, pp.106-13.

Moralities rise out of new definitions, of new experiences of what it is to be human. As you delineate the topography of the Other World, you are building the basis for the new morality that every sensitive person cries out for – not only the youth, but old men and old women. It has been a long time in the church since we have known what we meant when we talked about a "Christian man" or a "Christian woman." You are beginning here to define again what you mean when you talk about a person of faith, a person of Spirit in this world.

In working on the Other World, you are also building the tool for the new evangelism. I do not mean by "evangelism" anything that you have been programmed to mean by that word. I mean the means whereby you can elicit out of other people the decision that renders it possible for them to decide to live an authentic life. Years ago, when I was teaching in seminary, one of the problems people talked about was that they had no way for the new theology really to get down into the pews. It was not that the clergy could not articulate it. They could. But lives are not changed by intellectual ideas. The work on the Other World is the beginning of the creation of an instrument that will enable people to have self-consciousness about the states of being that define them.

We have talked frequently about popular preaching. You are going to see a lot of that going on in the world. It is the kind of spin you do with somebody sitting next to you on a commuter train – and they do not know until ten years later because you do not use any language that sounds religious – that new possibilities and new life flooded into their veins. I suspect that if you had 200,000 people located according to a rational grid across the world, you could design a popular preaching curriculum so that on April 28, in 1982, all 200,000 people would be spinning on "state of being #36." If the church is going to build a new society, this kind of tactical work needs to go on.

The Long March

Grace and peace be unto you from God our Father and the Lord Jesus Christ.

A little love poem, if you will:

> On a dark night, kindled in love with yearnings, oh, happy chance, I went forth without being observed, my house being now at rest. In darkness, but secure, by the secret ladder, disguised. Oh Happy Chance. In darkness and in concealment, my house being at rest, in the happy night, in secret, when none saw me nor I beheld ought, without light or guide save that light which burned in my heart.

I believe that the heart of St. John of the Cross is found in the fifth, sixth, and eleventh chapters where St. John deals with the *dark night of the soul.* In eleven he deals with what we call the *long march of love*. Both of these are the dark night of the soul.

In the section of St. John we call "the dark night," he emphasizes the intellectual. He deals with the dark contemplation. In eleven, he moves more to the practical, or what we mean by the "long march." There he uses the image of the strange fire.

Throughout the history of the church and Christian doctrine, there has been long, serious, and sometimes violent conflict between those who emphasize the rational and those who emphasize the volitional, existential, experiential, and practical. Though all of us have a deep appreciation for both contestants in this war, probably each of us shows up standing with the forces of the practical. So did St. John. This is to say that chapter eleven is more important to him than chapters five and six. In eleven he deals with the volitional, with the practical, with the cognitive or effective dimension of humanity.

In the dark night, behind the sense of humiliation, of weakness, of abandonment or resentment, and of suffering lies something like this: in the midst of life a happening happens in which you become aware of that which is other than what you have known all your life. This is the awareness of your own contingency, of the fact that you pass away.

It may be that your first awareness of this was at age three, or maybe two. Was I three when I wandered out into the street, saw the gypsies come by, and ran home screaming? That is the first consciousness I have of my life. Perhaps the first experience of consciousness, really, was when they yanked me from the security of my mother's womb into the God-awful world of pain and suffering, guilt and death.

Then weeks or months or years later, you experience the *word*, which has been expressed in a million different poetries during the past twenty thousand years. That *word* has always been there. What is important about the *word* is that a name is given. Nothing is taught; it simply gives me a name. When that name comes, there intrudes on my being a dark, strange, imposing, conquering image. It begins with a strange exhilaration, and also fright. Often, those who strike back at the bearer of the *word* are the most exhilarated. When that dark image comes in, one knows dread and fascination. Sometime later, a week, a lifetime, that image becomes filled full. I sometimes call this the experience of the ten-ton crane falling on me.

What happens in that encounter is held in the phrase of the East: "The one in the many and the many in the one." This is a phenomenological observation, an existential reality we all know about. The strange mystery present to you in the dark, imposing, conquering image is not "lo, here or lo there," but is the All, the Final, that is everywhere and is in everything. That is why to love God is to love everything. That is not a metaphysical statement; it is a profound, phenomenological confession. "He who doth not love All, doth not love God." This is what Augustine meant when he said, "Love your neighbor in God and love God in your neighbor." All fellow creatures, large and small, conscious and unconscious, are your neighbor. Look at how close that table is, or the chair you are sitting upon.

That is the ten-ton crane. That strange, very dark image – that imposes itself upon you and seems out to conquer all – becomes activated. From that moment on, there comes an indescribable warfare in the mind that is cut off from all temporality and focuses itself simply upon the Mystery. This is a long, dark night of humiliation that never ends. Nothing you ever attached yourself to is worthy of your attachment; yet you spend your whole life attached to it. You die. Out of this comes the deep sense of weakness. Your only strength is in your relationships and with the presence of this strange, dark image. You recognize that every one of those relationships shall pass away with you. The only strength is the strange, dark image of the All in All. This is the sense of utter forsakenness that is the core of resentment. Here is the key to life suffering.

The struggle is that another world is in my being at the core of my selfhood. The image is both deep within me and far outside me. It is the reflective part of my being. As St. John would say, when the Mystery intrudes, the effective, connotative aspect of being is impacted. Something different, but not inseparable from what I have described, takes place. This is the strange fire kindled within. While the dark image imposes itself, the strange fire in the practical, volitional part of my being is enkindled. The strange fire is the awe. The awe is not in us; we are in the awe.

We know about dread and fascination. But have you noticed that only when the ten-ton crane drops, only when you see the All in All, when you grasp that your life is only universal benevolence, then the awe is let loose within. At that point, you begin to paw away, trying to get rid of the awe because the small fire within you has burned away every emotional attachment you ever had to those things that pass away.

This is why those of you who run like scared sheep from trouble in your marriages are fools. Could you grasp yourself going to the grave aware that you had turned your back on divine grace? Mark you, divine grace comes with killing, ruthless pain. I told a young woman yesterday, "I want you to remember two things: one, there are not any personal problems in life (that is an empirical statement); and two, the divine activity is in every activity and it may take you ten years to understand that."

The presence of God is in everything. Have you noticed that once you have tasted the awe, every time you snuff it out, a new dose comes, no matter how far you have tried to run from it? It keeps on kindling and kindling. While you are fighting the dark image with every power, force, and troop you can muster, you find yourself ridiculously falling in love with the enemy, with God.

Rootlessness

You are falling in love with God, with the God in All. You are falling in love with the One who meets you in everything. The experience of falling in love is an Armageddon within: it tears you this way and that. I call it "rootlessness." When you fall in love, you begin to experience absolute ineffectivity. You experience total depletion. When you are falling in love, you also experience a strange, utter unfulfillment. This is the long march.

When you experience a not-at-homedness wherever you are, you are falling in love with God, who scorches away your attachments to either this world or the Other World. This God who wants you is a jealous God; and because he is the image of naught, of nothingness, it can never be said that he is a being. There is not the Other World and this world and then something else called God. And yet, this other-than, this totally other-than, only exists in the Other World that is in this world. This means that for the rest of your life you will be torn this way and that.

Ineffectivity

When you grasp that God has burnt from you any attachment to anything whatsoever, including your own spirituality, you are ineffectivity. You are the minnow in the whole of history. To fall in love with the All-in-All means that you sense only ineffectivity for the rest of your life.

It is a long, hard road to grasp that you and I are literally nothing; and to be God's man and God's woman is to be nothing. If there are to be any consequences to your life as a religious, they will come so many centuries after you are dead that no one will even be able to find your bones. You are building the City of God, not the City of Man.

Yet, there is no City of God except in the midst of this world. Suppose you finish Fifth City. Do you think God will allow you more than one moment of self-satisfaction? If you did one billion times more than you are doing with your life, it would not leave an imprint on anything.

This brings us to the question of the transparent life. Someone came in to see me the other day and did me a service by warning us that we had better be careful about the trap of quietism. Quietism ran more rampant in the Middle Ages perhaps than at any other time in the church's history. We must avoid that. In our day, however, activism, not quietism, has run rampant in the church. I see a far greater danger there as we turn toward the world. Let no one think for a moment that our greatest temptation is quietism. Our greatest temptation is that upon which we have been nursed, activism.

We are, however, beyond quietism and activism. Both have experienced transparentization. The issue is not quietism versus activism; it is quietism and activism versus transparent reality. To put it in more sociological terms, we are beyond the Roman Church; we are beyond the Protestant Church. Out of both of these is coming into being the new form of the church of Jesus Christ.

Transparentization means the dark night is always with you. The dark night itself is the light. The humiliation is the light, the weakness is the light. The resentment is the light. The suffering is the light.

In the long march, transrationality happens when you belong neither to this nor to the Other World. Pliny the Elder said, "These Christians out-think, out-love and out-die any other people." When you grasp yourself in relation to that which is present in this world, but is not contained in it, you become rational in such a fashion that you out-rationalize the rational. In the broad, when we say rational we mean civilization.

Civilization does not constitute itself. It is in relation to that which is other than the civilizing process. Otherwise, you do not have movement. That is why any new rational structure, which is aware of that which is other than rational, we call the irrational. Once one has visited the wellspring of the irrational, he does not dismiss the rational. The rational is intensified. Therefore, when the religious dimension or the irrational dimension of life breaks loose, a new construct of reason, a new vehicle for society comes into being. Wherever you smell intensified rationality, you have evidence that someone has visited the wellspring of irrationality itself. So when you are feeling sorry for yourself about being homeless, remember that this lovesickness you are experiencing is for the sake of burning you up in such a way that you can forge new structures of society on behalf of all.

Secondly, something like trans-actionality happens. In the midst of grasping your total ineffectivity, you are in fact capable of acting transparently, of actualizing impossibility. In Korea our colleagues have changed the universe in one year's time. Yet, if you sit around the table with them you see they are experiencing a deep dose of ineffectivity.

Thirdly, on the other side of the experience of dryness, of being all gone inside, comes a strange kind of sense that God is my friend. I realize this is next to impertinence, which I fear more than anything else, but I mean God knows I am his friend. He knows I will always be there and he is betting his future on me. That is what it means to be all burnt out inside.

It is hard for us to think the thoughts of God, but we must. We are not God, but we have to think the way God does. He is depending on us. That is why he burnt us out. I can hear Peter say, "I'd be glad to be someplace else, but where else can I go?" Burning you out is God's doing. He wants you to love him and him alone. So long as you have the least inclination to go out and make a name for yourself, he cannot depend on you.

The last category is trans-felicity, fulfillment. Socrates tried to say this with the word "eudaemonia." When you have all the satisfactions taken away, you know life is fulfilled, fulfilled in God. You are not fulfilled because the spouse is pleasing, because your children have achieved, but you are fulfilled in God.

It is precisely in the moment that you are aware of absolute rootlessness that you become aware that you are conceiving beyond your own capacity. It is in the awareness of ineffectivity that you know you are doing beyond your capacity to do. In the midst of grasping yourself burnt over like they burned over the plateaus of Africa, you know your staying power, a thrust that obviously is beyond your capacities.

Now, fulfillment is not something you define. My fulfillment is being in love with God, which love is born of God's wondrous love of me. Humans invented sin. God knows nothing about sin because he forgave me my sins before the foundation of the world. The Lord laid down his life for me, not because I was bad, but because he cared about me. That is my fulfillment.

What in the world is there to say after the dark night except "Praise the Lord"? What is there to do after you have been through the long march? That stillness is the stillness of God working; it is Being itself working in and through your being. I like the way the New Testament talks about it: you never can see God, but once in awhile you can see a leaf wiggle on a tree.

Now, you are going into the world to create a new vehicle for society. You will never see it. You will do it. You neither go into the world as a quietist nor as an activist. You go as a transparentized person. For our day this is a way to talk about trusting Being. Such trust is out over 70,000 fathoms. After struggling, you relax. Remember, however, relaxation is eternal rootlessness, eternal ineffectivity, eternal depletion, and unfulfillment forever.

I am not so sure we really want to go on such a long march. Yet, if all your life you have wondered exactly what was meant by the Kingdom of Heaven, then remember these words: "Blessed art thou . . . right now, right now . . . for yours is even now . . . the Kingdom of Heaven."

Hope

Recently, a few of us went to see a very wealthy manufacturer who is seventy-one years old. We went filled with hope that we could tell him about something that would really excite him. We took him to a fine restaurant in a fine old hotel and the four of us sat down at a table. This gentleman proceeded to talk for the next two hours straight. I barely had three minutes to bring up the subject we had paid for the lunch to talk about, and by the time the three minutes came up, I did not want to say a thing. I just wanted to leave.

For two hours this man spouted nothing but cynicism, cynicism, cynicism. He did not come up for air. The interesting thing was that he had us down under the table with him because everything he said was true. There was no contradicting him because he was right. He talked about business, about politics – there was scarcely a subject he missed. He was highly informed. I kept trying to muster a debate with him, but my head kept shaking up and down, affirming what he was saying. We were all in despair. We were grateful when he finally left so we could drag ourselves back to our hotel and sink into our misery,

This is an experience you have had. It was in the midst of this oppressive despair that I became aware of an objectivity called "hope." It is an objectivity called hope but it is beyond hope. Camus suggested that the last point on the journey to a person's waking up has to do with when s/he finally surrenders hope.

What have you got to hope about? There is no hope. The only image left you is a funeral director's office where you, naked as a jaybird, lie, as cold as his refrigerator will make you. It is that simple. Everything you spend your life for – your children, your nation, your fine company – the day after tomorrow they are not going to be there any longer. That is finally surrendering the last vestige of hope.

The old man we visited was spelling out exactly the way life is. He did not know it, but he was still reaching for hope. Kazantzakis calls hope the last temptation. When you grasp this, you have become a believer – and not in any religion – but just a believer. Camus, in the last page of *The Stranger*, called it a "benign indifference to the universe." It is like what the Arab people, the Semitic people, mean when they say "believer." To use theological language, it is a believer in God, a believer in the Mystery, a believer that you are relationship.

When you take that belief and grind it into your being, which is the dark night of the soul, and grasp that all of life is humiliation, weakness, and suffering, then you have entered into what I call profound belief.

When you have become a believer, sooner or later you grasp that you are responsible for the whole world. Belief and care are simply two sides of the same coin. If you are a believer you care.

Taking that love and burning it through every fiber of your being takes you through the long march, the sense of eternal rootlessness. You have no home, no home at all.

The moment you pick up care for the world you become aware of your final ineffectivity. You become deeply aware of your depletion. You are burned out at that moment, but you become aware of lifelong fulfillment. When that happens you are in the state of being called “profound love.”

When profound belief and profound love become realities in your consciousness, then “there appeareth hope” – but remember, hope that is beyond hope. As Paul put it, “hope against hope.” And it is not you hoping. You just find yourself with new hope. The difference between that old cynical manufacturer and a person of faith is that in the midst of participating in exactly the same world, the person of faith cares profoundly, finds herself hoping with an everlasting hope.

Do you want to know the very secret of the wellsprings of motivity? It is hope. It seems to belong to the Mystery itself. If you start out on the journey you have already started on, and are not aware of secrets like this one, then you are not going to make it. And if that sounds religious, then you will just have to make the best of it.

Section III

THE LIFE OF SERVICE

Commentary by George Holcombe

Talks:

A Call to Sociological Love (1972)

Human Motivity and the Reformulation of Local Community (1973)

Mission: Just Five Things (1975)

Sophistication (1973)

Forging Social Philosophy (1976)

Profound Humanness: *Integrity* (1976)

What Hath Been Wrought (1977)

SECTION III: THE LIFE OF SERVICE

Commentary

By George Holcombe

If you have an interest in a life of service, in building community, in caring for the poor, in development, local or global, then the next several pages are for you. Joe often said that the social methods were where the intellectual and spirit methods hit the road. Remarkable people's insights and remarks are always ahead of their times, and the world has still a ways to go to catch up to what Joe was saying and doing.

A double warning, though: two things are missing from these writings. The first is the context in which they were first uttered. The 60s and 70s were a time of great social change. Joe had decided to move to the ghetto on the West Side of Chicago and from there to learn how those cut off from the mainstream could not only rise from poverty, but could also become partners in the whole society. From there he went to the world in the form of twenty-four demonstration projects.

The second thing missing is Joe's voice and gestures. Joe was an orator, a preacher, who spoke with passion, even in individual conversation. His raspy, sometimes squeaky, baritone voice, the stuttering, the pauses, hearing his words explode in your brain are not here. There were also the images scratched on a chalkboard and the unexpected humor that made his speeches more like a symphony than a talk. Whether you liked him or not, or agreed with what he said, underneath was a constant drumbeat that threw you up against history and asked the unspoken question, Are you going to live your life on behalf of all, for all of history, or are you going to try to preserve your life for yourself? You never walked out of his presentations or a conversation without sensing you had your life on your hands and had to decide what you were going to do with it. So, these speeches were not given for a book such as this, but to inspire, provoke, discipline, and drive a movement.

For Joe, a life of service was not about doing good deeds or helping people. It was about a happening in one's life that connected one to every other human, to the suffering, and to the whole of creation. To serve meant becoming a profound human. It had to do with methodological and structural change that allowed the poor and disenfranchised to stand on their own feet. More than teaching people how to fish, it was a matter of learning the methods of fishing, so if there were no more fish they could continue on to what was next.

At that time the development world was focused on economic development and relief work. Joe had already seen through the failure of such approaches and was pushing for "comprehensive development" that he called "human development." These phrases have now become catchwords in the development community. Church organizations and charitable groups that wanted to help people were far too condescending for Joe. He called them "band aid approaches."

What was crucial for Joe was learning new methods that actually worked, be they economic, political, or cultural. Development was about local people, whose self-image was being transformed from victim to participant, who learned and applied the methods and owned the process. In addition, there had to be authorization and participation from all levels of the society to create the synergy that spells development. It was neither top-down nor bottom-up, it was both. To serve God and humanity means being embroiled in this process so that the whole world would be made new. Service was not something one did to feel good about oneself, or to justify one's existence, it was participation in the historical process of creating the new humanness, the new religious, the new society.

Joe was true to his middle name "Wesley." He practiced John Wesley's approach of pulling everything through scripture, experience, reason, and tradition (known as Wesley's theological method, the quadrilateral, put forth by the Wesley scholar Albert Outler). He was also deeply an ecumenical Christian and appreciated and found kinship with the religious traditions of the world.

Joe was not simply a talker. He was the driving force behind the Ecumenical Institute: Chicago and the Institute of Cultural Affairs. He led these groups to establish projects and programs in over forty nations on a shoestring budget, and the imprint of his efforts survive in countless organizations, businesses, churches, and individuals to this day. He testified twice before the United States Senate, first, on behalf of Fifth City following the riots in 1968; second, in 1975, requesting funding for the Marshall Islands, which aided their transition from the Trust Territory of the Pacific to becoming an independent nation. The list of his deeds could fill many pages.

Some of the treats in store are Joe's concept that a village be imaged as a nation with exports and imports so that a capital base could be created that could sustain development. Add to that his passionate belief that "culture is key," the notion that people's self-understanding, wisdom, style, and the symbols they live out of are central to any development taking place and the key to what is taking place in history.

I have arranged these talks chronologically, so perhaps the reader can detect the development of thought and action.

"A Call to Sociological Love" was given in December of 1972 to the gathering of priors (Order: Ecumenical leaders) from across North America. These were early days of expanding to the world. It was a moment of reflecting on the stretching of resources and efforts beyond what anyone could have expected and the preparation for taking even larger risks and seeking greater opportunities. Joe defined this as evangelism. This talk is a classic, especially for anyone who needs to issue a challenge to a group to go beyond itself.

"Human Motivity and the Reformulation of New Community" was a speech delivered to the Rotary Club in Bombay, India, in January 1973. It is a first-rate explanation of community reformulation and a sharp insight into what local people around the world are still attempting to create. It also includes a marvelous statement about the role of business in creating the future.

"Sophistication" was given to a gathering at the Chicago headquarters of the Institute of Cultural Affairs following Joe's return from a global trip in March of 1973. It has fierce humor and real instruction for any person or group who wishes to work globally.

"Mission: Just Five Things" was part of the Guardian Consult in April of 1975. The Guardians were a group of people of influence and affluence who shared their wisdom and efforts with the people of the movement. By this time social demonstration projects were on the ground and town meetings were in full swing. This was an effort to restate and update what the movement was about.

"Forging Social Philosophy" is a statement that carries the above speeches one step further, using the experience of the movement. It was also given at a Guardian Consult in October 1976 and is a form of accountability to those who were active supporters.

"Profound Humanness: Integrity," delivered at the Priors Council in July 1977, intensifies the level of seriousness, if that is possible. What could not have been seen or said earlier is made plain. From the external mission Joe turns to the inner journey and what was learned by "going global."

"What Hath Been Wrought" is one of the last speeches Joe gave. It was given at the Global Research Assembly in Chicago, July 1977. He made the listeners aware that he was finite, and in the conclusion he asks for forgiveness of his shortcomings. In between, Joe focuses on what is taking place in the world and the missional task. In one sense it is a plea for others to pick up the job of leading and an outline of how to do that. It remains a powerful address to those who would dare to participate in the vocation of awakenment.

A Call to Sociological Love

My report on what has been going on this quarter has to do with just three things: the new course, the guild, and the breakthrough in the practical understanding of sanctification.

I believe that this last year was the most productive year in all my life, and I believe this last quarter has been the most productive quarter in my whole life. That is something. But at the same time it was one of the worst quarters I *ever* had. This quarter I have been spoofed by TWEEU's. T-W-E-E-U is an acronym for "those who ever envy us." I suppose that TWEEU's have been around me a lone time, but it is just this quarter that I have noticed them. TWEEU's are somewhat like science fiction – but looking backward. Anyway, these critters are little. They have to be little because they do not even exist. They are green and have extremely sad faces. And they go around crying all the time. They ever envy us because they are the ones that did not make it. A couple of genes got crossed up and they did not make it. And they are green with envy just because you and I made it. And they are sad – I mean sad.

Sometimes they stop crying long enough to laugh at us when we are not being appreciative of this fantastic life we have to live. Their laugh is a little shrill, I think. On those days when you wish you were never born – do you remember the laughter? Those were the TWEEU's. Or on those days in which you are in despair, on those days when you say, "Life is too hard – I wish I could die," then the TWEEU's laugh loudest. They laugh because they understand that the glory of life is to have a life to glory in. That is why they laugh at us whom they envy.

Although this last quarter was the most productive quarter of my existence, it was an awful quarter. I say it was an awful quarter and the TWEEU's laugh. I have found out that not only was it a productive quarter for me, it was a productive quarter for almost everybody I bumped into in the movement. And yet it was an awful quarter for them also. So my guess is that all of us have heard the TWEEU's.

But you have to try to get to the bottom of it. You see, during our lifetime we have been consumed with time. In the church the only kind of thinking that you and I have participated in had to do with time, or history. When an age is coming to pieces, I suspect you always emphasize time. You and I have gotten very used to living under the rubric of time, especially those kairotic moments. But then as time began to breakloose, in the sense that the moments of life began to bleed their interior meaning, we began to break through the time barrier.

When you first begin to think under the rubric of time, it is the kairotic moment of death that first wakes you up. Then you begin through that kairotic happening to experience moments of *kairos* again and again. These are the revelatory moments in the midst of life, once you behold the final happening of death.

I remember, only about two years ago, I was shocked when some people came back from around the world and were not able to talk about the spiritual meaning of the happenings to them. I have never fully recovered from that. From that moment on my whole being went to work on that until finally the moments of life began to bleed. How shall I bear witness to the fact that now it is not a moment once a month or once a quarter or once a week or once a day, it is as if every little moment and facet of my existence is bleeding with spiritual meaning. Interior time has sped up so that I feel I have gone through the time barrier itself.

What you behold on the other side of the time barrier is space. It has been a long time since you and I have used the rubric of space to grasp seriously the interior dimension of our being. In one sense, Protestantism has known nothing about space. When it threw out the riches of Catholicism, it threw out the category of space. It became centered on time, and in our lifetime that has come to a climax. Take the idea of space and think of our own journey recently: the Other World space; the new social vehicle is about space; sanctification, in the sense of the life of presence in the world, is about space.

To flip from living in the rubrics of time to the rubrics of space is a traumatic jar to the spirit dimension of your life. Manifestations of it are like emptiness, but not the kind of emptiness we knew about twenty years ago when meaning appears gone. Now the meaning is there, but it is as if space is almost like the infinite. I would like to read again *The Adulterous Woman* by Camus. Do you remember, she went up on the wall of the fortress and she looked out across the endless desert and experienced infinity? Then, looking up at the starry heavens she experienced infinity. When she saw those two converging, it was almost like infinity squared. She fell back, sensing she was raped by the infinite.

Now you and I are experiencing space almost as if it were endless. You sense inside yourself that you have to fill that space. But there is a dread. It is a quiet dread filtering through you. The experience is something like being in a vacuum. That is the flip side of what people experienced twenty to forty years ago as suffocation from lack of meaning. Now it is like being suffocated by the rarefied air of meaning.

To take this out of the ethereal, you and I said we were going to give our lives to create a new world, giving until death. That is when you began to experience this sense of space. We could not fill the space. That does not mean there were not enough of us. We just did not know how to fill space full of Spirit. This is what is happening to Mr. and Ms. Everyone everywhere at this moment in history. If I were going to talk a long time, I would want to spell this out under the rubric of sanctification.

But to get back to the TWEEU's for just a moment. This quarter I have found myself screaming against my fate. It was not the kind of screaming that I had last year. It is not as if God has yanked the rug out from under us, but more as if a hundred-ton crane of responsibility was dropped upon us. There is a quiet nonchalance in this, but I think it is there that you scream. But remember, even if you scream softly, the TWEEU's hear you. And they cry because they did not make it. They did not have a chance for this, what they would call the wonderful pain of being alive, what you and I have had this last quarter.

How do we fill space? There is only one way, with "love." This is the first time in my sixty-one years that I have used that word seriously. This is the moment when people of faith fill full the space that can only be filled full with love. This love is not some kind of sentimental relationship that we have with one another, or with any other, but a very special kind of love. This special kind of love has to be put in concrete social form or it will not fill space. I am not off on a pseudo-individualistic understanding of love, nor am I after love in the sense of a kind of interior state. I am talking about a relationship that has the flesh and blood of the sociological.

I have been trying to say to myself what the shape of this is. I find myself going back to the "bug model." This is the model of the local congregation, with its interior dynamics of worship, study, and discipline; and the external thrust as witnessing love, justing love, and what I like to call "presencing love." What is ahead of us is precisely that kind of love. It is the love that is human awakenment; it is the love that is perpetual human development; and it is the love that is human fulfillment.

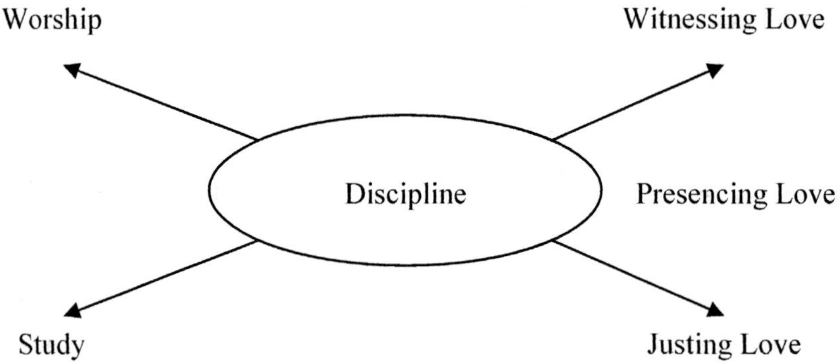

Figure 3-1: The Bug Model

We have at hand the concrete sociological form for *witnessing love*, which is the new evangelism in our day. But this is a radical evangelism. In our age you could not know anything about it. What was called evangelism was gone before you were born. In fact, I think you have to go back beyond the Great Awakening, which was not a radical evangelism, but a resuscitation of a Christian memory.

You have to get back to Cyril and Methodius, who in about the 8th or 9th century went to the Slavic people. Perhaps the greatest single church in the world is in Russia. How in the wide world did they succeed in that overwhelming task? Or, there is the other Augustine who went to England. That is radical evangelism. There are those who went to the northern parts of Europe, and you could go on and on. That is what I mean by a resurgence. We are living in that kind of a moment, but without a Christian memory to trade on.

I believe that the new course that many of you have been directly constructing for the past three years, and indirectly many years before that, is perhaps going to serve the fundamental task of awakenment relative to the masses. It is going to put sociological form on the kind of love that will fill space in our time.

This week I was out running a little experiment on my own. I went out under the guise of raising money, but what I was after was to put a thermometer in some mouths relative to the new course. I went to see George Romney first, and I did a little evangelizing. There he was, you know, about to be retired from Housing and Urban Development. He is about my age. I said to him, you have one more lifetime to live. "What's that? What's that?" he said. I mean he stood up and took notice. I asked him what is it you are going to do with that one more lifetime. Well, we had fun together. Then I went to the presidents of five companies in the small towns in Ohio, to Mansfield, Elvira, Oberlin, and talked to them about the new course. My gracious alive, they would come tomorrow. And they would send their executives, too. They will pay and pay dearly to take it. They will sponsor it. They are sitting there waiting for it. When I talked about the guild, they about came loose at the seams. I believe that the course is going to cultivate and draw together what I call the ground leadership of this country.

Now, I am talking about evangelism. Radical evangelism is not the superimposition of some dogma or doctrine or creed that you have people stand up and say "yes" to. Evangelism comes from the wellsprings of humanness itself. I am talking about how you go to the masses. A two-bit group like us cannot begin to get to the masses. The masses are going to have to be hit by those we hit. We must get tools in their hands. That is why this new course must be sheer excellence. This is the beginning of a hardheaded, practical, concrete, sociological way of filling the space of our time with love. And I mean love that has got some teeth in it.

The second kind of love is *justing love*. It is the love, practical and concrete, that has to do with the perpetual development of humanness. It is the perpetual revolution. If I were going to talk longer, I would talk about the guild. When I talked to those top-flight businessmen about the guild, they began to dream of having their counterparts take the course out in California, in Texas, and coming together across the continent. They grasp a body of colleagues who down underneath their differences manifest a common human concern. For example, one of those men was probably pretty close to an ultra-conservative. But there was no difference between him and another fellow who is the head of a new instrument factory and extremely liberal. It was as though we had tapped a common concern for humanity.

With these men you did not have to make a long speech about guildsmen. They understood that there were guildsmen in the Middle Ages. You reminded them that there were also guildsmen in Egypt and in ancient China and that guildsmen are really structural revolutionaries. They are the ones who occasion radical change within the structures. In every culture, in every moment in history, the guild takes a different form, but these are the ones who are the guardians of the structures, which means they must be revolutionaries, constantly altering the structures.

When you talk about the guildsmen, it makes your head swim to realize that you are thinking of the parish. Everybody here knows that there are 10,000 people in a parish. So you have a parish, an ecumenical parish, and it is exciting to be able to say that Fifth City is an ecumenical parish. In that case we got the parish done before we got the congregations renewed. In every ecumenical parish there are four congregations. Now let us suppose that in a congregation you could wake up five people. That would be twenty in a parish. Then multiply that by six, and you are up to the micro level. Then multiply that by another six for the polis, and another for the metro, and so on. The total is about 20 million ecumenical parishes around the globe. That guild person is going to be in operation not ten years from now, but the day after tomorrow, and s/he is going to be the most solid sociological reality you ever ran up against. The iron core of the guild will be historical church people.

The last thing is *presencing love*, and this has to do with sanctification. Sanctification is not some kind of experience down inside of you. It is the decision you make that you are going to accept responsibility for the whole world from this moment on and define your integrity in relationship to that kind of dedication, which will be the fulfillment of the only life you have. That is the presence that this world screams for.

I was kidding these businessmen that I went to see and said, "Now we are after seed money for this and that, and you have seed money." Then I would tell them a little bit about us. I said, "What we have to give is seed dedication." We are seeding dedication. The world needs people like us, to be the presence, to be sanctified people, people that live the holy life in the everyday going-on-ness of their existence. There is nothing pious about it, nothing religious about it, in the way most people use that term. It is the presence of people who square their shoulders back and assume responsibility for the whole world for the rest of their lives. That becomes their happiness.

This is to say that the movement is a sociological phenomenon. You are a presence which has already impacted history in ways that you and I never dreamed would be possible in our lifetime. I do not suppose that there is anyone in the room who thought that in his lifetime he would actually be dealing with the way that history was going to take its course in the future. Now you find yourself exactly in that role that is the presence that will bring about human resurgence.

Thank God we had our secular term for sanctification before we started using the word. The secular word is "resurgence." It is parallel to the word "insurgent," which means to rise in revolt. "Resurgence" means to rise again. The adjective is "resurgent," and that is also used for one who participates in resurgence. I say to you tonight that you are the "resurgents." You are those without whom restructured sociality cannot happen, because you are the sign of what is coming to be, and without that sign it could never come.

All this is what sanctification is, and this is what we have been about this quarter. We have been about evangelism. We have been about finding the effective tools for justice, the new justice that gives power. We have been trying to grasp the deeps of what it means to be God's man, God's woman, to be the holy presence in the midst of this world in our time.

During this next quarter, I believe we are going to find another kind of miracle happening. This may scare you, as I am sure it will scare me. We are going to find that space is literally beginning to fill. It will be filling with billows of this new whatever it is. I call it "love." It is beginning to roll, and by the next time this group comes together, you will know, as you have never known in your lives, that it can be done. It can be done.

Human Motivity and the Reformulation of New Community

I am deeply appreciative of the opportunity to be in India on her 25th year of Independence, because India is destined, doomed, if you please, to play a signal and very concrete role in the great human resurgence which has already begun. It is a strange experience, for I do not know whether you are 25,000 years of age, but certainly you are far beyond 2,500 years of age. I am delighted at this moment in history to tread this sacred land with you.

I am also happy to be here because of both the present and future role the international community, particularly the business community, plays in the world. The role it is going to play is the forging of a brand new civilization beyond our imagination.

It is almost trite even to mention that we are living in a critical moment in history. Since the dawn of consciousness itself, which produced human civilization, I do not believe anything like it has ever been. It is that kind of a radical moment. I believe you and I are living in a moment beyond compare. Would you not like, just for a moment, to get into a time machine and go into the future two thousand years. Or perhaps it would only take five hundred years or maybe only a century for people to understand the unbelievable drama in which you and I are participating. Of course, it is hard to grasp this, because we are it, we are the drama. We are a rare thing, for we have lived through the collapse of an age in global history. We have lived to see the emergence of the new. You and I are in one of those rare moments in history where we have experienced the bottom and the turn moving toward a crest on the wave.

You cannot talk about our moment in history as simply a cultural, economic, or political phenomenon. It is more radical, more foundational than that. It is an alteration in human consciousness itself. It is as if an implosion in the midst of the explosion of our day has happened. I think in the past there have been about five or six inventions of an image of man which have maintained themselves into the 20th century. One certainly came out of our American Indians, both in North and South America. Another fundamental invention of humanness came out of the Arabic lands, which now are made up of North Africa and the Near East. One came out of Black Africa. One came out of the Orient, or China. And one, of course, was invented in the West. Perhaps the most significant one of all emerged in this great land.

In our time people are inventing all over again, out of the stuff of many pasts, an image of what it means to be a human being; but, for the first time in history, it is being done globally. Whether you like it or not, the role the international business community is playing in this process, consciously or unconsciously, is rather unbelievable. You are fated to play a significant part in this breakloose of human consciousness. I can imagine many of you would like to respond, "Why doesn't that old man up there shut up and let us keep our eyes on our tiny little jobs?" Well, one reason I ought not shut up is because even if you keep your eyes on your little job, the impact of what you are doing will, nonetheless, go on. I believe what is happening in the business community is that it is beginning to see its inclusive effect. It is beginning to take self-conscious responsibility for the effect it is having across the world and in every aspect of our social existence.

If what I say is true, then this moment, as we start up toward the crest of the wave, is a moment of human resurgence. When you think of the signs of the social revolution today – the uprising of youth across the world, the feminine revolution, the revolt of the black people, the revolt of the non-Western world against the Western – they seem to me to be manifestations of human resurgence, a new kind of drive coming into history.

In ancient Egypt, almost overnight, a fantastic civilization was built, the remnants or symbol of which reside in the pyramids. I believe that behind that moment in history was a breakloose of consciousness issuing in human resurgence. You can point to the same thing in the ancient histories of China and India. Indeed, in every civilization you can point to the breakloose in consciousness that issued in a new invention of what it means to be a human being, and in a brand new construction of the social processes in which that humanness is appropriated and acted out.

When I look at those pyramids of Egypt, I am reminded of the thousands of people who seemed to be more or less slaves in building them. But that is the way you and I happen to look at it from our point of history. In looking from that moment's perspective, there was the farmer who, when the Nile overflowed and he got his rice paddies in, went to work as an unskilled or skilled artisan on the pyramids and other manifestations of a new society, putting creativity into the midst of it. What was behind that fantastic breakthrough in history?

At the time of Queen Elizabeth I, that little island we call England started out across this world and created four brand new nations far greater than Britain itself. In one sense, with all her mistakes and stupidities and brutalities, she prepared my country, your country, and many other countries of the world for this moment of breakloose. England alone did that. Just what happened in that country five hundred years before Queen Elizabeth II that gave humanness such unbelievable drive?

When the Aryans came through the pass and met Dravidians in India's great history, out of that meeting was created what, to me, was the greatest manifestation of a civilization the world has ever known.

I am reminded also of Confucius, who articulated a brand new understanding of what it meant to be human. He decided the way he would change the civilization of China with this new understanding was to go to the courts. He stayed there twenty years, but at the end of those twenty years he looked around and saw that he had accomplished nothing. So he went out into the wilderness, and he gathered around him a group of young local characters to train in this fresh understanding of what it means to be a human being. He then sent them to every crossroads and village and town in China. In dealing with local people they forged a brand new construct of primal community which altered the civilization of China.

Another understanding of humanness reconstructed science, permeating Southeast Asia, and spreading throughout all the Pacific Islands, westward into Persia, and on into the Arab lands. Quite unconsciously this was probably the route of the productive Western invention of humanness.

My question is What happened in that dim, dim past which released the vitality of these cultures?

We are now at a time in which, due to various forces, the worlds we have built have been collapsing. The British Empire is only one illustration of what I am talking about. But I mean something deeper than that. The self-understanding of the West has collapsed. And the self-understanding of China, India, Africa, and Latin America have collapsed as well.

But out of the death of this age comes the birth of a new age. I believe a new civilization is now being forged, and all of us who have been awakened have the choice of participating in it, or getting drowned by it. This is a rare experience for any person in history. I have very little patience with people who still despair over the future. I think they are not capable of grasping that the pains we experience and the complexity of human problems are but the birth pains of a civilization such as people have never dared to dream. Yesterday, the agony was death pains over the civilizing process. Today the agony is birth pains. Yet, if you and I resign, it will not stop the resurgence.

All these historical brush strokes focus our attention on human "motivity" (for me, a better word than "motivation," which too often smacks of individual self-help) in relationship to the brand new world coming into being. Often when you talk with people about human relations, they take a psychologistic approach. For example, how can you manipulate people in order to get the most out of your investment? When you live in a moment when civilization is exploding, then you have to drill much deeper if you are going to bring about human motivity. In the slums of West Chicago, we would not have lasted five minutes with the psychologistic approach to human motivity. We had to dig underneath it.

The Social Process

One of the great things the crisis of the hour has done for us is to force us to rethink the theoretics of inclusive human relations, or, to use technical language, to rethink the sociological manifestation of the sociality of people. Sociality of people simply means we live together because we have to live together. By the sociological manifestation I mean the forms we create in which we can operate with some degree of effectiveness and efficiency together.

What we have come up with in our day is dynamical sociality. In every social situation, in business and production, this new understanding is manifesting itself. No longer is society understood substantialistically. In the natural sciences of the world today nobody ever saw, or will ever see, an atom. The reality is the relationship, not the entity. Similarly, in the social sciences there is no substance called management, or a substance called stockholders, or a substance called labor. The reality in business is not the labor force, nor the capital force, nor the managerial force. The reality is the interrelationship of those. In society at large we call this interrelationship the *social process.* We are discovering that these sociological manifestations of human sociality are dynamical. They are a complex dynamic, not composed of interrelationships or social substances or entities, but a matter of happenings – dynamics – that are interrelated and interdependent. For instance, the social process as a whole is comprised of three major dynamics.

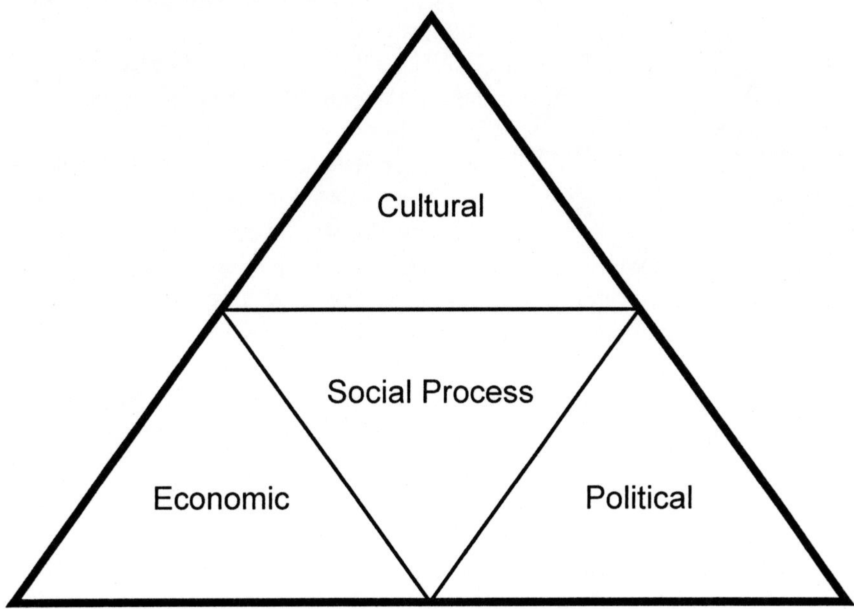

Figure 3-2: The Social Process Triangles

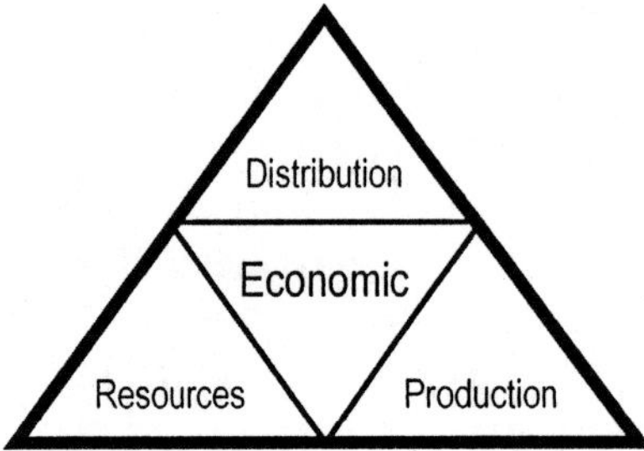

Figure 3-3: The Economic Dynamic

First is the *economic dynamic*, the means by which society sustains itself in existence. One level down, comprising the economic process are the obvious dynamics of *resources*, *production*, and *distribution*. Underneath any analysis, whether you go to Marx or Smith, you are going to find these manifestations of humanness at play. Through converting raw stuff into resources, converting those into usable goods, and then building a system whereby those goods are distributed, society maintains itself in existence.

The second major dynamic comprising the social process is the *political dynamic*, not politics, but polity, or the organizing dynamic of society. The economic process cannot go on if there is not some kind of organizing process in society in order for people to live and support themselves. The first dynamic of that process is *order*.

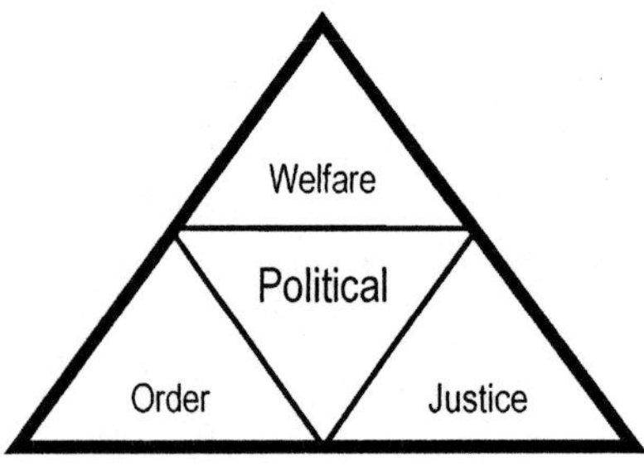

Figure 3-4: The Political Dynamic

The fathers that founded my nation said, "Provide for the common defense and promote domestic tranquility." There has to be order without and within. This is where we get our domestic and international ordering forces. In order to do that there has to be some kind of a covenantal relationship. People must come to some kind of a consensus, whatever its form. Our country has a written constitution. Great Britain has an unwritten constitution. But people have consensed together or these nations could not operate. This general consensus is the basis of a legal system. Without mores commonly consensed on, you would not have a people, you would not have a social structure. These same dynamics define every kind of social coagulation. A family exists by the same process. If you belong to a fraternity, a church, or any other kind of an organization, the same dynamics are there. You always have these dynamics.

The second dynamic of the political is *justice*. This, of course, deals with the problem of equity. Though no nation is or can be built upon ideal equity, justice is a nation's effort to keep some kind of balance of equity within itself.

The third dynamic in the political process is that of well-being, or *welfare*. The founding fathers in my constitution said we were to take care of people's physical and social needs, or their general welfare. They used that very ancient term "well-being" or "happiness" to indicate how the total person was cared for. When something happens which leaves me out, then it is the government's job to see that something happens to include me in. If welfare is not there you do not have an adequate political dynamic.

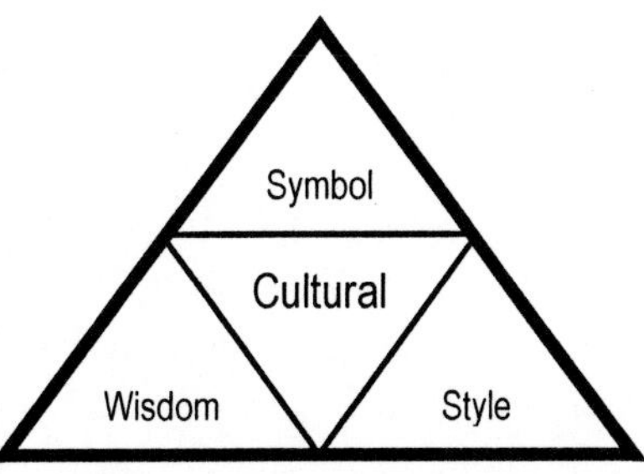

Figure 3-5: The Cultural Dynamic

There is a third major dimension in the dynamical social processes of any society, and I have put it at the top of the big triangle. I call it the *cultural dynamic* of society. By that dynamic I mean the basic images of a society are created and transmitted from one generation to another. What it means to be a human being is transmitted, along with the practical wisdom of how you go about spearing fish or running a nuclear laboratory, if that is what you do.

Education, or *wisdom*, is a part of the cultural dynamic. *Style* is another part of that dynamic. Every culture has its style. Usually, the more complex the society the more complex the style. A culture not only lives out of its rational images, but it lives out of its formulated postures. "Mores" used to point to a recognized style of the individuals, though that no longer quite gets at it, it seems to me. Every culture has to develop an individual style or it cannot exist as a culture. There also has to be a form for basic relationships. We call that "family." I am speaking of a basic community which has to do with sex, marriage, and the family, to use the jargon of the West. Other cultures might put it another way. There have to be forms that define the first community in which you wake up. It might be a multiple family. Then there is what I call "primal community." That is the basic cluster of social relationships in which a family exists. The family I grew up in was part of a little tiny town called Ada, in the state of Ohio, in mid-western America. In one sense, Ada, Ohio, was more primal than our family. Our family could not grasp who it was without existing in a basic community beyond our family. Every society has that form.

Or look at India's own primal society where you had that great social invention called the caste system. I want to come back to that for it was a creative invention. It was not until even as late as the 12th century that it began to deteriorate and really become a problem. Your panchayat, an unbelievable social invention, was also part of your primal community style.

The third dynamic defining culture is the *symbol* dynamic. No society has ever existed or ever can exist without a symbol system. It is the symbol system whereby any society communicates to itself who it is as that society. Probably the rudimentary symbol system in any society is its language. It is often taken for granted, but we communicate who we are through our language more than anything else. Secondly, there is art, not simply fine art, but social art. Then there are what I call the trans-historical symbols, or the mythology. Every society has its mythology or its stories. Some call that religion, though we often do not like to use that word today. For even when people do not have a religion, formally, they have some way to relate themselves to the cosmos. It may be down into the unconscious, but it in there. Without its story as to where it came from, what it is, and where it is headed, a society does not exist. Every society has a reference point beyond itself in order to have a sense of identity.

Now, when I say that these are dynamical, I mean they cannot exist by themselves. If you took any of these dynamics away you would not see anything, because it is the relationship that enables us to posit these realities. Therefore, what I am doing today is an abstraction. It is the function of the cultural to significate, to enlighten, give vision to the political and economic dynamics. The economic, without enlightenment or visioning, turns into nothing. The function of the economic, obviously, is to maintain these. Without it, the others do not exist. But if the economic begins to tyrannize the cultural, the political defends it by squeezing the economic. This is crucial in considering community reformulation. The function of the political is to defend society. Defense delimits, but its fundamental task is the nurturing, the fostering, and the defending of a society.

Social Process Analysis

When you move into the arena of community reformulation you have to do your own analysis. You have to know what you are doing. The reason I emphasize this, even to the point of possible exaggeration, is that every do-gooder in America who has a guilty conscience wants to go into the slums to do something to save his own inner being. Well, the slums do not need that kind of help; as a matter of fact, it does harm!

If you are going to be effective, then you have to be extremely objective. In the midst of deep involvement there must be this detachment, almost scientific. You must also be comprehensive. In other words, when you attack your concrete area to attempt to reformulate, you have to begin with a broad and deep understanding of the total social process itself. If you go into a black ghetto, or any other kind of ghetto, and pretend you are going to re-do humanness without being grounded in a comprehensive understanding of the dynamics of the sociological manifestation of human sociality, then you had better stay out. You

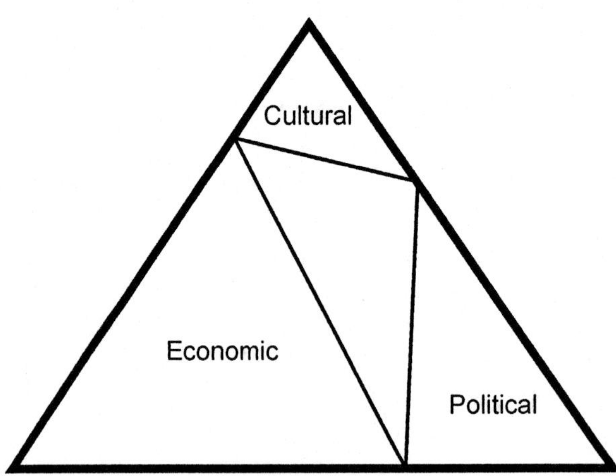

Figure 3-6: The Social Imbalance

would be better off and so would the people.

Since these dynamics are always moving and shifting by their very nature, they are not in equal balance in our day, or at any time. In every society they shift out of balance. Sometimes the *political* gets overextended and squashes the others; sometimes the *cultural* gets overextended and squashes the others. I suspect for the first time in recorded history, the *economic* is overextended. In previous times, the economic processes were taken care of in the family, in the state, and in certain organizations called the guilds, or your original caste construct. In our day, the economic has become an independent entity and has grown with a rapidity, a force, and a power that has made the political and cultural development in the world look rather weak.

The *economic dynamic* of society is the tyrant today. We are not talking about "nasty old businessmen." We need those businessmen, or we would not be able to live the way we do. We are saying instead that the economic dynamic of life controls the images which define our existence. In the West, and really, I believe, across the face of the globe, we are discovering that the economic images of life's significance are not adequate to freight the meaning of being human. That is where the malaise or despair of the West is located.

When the *cultural* collapsed, the *economic* moved in to fill that vacuum. I do not mean something from outside. Take individual style, for instance. What are the values that tend to rule a person in our day whether s/he be rich or poor? They are economic values, the values of success. Most families are built around the economic well-being of that family. Everywhere in the world the economic community has moved into education: the technological schools have become the most crucial dynamics in education today. What are the life symbols we live by? Take language. The jargon of technology has consumed every language. As a matter of fact, it is the closest thing we have to a universal language. In terms of the scientific, urban, and secular revolutions, economic values control our interior being.

And the *economic dynamic* has rendered relatively impotent the *political dynamic*. My country, perhaps more than any other, is an illustration of the *economic* rendering impotent the *political* in order to fill the vacuum left by the disintegration of the *cultural*. The economic forces of my country run it. People in the world criticize Mr. Nixon, and should. But Mr. Nixon is not running our country, nor is the common person. The economic dynamic is. I believe this is an accurate analysis of our time. If you disagree, that is all right, for what I am after is methodology.

The Cultural Revolution Begins in Local Communities

This brings us to the revolution in the world today, and guess what, it is *cultural*. Some of you young ones, you will live to see the cultural revolution happen. The economic community itself is going to play a signal role in the recovery of the cultural, which brings a kind of balance back into society. This balance will be the new civilization, which will also get out of balance. But it may happen in a different way. We are getting pretty close here to what I mean by "motivity." If this revolution is not brought to self-consciousness in every situation, then do not be surprised if you do not have drive in your outfit. You can see we are down about a million miles deeper than the psychologistic approach to human relations. If you are interested in productivity, primarily, then you are not interested in what I am saying. What I'm trying to articulate is the key to motivity in the emerging new world.

In terms of motivity in relation to the changes necessary in our time, one thing that I have come to believe with a passion is that the practical aspect of any such radical revolution within civilization is finally accomplished on the local level, not on the top, or bureaucratic level. Civilization is not reborn from the top down. You begin to look for it with local citizens. Indeed, you do not have a new civilization, a new social construct, until the mind of local people is reprogrammed, basically by locals themselves. Out of the reprogramming of the mind, locals begin to build those local structures that delineate primal community, upon which the pillars of the superstructure of any society is built.

I am an old, hardened, battle-scarred, structural revolutionary. By "structural revolutionary" I mean that I am out to occasion change within the structures of society. I have been in Delhi talking with gatherings of the Family Foundation, and with the faculty and sponsors of the Central Institute of Training, Research, and Public Cooperation concerning their twenty metropolitan areas where government and private interests, together, are running experiments in community reformulation in India. I suppose the reason they would have somebody like me come is because I am an agent of structural change back where I come from.

Fifth City

Let me tell you about a little hunk of geography on the West Side of Chicago in the United States. We call these sixteen square city blocks "Fifth City." It is a Negro ghetto, 100 percent black. The only white people who have been there for sometime are those of us in the Institute who work and live there. It is probably one of the worst ghettoes in the country. The crime rate is extremely high. I sometimes think there is a sort of carry-over from the gangster's period in Chicago, for this was Al Capone's territory. Perhaps if you are old and have gray hair you will remember him as the gangster who gave Chicago the reputation of being the wickedest city in the world. That is the kind of area we live in. We moved there because we believe if the United States of America was going to be changed it was necessary to move into local areas to begin to fertilize the situation such that local people could begin to be a sign that the future would be different.

I am not going to talk about that, except to say that the crucial problem in the reformulation of the slums in the United States, and I believe in the world at large, is the problem of human motivity. Any expertise we have developed has been out of the practical and difficult task of attempting to understand motivity in the midst of the black ghetto of our country.

You may remember in 1968 when the blacks revolted in our country, they burned huge sections of our great cities. One of the ironies of it is that they burned their own communities. Our section of Chicago was probably the worst hit of all the cities in the United States, miles of flattened ground. Our government, of course, became frightened. So did the white bourgeois suburbanites and the business communities. Our government set up all kinds of studies. They invited us to come before the Senate to make a report on the problems in the ghetto.

The first basic problem in the inner city, and I believe across the world, is the political problem. The people in Fifth City, and any local people in a slum area, have no way of authentically participating in the decision-making processes by which their own destiny is decided. In different societies this situation arises in different ways.

The second basic problem was that in this fantastically affluent moment in history, especially in my country, a vacuum of social structures exists in the ghettoes, such that there is no adequate way to funnel a portion of that affluence into the ghettoes. Frequently we call this the problem of poverty; that is not, however, the basic problem. I suspect the poor are always going to be with us in one form or another. But there have to be local structures whereby the basic needs of people are met in some way. Grassroots people in the slums have to have a way to participate in the master social structures for their own well-being.

The third and most important problem I tried to clarify with our government has to do with an inadequate image of self-significance of the people within our slums. Our black people have been brutally ill-treated for 300 years in our country. I am sure you are aware of the derogatory term the white man has used with black people. That is the word "nigger," a bad term in our society. What has happened is for over 300 years black people have been seen as "niggers" by white people – that is, as second-rate human beings; and many black people have come to see themselves as second-rate, as "niggers." That self-image is the fundamental problem.

We might try to look at the causes, but I am not interested much in causes, for we are geared toward the future. Fundamentally, we are after resolutions. Even if all white people should disappear, it would not solve the black people's fundamental problem, which now has to do with having an adequate image of their own significance in the historical process. Unless we attack that problem, we could pour in billions of dollars in doing new housing, and two years later that housing would be exactly like it was before we redid it. We should be giving them the tools whereby they can form for themselves a new image of their own significance.

This problem has to do with human motivity. There is little doubt that the slums do not need people from the outside to come in and do anything for them except to stimulate their motivity. When they are motivated in this fashion, they reconstruct their own community. External funds need to be poured into the slums, but only like priming a pump, only like yeast in leavening the loaf, to get the bread to rise. They then do the job for themselves.

Principles of Community Reformulation

In dealing head-on with community reformulation, it is important to clarify the basic operating principles on the local level.

First is the precise geographical delineation of the area in which you are going to work.

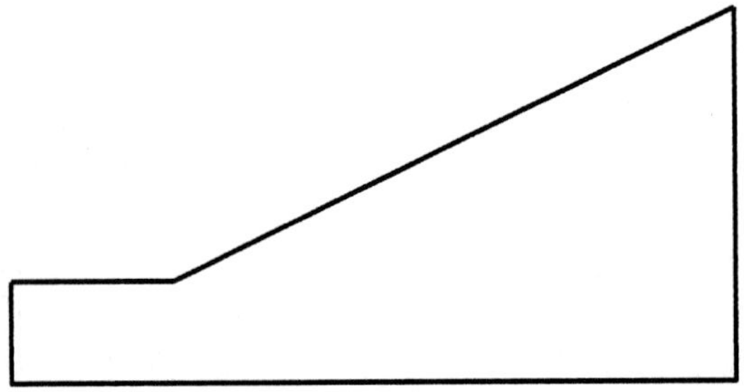

Figure 3-7: Fifth City – Delimited Geography

This is a picture of Fifth City and its boundaries. An expressway, which is a quarter of a mile across, is an ancient dividing line in the City of Chicago from the time the Indians created it as a trail. The park is about a half-mile wide. The diagonal street here is called Fifth Avenue. Within this section of Chicago there are 5,000 people. Actually, the area of Fifth City is broader with about 20,000 people. We believe, as an operating principle, if you mean to deal with these 20,000, you need to box off a bit of that 20,000 to get small enough where you can develop the kind of leadership necessary to move in on the whole thing. That is why we have divided it, and spent eight years working with 5,000 people directly and only indirectly with others. After eight years, you have a powerful local leadership that can move out and help do what we call "the flip side." They can themselves bring comprehensive community reformulation to a neighborhood, a small town within a great city. That is the first principle: be very clear about your *geographical delineation.*

The second principle is to do a *comprehensive job.* That is, you deal with all human problems at once. Those who go in just to help the youth might as well save their efforts. If you come in just to start a preschool, you might as well save your time. If you go in just to do adult education, we believe you might as well save your efforts, because you must deal with every human problem all at once.

How do you find out what those human problems are? You have your abstract model already. You have economic problems, and you have polity problems (I will call it polity rather than political, because you are not dealing here, at the moment, with the political parties). But you will soon notice that the real problem is in the cultural; therefore, we put three beats on it – the education, the style, and the symbol dynamics. When you go into Fifth City, using your social process analysis, you look for these problems. As an outsider, you do not try to tell the people of a community what their problems are. Instead, you give them a way to organize and delineate what those problems are.

We spent two years doing nothing but sorting out the latent hidden leadership of the community, getting them together and letting them articulate where the problems were. I think the first list they made was something like 913 problems. With that you have not the slightest idea where to begin; yet you have to deal with them all at once. If you do not rationally organize (we say "gestalt") those problems, you stand there paralyzed. It is like going to a library because you think you ought to read, and there are so many books you do not know where to start. That is why the library catalog system came into being, to overcome that paralysis. You must comprehensively attack *all human problems at once*. That is the second principle.

Third, you have to *deal with all life phases at once*. You deal with the young ones, the youth, and the adults all the way to grandma. In our educational program we started with youngsters six months old. It was not just to take care of them. We have a school for them; and in those first eight to ten months they probably learned more than you and I learned in the last forty years. It is amazing how they can identify African music. It is amazing how they identify certain kinds of symbols – the kind of symbols you want them to live out of when they grow up. The color black is going to be crucial to those people as they grow.

We start with the babies and then we have mini-school before preschool, and then they go on to kindergarten. When they go to elementary school we work with them after school. At high school level they begin dropping out, so we have a special program for those who drop out. It is necessary to have a program for those who can go on to higher education. When we first went there, there was not a single college graduate in that area; now there are fifty. If we had not started community reformulation, maybe there would not have been a college student there for another fifty years. The leadership is coming. You also need to work with the adults in education. That is a crucial need. Those who say forget the adults and teach the children are wrong. And the elders must be included in this. In a black community, the grandparents take care of the children when they come home from school. If grandma and grandpa have an image of self-depreciation, they unintentionally undo overnight what you taught the children that day. You therefore get nowhere unless you change the image of grandma at the same time. It does not do any good to have a preschool in the midst of the inner city unless education of the elders also goes on. That is what I mean by working with all phases of life.

The fourth fundamental operating principle is the *image of community significance*, or community symbol. The very fact that you build a model delineating a neighborhood is the beginning of creating symbols that change society. To live in the ghetto, in our nation at least, is to live nowhere. You have no place. Can you imagine living in no place? Those people are constantly "socio-spatially" lost. The beginning of creating the symbol that starts community is to delineate the area in which you live, to give it a name. "I live in Fifth City." Barely had that been named, when the people of Fifth City began to create songs about their community: "I live in Fifth City; Fifth City is my home." You would not believe the enthusiasm that came out of those songs and symbols. Then they began to have festivals. It was interesting in those early days. I would not have walked twenty feet at night out in that community, because you might not come back. But it was not long before one could go out and walk around on the streets. When community symbolism began to flow, then the roots of community began to grow.

This was Fifth City's community reformulation. There was a part of it that began to build economic structures, part of it that began to build polity structures, and a part operating as the Cultural dynamic, that began to build the educational, stylistic, and symbolic structures of community. With the people, using the problems they delineated, we began to work with them to build four major structures under each one of the basic problems. I will not go over them all for you, though I have some charts to hand out. For instance, under the economic is the problem of housing and employment or income. Then there is the problem of health, which is also crucial. We put that up under the sustaining dynamic of society. The Fifth City community built a health outpost that relates to the health structures of the city. Hundreds of people a day, coming from all over the place, go through that health outpost. You try to build the structures which give you ways to handle your local society.

Fifth City Operations

How do these structures operate? To run them they built a *guild system* of awakened neighborhood people who took responsibility in the community. One group was responsible for the economic: the Economic Guild. Another group was the Education Guild. Some took responsibility to be the Political Guild. Others were responsible for Style Guild and the Symbol Guild, so you have five guilds, led by the awakened neighborhood people.

A second master construct to care for the whole community was called *stakes*. A body of awakened people would be the force in each geographical unit or stake. Their task was to move out in the neighborhood and care for every person who lived there. "To care for" meant that if anyone was sick s/he would be taken to the Health Outpost. If anyone was not making as much money as they had to make in order to live, they were put into the structure dealing with income. If children were not in preschool, they were signed up. If there was a child who needed to get into high school, s/he would be assisted. In this way the community cared for itself. The guilds thus mediated the comprehensive structures of society down to the local community of stakes. The way the people were put into those local structures enabled all of society to minister to itself.

They found they needed to have a *council*, so the interested people in the community could meet every three months and make decisions together. Their attention span was very short the first couple of times they met. You had to write out speeches for those who could read them, and with great labor they did so. You may not believe this, but now there are leaders in that community who can give a talk far better than I can, and have been invited to universities to speak. The talent is there. What you provide are the tools and help to develop the skills. The charismatic leadership power of our outcasts in America is fantastic.

Then they have what they call a *presidium*, a few of the citizens who have become leaders, who constantly watch over the whole construct. The presidium now has what they call a *board of managers*, which the community supports, giving them just a minimum amount of money to live on. They spend their full time ensuring that the structures they set up work.

One day the statistical sociologists of our country are going to get their discipline straightened out so that it is human sociology they deal with and not abstract statistics. When they are brought in to evaluate the work of Fifth City, I am appalled by the criteria they use. Perhaps this is my eccentricity, but I want them to ask whether human beings have been changed.

I am not just interested in the particular people in that particular community. I am interested in our whole society. I am interested that local people everywhere find a way to release their creativity into the civilizing process. I believe that in the experimentation of forging new community the "guts" of human resurgence are found, and, indeed, the rock-bottom foundation of a new and effective social process.

Sources of Motivity: Space, Time, and a Sense of Being

I stopped by Ahmadabad the other day and for the first time went to the Gandhi ashram there. As I walked through it I asked myself, "Where did that little man get that drive?" He moved out into the impossible and did it. We who are not so forcefully driven would have buckled under the first wave of opposition. Where did he get that motivity? I believe that rudimentary and radical motivity comes from interior space, interior time, and a sense of being.

I am convinced that when people's interior *understanding of space* is small then their motivation is small. If I only thought in terms of Ada, Ohio, that small town I lived in, my motivity would be about as big as Ada, Ohio. Can you apply that to a factory? In direct proportion to a person's interior space is motivity. If I live simply in terms of the United States of America, then I have motivity that size. If I begin to live in terms of relationship to the whole globe, then my motivity expands. Where did Gandhi get his drive? All over those walls he says, "Sure, I am interested in my people, in my nation, but I am interested in humanity, in mankind." You and I who go around with our interest centered in our family, in our work, in our own village, or in our own country, when the hard times come, we collapse. Like a car we have sixteen cylinders in us but they are only hitting on about two. We are missing on about fourteen. When our sense of interior space expands, then all sixteen begin to hit and we accelerate.

When I was talking about this to a group of sociologists in Delhi the other day, one of the professors asked me, "What about motivity in the village life one or two hundred years ago in India?" That is a simple question to answer. Did they live in space? Certainly they lived in space, cosmic space. Back when trans-historical symbols had relevance and power in life, in principle, the most ignorant, the most remote person in India had a sense of participating in the universe. Though that may be hard for us in our urban society to understand, it was true of rural people. I think of the early history of my country when we were winning the West. All castes of Europe came to our shores – some out of prison, the ones European countries wanted to get rid of. They started out in wagon trains across the West, facing unbelievable hardships, the kind of hardships that would make us in the 20th century collapse. But they moved on. Why? It is as if space was opened up for them. There was the drive.

Secondly, if you want to think about how you are going to get drive out of people, you must think in terms of *expanded time*. Every person not only has a sense inside of space, where s/he belongs, but a sense of time. If you and I are only able to think backwards a short distance or forwards a short distance, then our motivity is just that much. The trouble in Fifth City was that they could not think beyond the space of the ghetto nor beyond that day in terms of time. They were concerned about where they would get their next meal. They could not afford to think two days down the line, to say nothing of ten years.

As you begin to get a broader view of time in your own personal life, you begin to get a picture of what could be in ten years from now. If you remember back to your grandfather, and further back than that, then that motivity begins to increase and the drive comes. I like to think in terms of the whole journey of humankind through history. There was Gandhiji. He thought of the total journey of humanity, not simply the 20th century. He thought far beyond independence from Great Britain. There was his drive to bring about independence, the 25th year of which we are now celebrating.

The third category is difficult. I do not mean this to be abstract philosophy. To the degree that I participate in my interior space and in my interior time, I have a sense of being somebody, of *being significant*. I have a sense that my life is a manifestation of that which is far beyond me and therefore gives me a sense of my own worth, of my own significance.

I am back to the fundamental problem in the black ghetto. One way we dealt with it was to work outside to create inside space. We took the people out of the ghetto for visits to other places in Chicago. Some of them had never been out of that ghetto before. Then we even began to take them to other cities, to New York and Washington, D.C. You do not have to take them all. You take a few out of Chicago and they bring back New York to the rest through their stories. They bring back New Orleans. Even though we did not have much money, we wanted to take them outside of our country. As you know, the closest country different from us is Mexico. So, we took about fifty from the ghetto on buses to Mexico. They saw that there were other poor people in the world, and they brought that back. They paid what they could on these trips so they could really participate. We went to the community, took up a collection, and sent three of them around the world. That was expensive, but they paid a good bit of it themselves. That did wonders for the dramatic reformulation of that community, the stories they brought back. The motivity was released not only in running their community, but also in having a social milieu that released the creativity of the individuals within the community.

Business Motivity Methods

Now, in terms of motivity in the business world, we want to talk about human relations. You may not get around to it yourselves, but if you do not, be sure that the day after tomorrow the business community is going to be doing something like this. I do not pretend to be an expert.

First of all, whether you have a large corporation or a small business, you have to engage every employee in your master or inclusive vision. What I am talking about here is common participation in the *vision* of the company, or the vision of its outreach. I can be a sweeper and be relatively content. That does not mean I would not want to get ahead in life, if I had a sense that I was participating in a broad vision. This is a bit of a problem for some companies. Some companies have not gone to the trouble to spell out their inclusive vision. Their inclusive vision must be their own understanding of how what they are doing or what they are selling is a contribution to society. Suppose I make automobile tires. It would not take an overly bright person to begin to relate this fact to the total needs of the world. Without that vision you cannot expect the human relations in your outfit that you want. The last sweeper in the place must be given an opportunity to participate in that vision.

This means that businesses have to reorganize themselves. You have team operations. If you have a sales division, that whole division would grasp itself as a *team*, including the sweeper. And there need to be *teams* within the division team. I do not mean anything sentimental by teams. This reorganization is built around the discernible activity that has to go on in the total enterprise. The vision must go up and down the organization. I believe that any moment you take away from actual production to communicate the vision of your total enterprise will be more than made up for in increased production. I know of groups where a team comes to work and spends the first fifteen minutes looking at the whole vision of the task and the immediate jobs that have to be done. Every person there feels they are participating in their team.

This means you are going to need to create new kinds of methodologies, such as *brainstorming sessions*. By brainstorming sessions I mean the units on some level would get together and identify the primary contradictions. Suggestion boxes hint at this. They are not adequate because you do not have a sense of participation. We have discovered that when even the most unlikely person within a group has had an opportunity to get her/his wisdom in, something happens to the whole production scheme. Without this method, I do not think you can operate effectively.

This is part of the *workshop* methodology. A workshop methodology takes the contradiction and rationally pulls out the wisdom of every single employee relative to the resolution of that particular contradiction.

A third methodology is *consensus-making*. Suppose I am a foreman and I have ten people working under me. If I am going to do something about radical motivity, I have to find a way to get those people together. Together we have located the contradiction and its possible resolutions. We have sent it on up the ladder and the solution sent back is based on our research. I have to have the team believe that their creativity got into this decision-making process. Through a participatory method, I have built that motivity inside those people.

The last method is *proposal writing*. You can put quotes around "writing," because you do not even have to be able to write. Somebody else can do that. I have discovered that in the black ghetto. Those people are capable of beginning to draw pictures of the future for their community. The whole business world is going to be surprised by the janitor of a factory who is capable of articulating the vision of the whole plant.

Conclusion

I believe this is a moment of resurgence in history, such as has never been before. It will not come by magic. It will only come when bodies of individuals on this globe of ours, from ghettoes and local communities – villages – to teams in the workplace, finally decide self-consciously to participate in its advent. And somebody has to give them the human motivity methods whereby they can participate creatively. New communities are emerging in our time that will reformulate the globe.

The Mission: Just Five Things

It seems to me that we get fuzzier every day about what we concretely have to do, and clearer every day about the inclusive and profound task that we are about. I want to try to say what I mean by that. I know now what life is all about. That is sort of silly, isn't it? It is not so silly, in a way, when we are trying to think about what we are up to now, what it is that we have to do, and when we try to push those questions into the dimension of profundity.

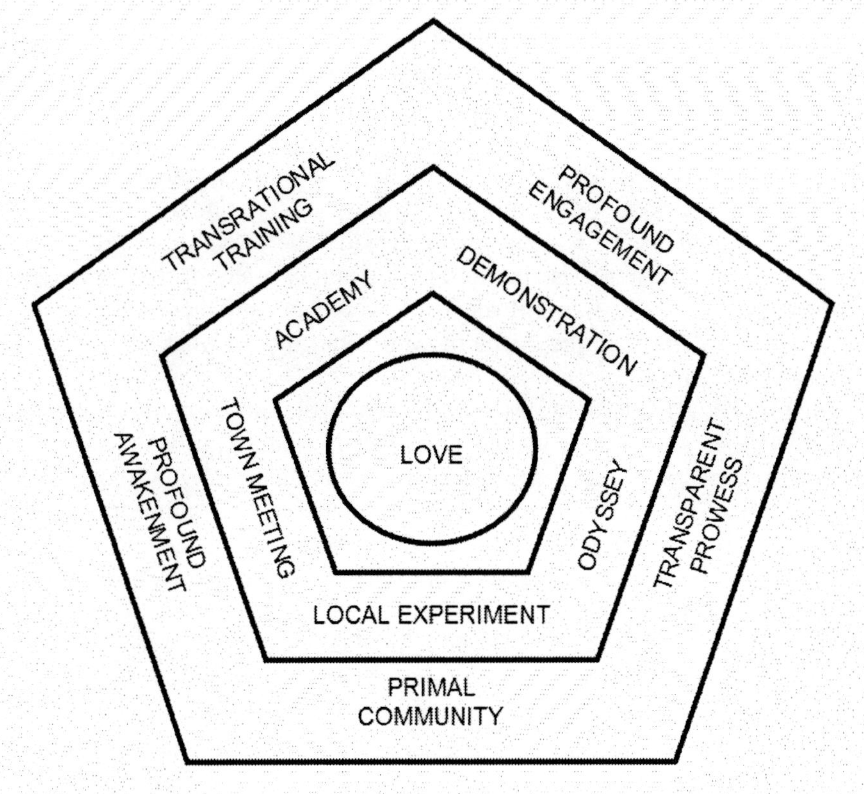

Figure 3-8: The Pentagon of Love

As I began to look at my life, primal community started me thinking. By *primal community* I mean something other than what you can bite into. I am very clear that the family is not primal community. No family by itself can open up the deeps of what I mean by the primal. Ada, Ohio, the town I grew up in, was far closer to this than my family. In one sense, my family did not have the slightest idea who it was, save in the context of Ada, Ohio. In our day, that neighborhood sense is gone. Yet, I do not mean simply that the neighborhood in which a family exists is primal community. As a matter of fact, as a little boy I did not know about primal community in the sense of a thereness that you could point to; however, the dynamic of primal community was truly working on me.

I can put it very simply and in sociological terms: a dog only grasps that it is barking when another dog barks back at its barking. That is, there is no such thing as individuality except inside of community, or our sociality is prior to our individuality.

Later on I grasped more concretely that primal community in abstraction is the People of God, whose fundamental intent is to be primal community. But by the time I woke up to that, the People of God had lost their sense of being people of God, and therefore primal community did not exist there. This is all by way of saying that what we are about is the recreation of primal community.

The second thing I stumbled upon when I began to relive my experience is what I want to call my solitary awakenment. I had been well conditioned by Spock and everybody else who said that one way or another you are made what you are by the neuroses of your mamma and your papa. About two miles south of Ada is Grass Run Creek. It is about four feet wide and maybe four feet deep in places, but most of the time it is six inches wide and two feet deep. I never cared much about fishing. I did fish but mostly I would go out there and sit all by myself. When I try to grasp the deeps of who I am, that is what I think of, just being alone by the creek.

I remember Walnut Grove. I used to go by myself and pick up walnuts, then get a board with a knothole in it. Did you ever do that? You could not get the stain off your hands for weeks after you hulled walnuts; and you know what, I was proud of those stains. I also remember when we lived on Main Street in Ada. I would get up in the morning before anybody else and go out and sit on the back stoop and look out towards the sunflowers on the side of the woodshed in the back of the lot.

Did you ever wake up in the morning, as the sun comes up, and watch the sunflowers wake up too? Alone? Solitary? But you are not interested in my life story. I could tell you about the sibling squeeze of one brother before me and one after me, of two sisters on each side of both of them, and how my older brother was sort of the wayward one. My mamma used to pay too much attention to him, and all of us knew the young one had the brains and had to be taken care of. But the way mamma took care of me was to just look at me sometimes. That was all she needed to do. She was enabling my solitude.

I am talking about awakenment. Yet, I was far into my manhood before *profound awakenment* happened to me. I am trying to grasp our mission. I am talking about the early church. I am not talking about Christianity, but about an instrument, a means of how something happens. Who thought up that fantastic phrase "good news" for evangelism? We think of it as some silly piety or some abstract theology. No, the good news was what people were trying to talk about when they experienced some kind of profound awakenment in their lives. I do not know what I would do if that happening that unveiled the deeps of consciousness about consciousness had not happened to me.

Let's move to the next part of our journey on this pentagon. I went to school a long time. I went to college and did graduate work. I did not get an education. It was not until World War II grabbed me and turned my being inside out that I got an education. Before that, I got what we call a classical education. But I really am talking about *transrational training*. I did not get an education until I grasped what I mean by transrationality or, simply, methodology. No person is a real person until s/he has not data that is poured in but the methodologies that make life creative. What is creativity? What are we about? To communicate methodologies to individuals, groups, and communities that will enable individuals and groups to be themselves, to release their creativity, to genuinely participate in this strange, mysterious process we call history. Why did that come so late to me? As a matter of fact, I believe that the whole revolution in education in our time pivots around becoming aware of precisely this.

Now, when I look again at my life and try to think what it is about, I come to words like *authentic engagement*. It has something to do with vocation. The general understanding of "vocation" makes me sick at my stomach these days – so superficial. I am a clergyman, and I think I am a pretty good one, but that is not enough. That is not what I am talking about. When you read the news these days, you know you are living in one of the most remarkable moments in all of history, and sometimes you wipe the sweat off and think, "My God! What if I were a good clergyman and died a good clergyman, and, some way or another, had *not* stuffed my creativity into what was happening in my time?" You can ask that question as a clergyman, as a lawyer, as a businessman, as a surgeon. It is the question of authentic engagement. What are we about? Answer: in some way or other to enable authentic engagement of the masses. I am not interested in Fifth City and Majuro for their own sake. I am interested in some way of getting something done that can be a sign for anybody in this world of what is possible for them to do if they choose to do it, as a doctor, a lawyer, or a businessman.

Now comes the fifth dynamic that is even harder, if you try to get this into secular language. You are going to laugh, I suppose, at the name *transparent prowess*. How is it that a person knows the way to that Other World of consciousness which is always present in the midst of this world, which is the only world you and I know anything about, really? How do you find your way through the humiliation of contingency, through the weakness of contingency, through the resentment of contingency, through the suffering of contingency, through the rootlessness of contingency, through the ineffectivity of contingency, through the poured-out-ness of contingency, through the unfulfillment of contingency, and find precisely in the midst of these – without the contingency ever going away – the glory of living and dying?

This is when hope appeareth. How do you find your way around this world that is the Other World that is only present within this world? When I taught at Colgate, we were still talking about the "well-rounded man," but people were pointing to the moral level of life. When you push that to the profundity of the ontological, this pentagon is what it now means to round out your existence. When you walk around this pentagon and come back to primal community, then you know what real living is all about.

So, what is it that we are about for the next forty years? There is nothing religious about these five dynamics. We are out to build *primal community*. In some places we call it the Ecumenical Parish Experiment, in others the Local Church Experiment. We are out to establish programs of *profound awakenment* through Town Meeting '76. We are out to do *transrational training* through University 13 and what we call our eight-week Academy. We are out to do *authentic engagement* through Social Demonstration Projects. And we are out to do *transparent prowess* through spiritual Odyssey weekends, which we have pretty well bracketed for now, but day after tomorrow, men and women are going to come together for no other reason than to find their way to the deeps.

This is my picture of what we are about. There are just five things that we're about in our mission and I do not know which is the greatest. Social Demonstration Projects are important right now for us, but they are not as important as awakenment. For awhile, you know, we thought of Town Meeting as social demonstration, because everything that is serious is a demonstration. But Town Meeting is awakenment. Those of us in the church get all mixed up on this point. I almost hesitate to say this because I love the church, but we in the church have reduced awakenment to believing a set of ideas. The New Testament talks about being born all over again in such a way that you can see it. When the New Testament writers talked about someone's becoming a new creation, they did not mean believing some special ideas. They meant that the person's whole style was profoundly altered in the concretions of living. By the way, Buddhists have done the same thing with the category of illumination.

Enough! I am making another speech. . . .

Finally, why put the word "love" or "care" at the center of the pentagon? If somebody were to ask me now what it means to profoundly love or to profoundly care, I would have to answer this way: being about building primal community; being busy awakening people to the deeps of consciousness; giving them methodological skills so they can creatively engage; globally pioneering with social demonstrations; and finding ways of nurturing people in the world of transparentization, or the Other World in this world. This is why this body is called to be, to be of service – as they used to say when I was growing up, to be in the "service of love."

Sophistication

To cultivate the establishment requires sophistication. I am not interested here in defining "sophistication," but rather in describing a dynamic that can be pointed to with that word. I do not believe I have arrived at the kind of analysis of a dynamic that I think has to go on if we are to permeate the establishment. I am not even remotely interested in artificial sophistication. Most of what I have seen in my life has been that.

Sophistication is that invisible dynamic which produces the unobservable courage to do. I think it has to do primarily with the male rather than with the female, first of all, although I am aware there are exceptions to this. It is just that most women I know do not have to worry about sophistication so much as effervescence. These two are very close. Perhaps clarity on this comes first in dealing with sophistication; and then, in what "X" is for the male and what effervescing sophistication is for the female.

One of the wonderful and humiliating things in my life is that from the time I met Lyn, she was sophisticated, but I have never been. I still intend to do something about it, however. Some people are born into a family structure where authentic, invisible sophistication is just there. I think of the Kennedy family, for instance. Whether you like them or not, part of what I mean by sophistication is there. Other people are clothed with it early in life. Some are thrown in certain circles that provide the setting for learning sophistication. Lyn did not come out of a sophisticated family, but fate threw her into a sophisticated circle in Wilmington, Delaware. I never had that. This is part of my shyness. I am a shy man. It takes guts for me to walk into a new situation or to make a speech or a formal presentation. I was born a shy man and my background intensified that.

I still think, however, the sophistication I am after applies mostly to men. Women have it, though not all of them, perhaps. There is an area of courage that I believe women have that we men do not have. Sometimes when Lyn and I have gone to a hotel, I have sent her to make an inquiry, which I am aware I should have made, but did not have poise and courage enough to do. When I think back on that, it hurts to remember I was that childish, that boyish. What really surprised me is that when Lyn would do so, it did not seem to bother her one bit. She just went and did it, as though anybody who is an adult should just go ahead and do that. That offended me.

In one sense, our "ugly Americanism" overseas is not simply ugly Americanism (though I do not want to take anything away from hitting that hard). It is our "little boyishness." It is our lack of sophistication. I do not know enough about other cultures, but I wonder whether what I would mean by sophistication (which has nothing to do with a particular culture) is not more of a normal reality among the men of those other cultures than it is in the West. It would have a little bit to do with whether or not a culture keeps its men little boys.

The time has come when we men have to be sophisticated, because we have to cultivate the establishment. I have polished the shoes of people in the establishment all around the world. I do not mean by that that I am trying to get the establishment to like me. I do not mean that we have come to terms with the establishment. I intend to communicate to the establishment, with my being, that they are going to change. I am out to see that they change, while I am polishing their shoes. That is, I am an unabashed revolutionary. And as an unabashed revolutionary, I carry their suitcases and shine their shoes, not as a lackey, but in sophistication.

I do not know quite what I mean by sophistication, but I do know that certain little things are necessary. To start with I am talking about your presence on the most mundane of levels: *your appearance*. If I were the wife of any man in the Order, I would see to it that he had a dark blue suit. If necessary I would treat him just like a little boy until he got it on; then I would start treating him like a man. He needs a traditional suit, but he doesn't need to look like a broken-down Methodist minister of twenty years ago. I do not mean that. And, if I were that wife, I would see to it that he had one shirt that was out of this world. I never knew much about dressing, so do not take my details seriously, except that dark blue suit. Two years ago a striped shirt seemed to be the thing, and a few years ago, a dark blue tie. I would also have a dark blue shirt that was clerical. I probably would not wear it, but I would have it.

I am speaking of intentionality. The way I dressed today is what I mean by intentionality. I had a little mission to do. You dress according to the mission you want to do. I find a great deal of real excitement about having a uniform. When you wear your uniform, you intentionally wear your uniform. We men have never had the type of flexibility you women have had. The way you dress is for a purpose. That is crucial. That is sophistication, but if your intention shows, then it is inauthentic sophistication. Yesterday it did not make much difference in the movement. But the mission now requires a kind of sophistication.

Another dimension of sophistication is knowing what to do and how to do it. This has to do with *exposure*. Therefore, we should welcome every exposure. This has to do with registering and moving into a hotel, without anybody seeing you register. This has to do with paying the hotel bill without anybody seeing you pay it. We have a colleague who is one of the best I have ever seen in my whole life. You would be having dinner with some guest, having decided beforehand who is going to pay the bill. Missionally, you intend that someone else pay the bill. Our colleague does not do so well with that. He likes to pay the bill, and therefore grabs it first. But, when we decide we are going to pay and it is time to leave the table, we find the bill all settled even though we never saw it and we just walk out. All we remember is that our colleague left briefly somewhere in the middle of the meal. That is sophistication. He is an expert at that kind of thing and I envy him. I never had that. I worry too much about how much it is costing – not when I am ordering something, but when I am paying. This sophistication comes from exposure. This kind of smoothness has to be there. Some people go up to the airlines to check in and have obviously left their poise outside. You have seen people sweat over paying a taxi driver. It is because they did not have it all thought out while they were driving along; they were looking at the tall buildings. You need to know what it is going to cost, to know exactly where your funds are, exactly how much you are going to tip, and you settle that inside your being so that at the end you are not there sweating over whether you are going to give him 10 percent or a quarter.

This brings me to the next part of poise, which is *planning*. You wish people would learn around here. It was two days before we left for the global trip and one idiot did not have a passport! Frankly, I have just enough of the devil in me that I was hoping he would not get it. He had just two days. I was hoping he would fail, and at the last moment we would have to call around and see who did have a passport. Sophistication has to do with having your passport. The guy who has not thought himself through is always trapped. Tactical thinking is not something you do when you want to start a revolutionary movement. It is having your passport. It is something you do before you go in to register at the hotel. It is always sizing up and casing a place without anybody seeing you do it. Your eyes go every which way. Nobody knows what you are doing, but you are building your tactical model. I am talking on the very crass level of this subject, the mundane things of life.

The third thing about poise is *detachment.* What I just described gives you detachment. It is the embracing of your detachment. This is the meaning of "cool." The way I come at it is to say inside myself, "Now your destiny is not wrapped up in this little thing-a-ma-jig you are doing," even if it is going to see the Cardinal. You cannot be detached, however, if you do not have a tactical model. You would be a fool to walk in to see the Cardinal without a tactical model. Only when you know where your are going to move exactly can you be free enough to field a hard-hit ball coming at you.

In addition to that, what I would talk about as prayer is that of making the decision that your destiny is not tied up in that moment. When somebody walks me into what I would call a tiger trap, I become angry. When I went in to see a Cardinal last year, the people with me did not inform me that he had visited us on the West Side of Chicago. Nor did they let me know that he had been misused. Let us assume that these people did not know. But when I get upset I do not think of these things, I just get upset; and then later I find out that they did not know it either. You see, however, that I would not even have to get upset if I had seriously made the decision about detachment before I went in there. That is not quite the right way to put it, for I intend to be upset when I walk into a tiger trap.

But I do not want to act out of the up-set-ness. It is that kind of detachment that I think of as a part of poise.

Another has to do with *etiquette*, a prescribed method of action that has to do with bestowing the kind of honor without which you never have a society. For instance, I would not think of going into any Bishop's presence without calling him "Your Grace," even with those who haven't made the decision to be the Bishops they are. I remember one of the finest speeches that I think I ever made was to twenty-one Methodist Bishops at a meeting in which I told them that one of their biggest problems was that they were not willing to be Bishops. And that, whereas they thought we every-day preachers want them to be nice, friendly fellows, we want exactly the opposite. We want them to be our symbols. We want them to be our Bishops, not one of our buddies. I enjoyed that, and it was very interesting to me that they found that helpful, for it cut across what most of them thought. I had a hard time working out what to call an ambassador. "Your What?" None of us knew for sure. We finally decided that "Your Excellency" was right. That is a hunk of etiquette I should have known in terms of the job ahead of us.

For several years I have been trying to learn from the Koreans how to address people. But they would not help me. The Westerners had so conditioned them that they would say, "Just call me Henry." They get a Western name and put it before their surname. One of my concerns was David Cho, who has a church in Korea like Harry Emerson Fosdick had in this country. When he came to Singapore where I was preaching some years ago, I treated him like I would myself, just a country preacher. It was not until over a year later that I found out that the very minimum anyone would call him is "The Right Reverend Mr. Cho." This was a lack of sophistication on my part. I finally learned from the Koreans the way I would address Kang Byoung Hoon, who was here for some months. Every time you speak to him it is "Kang Byoung Hoon, Moksanim, how are you feeling this morning? Kang Byoung Hoon, Moksanim, I am glad you are feeling well this morning." I said to some of them, "Shouldn't I call him just 'Byoung Hoon' because I know him so well and because I am older?" "No." "Well, he calls me 'Joe.'" They said, "That is because in your country that is the thing to do. And he is trying to do what you do in your country. In his country he would be called 'Byoung Hoon' only if he were a kindergarten student."

I have no desire to give in to the phony kind of liberalism that is afraid to make a mistake overseas. They will forgive you if you make a mistake. The problem is when you do not know enough to make a mistake. When you go in to see His Holiness and His Beatitude Theophilis, the person who enters his audience first is the one who has the most status; if he does not have obvious status, then it is the one who is older. The youngest, with the least status, goes in last. When you leave his presence, it is exactly the reverse. The youngest goes out first and the person with the most status or oldest goes out last. You would not think of being in that room in the presence of His Beatitude with the status figure having already gone out the door. That is just crucial.

Or I am talking about such things as when a President of a country, in his office, makes the slightest gesture of looking at his watch, or standing up, or reaching for his papers, you are on your feet in a flash of a second. You sense when that is coming, and you are on your feet just before he does it. This is what I am after here in terms of deportment.

The last point I have to make is a hard one. It is something like *being of service in every situation*, or being a guru. I am a little afraid of this. For instance, a colleague backed a Bishop's wife into the corner and began to give her a pedagogy course on the meaning of prayer. Later, when the Bishop got up and walked out to his car, wanting to take one of the guests home with him, our colleague still had that guest pinned on the porch explaining some last eternal truth while the Bishop waited at the car door. The Chinese man he was talking to was doing his best to tell him to "Go to Hell!" while trying to be a polite Chinese man at the same time. If you ever wonder why we get in any trouble overseas, it is that we lack finesse. Up to now, that has not been such an issue, but from now on it is necessary that we have finesse. If any of you think I am not dealing with revolutionary tactics right now, then you just do not understand.

This all has something to do with being the guru. But your guruing must never stand out. We had a good time when we saw George Romney, because he is a Mormon and we enjoyed spinning about the stakes and the guild. We had fun because we were not trying to teach him anything.

Rarely do I ride in a taxi when the driver is not glad that he had that old man in his cab. Those of you who know me know I exercise this gift in myself even though I may be a bit corny at it. I do not always do it because I am lazy and because I like to pretend I am tired. What I am trying to say is that everywhere you go you owe these people just a little touch of yourself. Frequently I think, "What do I have to give him?" But when I become a little detached, I discover I have a lot to give most everyone I meet. And so have you. You can leave just a little bit of yourself behind with a hotel clerk; with a stewardess on an airplane; when you go to see the Cardinal, you can have fun with leaving a little bit of yourself behind. I believe this has to do with sophistication. You unobtrusively be sure you give a hunk of yourself. Most of the time, when we go see people, we are after something. It is the sophisticated person who leaves a little behind. Winston Churchill, in the midst of the unbelievable pressure of unbelievable problems, had time to speak to the lady who was sweeping the floor. These are crude illustrations, I realize, but I have had to say them to get to what I mean. We have to become sophisticated people.

Most of what I have been saying has been more to the men than to the women. I tell you women that when one of you does not stand up like a queen, I get a little pain down inside. When one of you does not get up in the morning and dress like a queen, I get a little upset down inside. I like nice looking girls at any age: little ones, big ones, old ones, and young ones. That has to do with effervescence, sophistication.

What I am talking about has to do with the unconscious dynamics which create unobservable courage. This exercise I have gone through is what gives a man like me, who is neurotically shy, the strength to move into most any situation with people and get that job done. I guess what I am saying, finally, is that sophistication is something you are constantly creating in yourself. One of these days I hope some of you will get up and be able to give the talk I have just given, and do it well, pushing it much deeper. For the next forty years that kind of almost sacred sophistication is going to be required of each of us. I see no hope of our being global, of our going global, save that which I call sophistication develops among us.

Forging Social Philosophy

When we were last in Maliwada we were with Mr. Dethe, who is about 65 years old and a Guardian. He is a very renowned architect in India, now retired. He had suffered three heart attacks, and his family and his doctors all convinced him that he ought to sit at home and have a fatal heart attack in ease. However, your colleagues persuaded him to use his expertise and go to Maliwada. He is the man who, with the wisdom of the local people, designed that unbelievable three-room house. They now have some twenty of them built out of local material – rocks that grow like mushrooms, local labor, of which there is plenty, and a not very satisfactory roof. That is one of the issues of the Repository, finding the roof for housing around the world.

Anyway, he has also done the master plan of Maliwada. He designed the two industrial sheds there that are out of this world. Subsequently he has gone to the other villages in India and has already started to do master plans for them. He was the senior architect in the design of the town of Chandigar, which is a fantastic new city built north of Delhi, and he has developed a number of the significant industrial buildings and commercial office buildings in Bombay, plus temples. We were talking one night in his room in the religious house in Maliwada. We asked him, "Of all your projects, which one do you wish that history would remember you by?" I frankly was expecting the Chandigar one, but he shocked us. He said, "I hope I am remembered by that," and he pointed to the model house in Maliwada. I do not know why I was shocked. I guess one of the privileges of humanness is that you can be constantly shocked by what encounters you. Mr. Dethe has never been in finer health, by the way; whenever they have a celebration he dances with all the ladies.

Mr. Dethe made the remark that India had been invaded some thirty-two times in its history. He said each time there was an invasion local people gathered and built the great palaces and forts, the great temples, the great mosques that today stand as wonders of the world. Mr. Dethe said that in his experience in the last six months he now was persuaded that for the first time local people in India were going to build their own dwellings. The things that have stood are the Taj Mahal, the Ellora Caves, and the Red Fort, but the dwellings are in shambles. He has talked to his fellow architects about participating as Guardians in the rebuilding of local people's dwellings. There are 700,000 villages at about 100 houses per village – that would be 70 million houses. Can you imagine? And he has committed himself and his colleagues to design those houses as their participation in the replication movement.

The 85 Percent and the 15 Percent

This has to do with the fact that 85 percent of the people live in an entirely different universe than 15 percent of the people. This is not the simplistic division of the haves and the have-nots. It is not the simplistic division which says the West has the money. Many of the richest people in the world are in India. That is a fact, and our people have done well in getting money from them. I am talking about the fact that 85 percent of the people live in an entirely different universe than you and I do. This is not a statement about hunger. The shocking thing is that to date in history only 15 percent of society have gotten their creativity into building society. Just think if the 85 percent or even half or a third of that number found a way through town meeting, social demonstration, or awakened community renewal to get their creativity into history. We would have the greatest explosion since the dawn of consciousness itself. Somebody pointed out that the art of tactics to date had been the special privilege of the military tacticians. In this explosion of the 85 percent you would have on your hands something that is beyond imagination. We are participating in something that is far beyond any institute, any group such as the Guardians. It is the most profound trend in history today, the resurgence of local people.

As you know, we have spent our lives trying to evolve the philosophy of the local approach, and we have come a long way. The social demonstration documents represent the unbelievable creativity of given communities. In the last year or so we have been in close dialogue with the superstructures of the world, the European government agencies, the World Bank, USAID, and so on. We have started to talk about the local approach. It has been fascinating. Each time we say, "Only in the 20th century have humans been able to do the inclusive planning that the World Bank is a symbol of. Before then there was only local economics. But once again the local is coming into being. We underscore it with our lives." We say, "If you think of the broad approach, the figures dominate. The figures say so many people will die, and the figures are right. Even the Club of Rome, the Cassandra outfit that publishes the yearly doomsday report, or the latest liberal echelon forecast is right in that sense. However, if you think locally, village by village, there is no reason for anyone to starve in the world." The funny thing is that when we say all that, the people like McNamara understand. When we talk about local economics, local social infrastructure, and local motivation, they understand. When you think from the perspective of a village, they understand that the local economy can generate enough so that people need not starve.

We are being forced to articulate our social philosophy. No longer do they ask, "Who are you?" They ask, "What do you do?" Really, what they are after is the $64 question: how does motivation take place? I want to talk about that a little. We are finding, as we have done twelve of these social demonstrations, some remarkable constants that occur in each one. These constants represent a social philosophy, a screen by which you could gauge a community while at the same time dramatically insisting that each community do its own planning.

Three Arenas of Our Social Philosophy

There are three arenas of this evolving social philosophy. One has to do with the economic, one has to do with the social, and one has to do with the spirit. We have received very little criticism as we have talked about using such a word as "community spirit." We are after social self-reliance. We are after local self-sustenance, and we are after local self-confidence. There are five categories in each one of the three, and the third one is by far the most important.

Under the social dynamic, the first one we have entitled *complete and immediate nutrition.* A more rational approach would be to put nutrition under health, but it is a shocking thing what we find in nutrition as we go into these villages. We believe that when you do a site selection you first look at a village from outside. Only if you think that there is a remote chance that this could be a village project do you get out of your car and then you walk, and you walk fast, because you are after an art form of that village, not details. You are after the intuitive impact on your consciousness. The village people in Kelapa Dua had a hard time. One village guy was always behind and was trying to keep up, and he finally came up and said, "How old are you?" He thought I had premature gray hair. I said, "I am 65." He said "I am 50 and I can't keep up with you."

The fact is that you go into a village like Kelapa Dua and you are impressed with the physical lethargy of the people. I am not talking about a bigoted laziness. Their bodies have for centuries been undernourished; therefore, we believe nutrition has to be complete and immediate. If it is a long term process you might as well not do it. What we do is start a community kitchen. It took a while to get the community kitchen started in Maliwada. This is a kitchen where not just the kids but everybody gets one nutritious meal a day, cooked by the community people out of both donated food from the UN organization and locally grown food out of their corporate garden, which ultimately will replace the donated food. They eat like mad, and the kids drink like mad. If you went around house to house with a home economics course, it would take years. This way, with a community kitchen, the vitality that they now have on their faces is a shocking thing. We believe this is one of the keys to rapid socio-economic change.

The second has to do with preventative *health.* One of the things that is absolutely vital around the world is water. In Kawangware this is because of parasites. They have got to find deep water bores, they have got to drill until they get good water that the people can not only drink but wash their clothes in and bathe in. Then they can use the high table water for irrigation only. Where this is not done you might as well not do health. The doctors come in with immediate immunization and preventative health structures. In Kawangware they went down 450 feet to find good water. Ingersoll Rand came in and it was a $7,000 expense. They just drilled and drilled until they found water. They got it. In Maliwada, 250 feet down they got water. I prophesy they are going to find water even in El Bayad. It is just a matter of going down far enough. The health team is right on target in that arena.

Third, and most important under the social, is *local social framework*. What I mean by that really is the local social infrastructure. In each developing country there are unbelievable cities, unbelievable regional infrastructure, unbelievable airports and highways. What has got to happen is development of the local infrastructure. In our terminology there are "stakes" in terms of community care, "guilds" in terms of community action, "assemblies" in terms of the whole community, "congress" and "commissions" in terms of the administrative, and a "panchayat" in terms of the symbolic leadership in India. We would be fools if we went in and did not consider that a priority, because we want to get out of those villages. If you do not build the stake, guild, commission and assembly structures, you are there for twenty years. Those structures are working everywhere. Maliwada, after only ten weeks, had everything going except stakes. These are not organizational structures. We insist on saying that we are doing local socio-economic development. Now we could say "community development," however, we are not doing community development. Community development is bureaucratically superimposed renewal. Stakes and guilds are the extreme opposite of local bureaucratic structures. They are that without which the social cannot be done.

Fourth is *functional education*. This has to do with skills relative to total community renewal. It has to do with basic literacy. It has to do with English, and a liberal will tell you that you ought not teach English; but if a person is going to survive he has to have some basic capabilities in English. Then they must have technical skills. They have to have functional education that is relevant to their lives rather than four years of college.

Fifth, and last under the local social dynamic, is *family development*. This is not just family planning, though that is a part of it. We have found some unbelievable things in these villages. If your body is enervated by parasites and therefore lacks vitality, you could care less about a message that has to do with tomorrow. Only when you have engagement of a community and only when they have the physical capability to hear will the message of "we can do our own development" be understood.

Under the economic dynamic, the first item is *total employment*. That is an audacious statement – not half, but total. What we are really talking about is total engagement. In the mud in Kawangware they have 1,972 people, from the kids and the adults, involved in the training. I would like to describe the Maliwada factories a little more. One out of every family in Maliwada is employed in either of the two factories or the construction program. That means that they are spreading income. The rest are farmers. They are about at total employment or engagement now after eight months. These factories are the most incredible things in the world. One is a food processing industry. They have 130 people working. They take soy bean stuff and make a little lunch pack for the school lunch program in the state of Maharastra. They have to improve the taste of it, but you go there and people are working. They work three shifts, 24 hours a day. I was standing there and all of a sudden a whistle went off, and I said, "What's wrong?" They said, "That is for the next shift." Can you imagine a little village having a whistle that blows and out goes one shift? The ladies are there on the floor crushing this stuff and singing songs. Next to it is another shed where they are creating boxes. They are going to do more industries, but it is total employment that we are after. The vital thing is that they have stressed that the landless be employed there. They are getting a tremendous distribution of income within the village.

Secondly, *local commercial structures* are to be built. This is the direct input of the principles of local economics where, with an injection of outside funds, you re-circulate a dollar within the village. You consider the village an economic unit in and of itself, as if it were a nation. You talk about imports and exports and so on. You get a dollar or a rupee or lots of rupees into a village and then you re-circulate the money as many times as possible before you let it seep out into the larger economy. What do you build? You build structures that have to do with corporate buying of goods, corporate retailing, and inner circulation of the funds. It is phenomenal what such structures can do.

Thirdly, we build the *local economy*. We are interested in sizeable income upgrading. If you just do cottage industries you are creating structural under-employment. We are after people having a dramatic increase in income. Our goal within two years is to triple the income of that village. When we saw McNamara at the World Bank, he said their goal was to double income in five years by using the regional approach of impact through projects like their command area irrigation and so on. That is not a bad goal through that approach, but we are out to triple the income in two years. We are persuaded that it is possible. Again to illustrate from Maliwada: in eight months they have gone from $100,000 gross village income to $280,000 gross village income. In eight months they have almost tripled it. The actual net cash input was $25,000 over six months. They got a lot from the government but that money was sitting there anyway. They got a lot of loans but that is locally assumed. It is a shocking thing when you see how they have spread their income. There are similar figures on Kawangware and other projects.

Fourth, we are concerned with *local agriculture productivity*. That has to do both with expanding and intensifying the agricultural effort. What they have done in Kawangware in farming is just amazing. They raise green beans which they export to London, and they are able to make a fantastic income off a corporate demonstration farm. On the demonstration farm they are trying every crazy crop they can think of that would grow there. The farmers are using hybrid seeds to intensify the yield of their small plots. Irrigation is another factor. You go to Maliwada where the Great Fort sits. It is very easy to visualize how it was once a Garden of Eden, green, plush beyond all imagination. There is a big hole miles long that was a fantastic reservoir built 700 years ago. You can see the tracings of small irrigation lines. Maliwada is in what the World Bank calls the drought prone area. What happened? Did God have his way? No, they just stopped irrigation. They once did irrigation and now they don't. But they are doing it again. It is getting green again. Barring natural catastrophe the irrigation locally is easy to do.

Fifth under the economic is profitable *light industry.* I described those industries that they have in Maliwada. First is a cottage industry. I am not against them as long as they are not the only thing. I do not mean handicraft per se, but things that people can do in their houses, such as rope making. Second is a processing industry. That is where you take a crop that is locally grown and you push it one more step down. You take the guava that is grown and make it into guava jam. Third we are calling ancillary industry, which is trying to point to the factor of a guaranteed market. Any minority or entrepreneurial business that has failed has failed at the marketing issue. We have had unbelievable luck around the world in approaching the national and international corporations in the nearest city. We say to them that we are after employment. If they have a product that is relatively low skill or easily learned skill, we would create this product. They get started off with a guaranteed market. That is what they have done and why they did extremely well in those two industries in Maliwada.

I have talked about the social and economic dynamics of community reformulation. Quickly, onto the third, the dynamic of spirit. We believe this to be the white hot heat of motivation itself. First is a *meaningful context.* This is a crucial one. You know in our first projects we picked some villages where the story of the village was relatively easy to discern. Just think of a village sitting at the foot of the Dulatabad Fort, carved out of sheer rock. It is easy to see that once upon a time they had a fantastic story about their village; their ancestors built one of the great wonders of the world. What we are finding is that every village has a great story about its past. The story of the village at Kendore tells of a sacred well. Every village around the world has in the deep recesses of its past an unbelievable story, and all you have to do is ask enough questions and it comes out. What a look on the villagers' faces when they see their story in print. Once they remember their past they have a chance to envision a future.

Also, under a meaningful context, you are charged with discerning the fundamental human issue that is there. This is not easy. It was hardest perhaps in Kelapa Dua where you had to discern what the deep underlying human issue was. They had an unbelievable physical lethargy but a deep motivation. We had a hard time stating that one, but in each project if you do not discern what their fundamental human issue is, you cannot help them in creating their story.

Second under the local community spirit is *revitalized symbols*. These are not symbols that you import, they are their symbols. Every Indian village used to have festivals, but they stopped. You encourage them once again to use their symbolic life and their stories and songs. When they started the preschool in Maliwada, we went over to the outcaste community. When we first went in, they hid in their mud huts. When we went there again they came out and brought their kids. The lowest of the low brought their kids out. They had their kids sing songs in Hindi to us, and then songs in English. Not just the kids were vital and alive, but you should have seen their parents. They were so proud of their kids. Anyway, the symbols have to be songs, rites, and festivals. Without that you do not have a local community spirit.

Third, and most important, under local community spirit we are building a *new living environment*. This is best illustrated by the housing. Everywhere around the world housing can be built out of local material and local labor. In Kawangware they have their drain ditches. It is a lot easier now to walk down the street without hip boots. It is fantastic the way those kids get out and dig those ditches. The city council has come in and has laid half of it with stone, which is a fine example of working with the city structures. In addition to housing there is the community itself. They have cobble-stoned their streets in Maliwada. Can you imagine? They have set white rocks around the road. They have named them Mahatma Gandhi Avenue and Jawarahal Nehru Avenue. Isn't that great?

Fourth, *corporate effort*. We believe that such renewal of a community is impossible without intensive corporate efforts. As you would well guess, we first go out there and we are a sign of corporateness itself. People can laugh at our blue and we do not much care. We roll up our sleeves and we start the first work day. Then the next thing you know the people are joining in. Age-old taboos disappear overnight. It used to be in these places that water could not pass over one man's land to go to another. That is no longer an issue in Maliwada or Kawangware. Age-old taboos disappear with the corporate effort. It used to be that you had the outcastes, and overnight you have all classes working together with significant engagement, community corporateness. That does not mean that they truly like each other. They sense with the engagement that they can work together and get their community renewed. It is fantastic to see.

Then last, as you would well guess, we are after *individual creativity* coming out. It is the flip side of corporateness. We have seen it not only here in our Order, but we have seen it with villagers. You and I could not do what we are doing without Kang in Korea, Parekh in India, Fishel in Majuro, Campbell and Kameme in Kawangware. The individual creativity comes out after that.

Town Meeting re Replication and Local Care

We are going to keep working on articulating our philosophy, but this is not something that we are going to superimpose on a village. At the height of replication in India, the first four villages are going to do a consult. Then, when we do the 25, all the work will be done. They are going to go in and instead of having a week-long planning consult, what they probably will do is have a one-day town meeting, and that will be all they need. Then they can take the experience of their fellows. With the 250 villages, they send leaders to the training school and then they have a town meeting in each village. What I am trying to say is that the town meeting is key to replication.

Now, to you in North America, I would like to charge you with two things. One, your colleagues around the world are impressed with what has been done with town meeting. Moreover, they are depending on it because they know that what local people did in North America will make it a lot easier for them. Why would this work? There are two reasons, I believe. One has to do with the local people themselves. Any of you that have gone to a week-long consult know this. Integrity bleeds out of the local people. After one day in the consult, visioning the next five years for their community, they are standing up straighter. They are not encumbered with education. They are willing to move. They are not after some dole; they know that depreciates their own selfhood. Some of the finest associations that we have made the last few years have been with local people themselves. I believe it will work because of the integrity of local people. The second reason I believe town meeting will work in the replication of village development is because we are finding a pool of people around the world where voluntarism is not a dead issue. They happen to care. There are local people in the 85 percent who care and people in the 15 percent who care. Down underneath the social philosophy of this social demonstration movement I've been talking about is human care. All we have to do is release it and give it form.

Profound Humanness: Integrity

Integrity is not what we used to say it is: rules, some kind of quality or merit you might have, or values and principles. Nobody has integrity.

There is only one kind of integrity, and we have grappled with that for a long time. We called it secondary integrity at one point. It's the integrity that is not you, but you are of it. The integrity that is profound humanness is a tent. You go and live in that tent and you feel like a human being. You are a human being. If you go outside that tent, you are a man-dog or a woman-cow. I think this year most of us have met strangers that lived in the tent. You worked with them and did miracles with them. There were people that you woke up in a Town Meeting or a Social Demonstration Project. They came right out and said, "What is your secret? How do you keep going? How do you live like this?" In the past when people asked us that question, we used to give them a long context. You don't have that kind of time anymore. I believe this is really what we have been starting to work on here. Maybe later we will come out with the "Sayings of Profound Humanness" that you just say and people understand. Until then, you really have to give sort of an answer-unanswer.

There was a fellow named St. Augustine who tried to say it: "Love God and do what you please." That's an answer-unanswer that allows you to take in a lot at once. We know enough about theology and temporality to know that we have got to do that job ourselves and say for our time what that is. We are left with the question, "How do I be a human being? How do I be a person of integrity?" We all have to find a way to get our insides out. That is, to get inside profound humanness and know we are also issuing a call for people to deal with the great global divide between the 15 and 85 percent. This line has to do with the seven revolutions of our time.

Integrity as profound humanness is about *keeping your own conscience*. You really can't say much more than that. But beneath that there's a whole lot. There is an awakenment when you find out you are headed for death. You only have one life to live and you have decided to straighten up and live it right. You find out that there is criticism in life and some think this and some that. You begin to shape your life that way, and it becomes a ping-pong game and you are the ball. You close that game down. Then you decide what you want to do. You create a private conscience. What you find is that you've turned your life over to your appetites or some abstract goal or principle. Then comes along a profound moment in your life. Sometimes it is remembering the moment. I've been struck this year at how many people in the course of a conversation say they knew deep stuff when they were four, five, six, seven-years-old. But it comes over and over again. Hammarskjöld has a tremendous piece of writing in his book *Markings*.

He says something like this: You told yourself you would accept the decision of fate, but you lost your nerve when you discovered what this would require of you. Then you realized how attached you still were to the world, which has made you what you were, which you would now have to leave behind. It felt like an amputation, a little death. And you even listened to those voices which insinuated that you were deceiving yourself out of ambition. Why, then, weep at this little death? Take it to you quickly. With a smile die this death and become free to go further. Become one with your task, whole in your duty of the moment.

Whatever it is that stirs that moment in you is what you watch over and be careful about because it leads you to being a human. You start "keeping your own conscience" just a little and you know what happens. Everything inside of you gets torn up and you fall into a perpetual state of self-criticism, while outside the haze of life lifts and you begin to see things with particular specificity. Keeping your own conscience binds you to humanness. It's your ticket. You really have to give sort of an answer-unanswer. It's the only way, finally, that you have of seeing that what you are doing is real.

There is a story about an old man who had two sons and he told them something to do. You remember one of them said, "No, he wouldn't do it," and later ended up doing it. The other son said he would do it and then didn't go do it. The son who said no, when he was encountered by a profound moment, took care of his conscience. When the jarring moment came, he knew what he had to do and he went and did it.

But there is more to this. Integrity as profound humanness is *hitting the moral issue of our time*. This line is drawn across our moment. On one side is the big haze. The big haze is everything. On the other side is this 15-85 percent. No haze. Very obvious. I have begun to talk about both the 85 percent and the 15 percent as the poor of spirit, the poor of body, the poor of mind. It's humankind that suffers. When you see that, you see that the issue of which side you are going to be on or which is better or which is more loved is not a question anymore. That has already been dealt with. The only question that you've got is, "Where are you going to put both feet?"

We've tried it all. We've tried putting one foot on one side and one foot on the other and both on either side. You found out certain things. You found out that whenever you keep your conscience just a little, and you care about it, somewhere, somehow, there's a power that comes. You've seen yourselves and you've seen others do miracles. Do one hundred Town Meetings in a single day. It's hard to get hold of it, hard to understand it. After that, people have come up and said to you that the course of the community is changed, that this place will never be the same again. When that's occurred, you've sensed (that's not a strong enough word) the weight of history has come to you as your life. You've also known that as soon as you put aside this taking care of your conscience, you pour cold water on it. You forget it. You don't tend it.

It starts off something like this. You say to yourself, "Now the reason I did this, or the reason I'm going to do something else. . . ." You learn fast that the failure mentality, despair, negativism, cynicism, fillyism – and whatever else you want to add to that list – are rooted in a refusal to keep your own conscience. When you get both feet on the other side of that line things start getting clear. You see the human suffering of the world. It's not just seeing it. It penetrates your being. You are profoundly addressed by how much there is to do. You go out into a village and you know that beyond this village there are millions more. You enter into the suffering of the world. The issue you face is not how little or how much you can get done; how effective or ineffective you are. The issue is there's a lot of work to do; let's get to doing it. I think you step across the line and call your shot and carry it through, or you join the reactionary un-society.

You've all been given answers to how we got sustained this year, or what sustained us as a body. I think mine would go something like this: we got sustained as a body because we lived out of and we lived off of the suffering of humankind. We saw through a village or Town Meeting that there was another and another and another. The preoccupation that came over us was, "Let's get this one done so we can get to the next one, so we can get to the next one."

You don't notice at that time, but I believe that's the point where integrity begins to raise its tent over your head. I believe when you wake up to integrity, you wake up to integrity's over-shadowing you. That would be another way I'd say integrity as profound humanness is *constituting the new image of humanness*. It's sort of like the training thing. Somebody comes to a project and says they want to get trained. They bug you and all you can think to say is, "Would you get that chain over there? Put it in the car. We've got to go get the truck out of the ditch." And they show up again wanting to get trained and you have them going after other chains. A few weeks later they come up and you notice that they are trained. They're leading a group. They're doing things. They're building models. All this time you've been worrying about how in the world you'll get them off to an ITI [International Training Institute]. I think integrity is a little bit like that. The locus of integrity is where the rubber hits the road.

We've all come to know about this business of nobodies. A "nobody" is anybody who's going so fast he doesn't have time to be somebody. There's a global command. It's like the rule of the Order. It's not written, but you know for sure when you're around it. It's doing this global command — not doing your project, nor your Town Meeting, nor your business if you're a businessman. It's doing this global command that allows a person to be a nobody. Blame and praise don't count much for motivity at that point. It's getting this global command actuated that becomes motivating. Or a way someone else said to me, "It's really exciting, now."

Winning is doing it all at once. This gradualism and doing it one step at a time belongs on the other side of that line. Winning is doing it all at once, doing what you say, delivering, living out beyond the border. Several of you commented that you go into offices where people are supposed to be caring for places, and the one remark they make is, "I don't know how you guys go out there and live in that village and do that kind of thing." They have been addressed. It's going like a freight train, never slowing down. Then when the awards are being passed out, you beat the Lone Ranger because you're not even there to say, "Hi-ho, Silver." You're off doing the next one. It doesn't feel much like integrity, I must confess. In fact, you don't feel like you've done very much. You feel like there's just more to be done.

I even heard that the village drunk, who always hung around and caused trouble, got out of his bed the other day. He had the flu. It began to rain and through his laryngitis he cussed out the whole village and motivated them to finish the wall in the rain. Somehow integrity was in the midst of that.

Or you get one of those invitations from some patron, who has given a big gift, to go to dinner. I always worry when I'm the one who has to go. He fattens you up, you know. He kills you with praises about how tremendous you are and all the things you've done. You know what's coming. Things get quiet and the martinis go by for a while. You see that he's hiding behind a lampshade a little bit. He says in a very quiet voice, "I've always wanted to do what you're doing." Then he asks you if you want to have another martini and you're glad to get out of there and go about your business. You hear from this guy. He starts sending you things you didn't ask for. And he's getting you out of trouble you didn't even know you were in. Some people say he's gone a little nuts. He's gone beyond what a businessman should do and lost his objectivity. He's getting other people to come and see. Then you hear that other businessmen are joining him in this. I get a little scared and I tremble a little bit. What kind of power is getting loose here? It's about that time you begin to look at your colleagues and see this integrity showing all over their faces. That gets you a little scared, too.

What is integrity all about? Integrity is about *keeping your own conscience, hitting the moral issue, constituting the new image of humanness*. And it's all tied to making a new picture of what a village looks like, what an inner city looks like, or what a town looks like. Finally, integrity as profound humanness is *creating new community*.

A long time ago we said that the center of civilization in our time is the cities. It's an urban world, and that's bothered us a little bit about going to the villages and to the small towns. But, you see, Bombay doesn't know how to build a human city until the villages of Maharashtra give it a picture of what it looks like to be a human village. Bombay, Chicago, and London don't know what it is to build a human city until the inner city gives them a picture of what a human city looks like.

It doesn't work the other way in our time. It comes from the ground up, the rising of local people. That's how we get clear about what humanness is. The new neighborliness, the stakes, the new economic functions, the guilds, this global band – we don't really know yet what we've got on our hands. All these pictures have got to get delivered up to where people can see them in order for anybody to begin to be human.

You step back a little bit and you look at all the faces. You see all the faces of the villagers and people in Town Meetings. You see all those picture books that *Life* and other magazines used to put out, all those faces. They're human faces. What you know is that they live like man-dogs and like woman-cows. In those faces (they're our faces, too) you see they want to be told. They know it, but they've got to be told in order to know it, just like us. We've always got to be told what we know in order to know it. And that's not enough. They've got to see it. Everybody in our time knows that this is what life is about in our day. Somebody has got to go and tell and show in order for any kind of humanness to happen.

The integrity we've experienced is really what is on our walls, the décor. When you look over here and over there, you know about the presence of integrity, and about this being the tent of integrity. I think that's why we feel like human beings. It's strange because this is really not what we've done. Though you know we've done it. Like Oklahoma 100, somebody said that it took half the Order and the whole state of Oklahoma to do it. If you think that's bad, it's embarrassing to tell you about Kwangyung II. It took the Navy. It took two acceleration teams. It took the Guardians. It took the whole village. Finally, it took all of Korea to do it. I imagine we could share some stories around the room about what it took.

In everything I've said, integrity as profound humanness is a social reality. You don't get to participate in that save you bring the whole show within the tent. I'm looking forward to the day, and maybe before I get to the grave, I'll see it or hear it. People are going to say, "That's a community of integrity." They're going to say something like, "Now, there goes a person of integrity. How do you know? Why, she's from Maliwada." They'll say it because they can sense integrity when it goes by. Integrity is like a fast train going by. Deep down everybody wants to be on it because they are human.

What Hath Been Wrought?

My beloved colleagues, I bring you greetings from the globe-at-large and from all of history. Forthrightly, I intend to be a bit tedious relative to time, and I intend to talk about the kitchen-sink, as we say, but I do not intend in any way whatsoever to be practical. I must begin by confessing that a year ago, before this Assembly, I misstated the truth, unintentionally. It was not the truth when I said that the greatest year of my life was my 65th year. The truth of the matter is, the greatest year of my life is my 66th year.

You can't keep things quiet around here. Most of you know that for some five days of this Assembly I was in the hospital, and there wasn't anything really wrong. They found certain things that disturbed them about my kidneys, my back, my heart, and my lungs. They summed it up as normal deterioration along with age. I feel like a young man with something gone wrong. But I have not told you the good news. They must have taken my blood pressure twenty times. I began to get curious, not to say a bit frightened. So I asked them about my blood pressure. They said, "Every day it shows up normal."

Then my mind went back to this past year. I have never lived through such a hectic time in my whole life. I have been humiliated more deeply this year than ever before, and I am an old pro at being humiliated. There were times on an airplane when I thought, literally, that I would get up and start screaming, but I did not. Time and again I considered just getting myself lost in Bombay, never to be seen again. I experience my insides as just ground to pieces or as if they were an atom bomb just about ready to blow me and everything around me into kingdom come. But my blood pressure is normal.

I asked them what blood pressure meant. They said, "Well, first of all, it determines whether enough of the waste matter has been eliminated. Secondly, it tells whether, at the moment, enough blood is being forced through the body to maintain the mind and physique. But, most of all, it checks on your state of anxiety, or the effects of strain." And I was normal. I read into that what I'm not sure they would have read. In the midst of the agony of this last year, my total life has been one of effulgence. My life has been one of fulfillment. That is not because of anything I've done, because fulfillment is a state of being over which you finally have no control. And if I have been under strain, what in the world have you been under? Not once during this year have I ever come within several miles of a live bullet. I have not been in a fox hole. I can tell you from experience that being back at the command post in a war has a certain calm about it that even visiting the front lines does not have. As I sat here this morning I was overwhelmingly impressed. I thought, if they took our corporate blood pressure, much to our humiliation and embarrassment, it would be normal.

I want to remind you why it is necessary to take good care of yourselves. You and I understood two years ago when we started out to move the universe that we would have no time to take care of ourselves. We do not have time to train ourselves. Whether you know it or not, you are on what Sun Tzu called "death ground." You have no time to train anyone to use a rifle. You just hope s/he shoots out of the right end, that's all. That will still be true this year. You don't think for a moment we could have possibly done 24 Social Demonstrations and 1500 Town Meetings in 23 countries if you cared about whether somebody else got proper training or got proper care. No. There comes a time when you are on "death ground," when you just have to move.

Two years ago when we probed into the deeps of profound consciousness, we found that there was no way to be of assistance to each other, that finally every individual is all alone before the Final Reality. Husbands, wives, children, colleagues, and friends are of no assistance. We have to learn for ourselves, as unrepeatable individuals, to walk in the Way; to live in the Other World in the presence of this world. That can only be done in total and absolute solitude. In anything else we can assist each other. But in the profound deeps of consciousness we walk alone. It is a quality of consciousness itself. In the last two years, if you have not learned to walk alone, you either built an illusion around yourself, or you got your two suitcases and left the front lines.

Sometimes I hear people talk as if five years ago we should have had the practical wisdom we have today. You get that kind of wisdom only through raw experience. I am trying to say that God knew when to send the "death ground." And you either learned or you didn't survive. The kind of know-how that went into your reconstructing the weaponry of our task this summer did not come out of textbooks. Experts were of little use. It was learned in the raw experience of hell in Kwangyung Il, Kawangware, Maliwada, Majuro, and Oombulgurri. It could have been learned no place else.

The last reason why you have to take care of yourself we'll be able to explain better a year from now. You see, what we never intended to stumble onto, we stumbled onto. That is the awareness that humanness is universal. If you think that is not a profound statement, you did not even hear me. Our bigotries have been assaulted. The most profound bigotry in me, as I have admitted to you, is my religious bigotry, and then there are several close to it. It is with a sense of pride that I can say that I do not experience myself as an American these days. I experience myself as a human being. I do not experience myself as a white man. I experience myself as a human being. I do not experience myself first of all as a man, but I experience myself as a human being.

Now, moving into that depth beyond all depths of life is a kind of wrenching of the spirit. For what it requires is that you tear yourself asunder, not from the external, communal relationships you have, but from those relationships which are buried, rooted firmly in the deeps of your psyche. We have been alone in our togetherness and we have had no other course.

A few months ago, when I first began to see that the life force was coming, I tried to draw together the statement of what it was that we have wrought, and then quickly I changed that into the statement of what has been wrought in us. Or, what have the powers that are beyond our activities and efforts made of us. I listed these. First, God has made of us a global service network. Secondly, God has made of us a global corporate style. Third, God has made of us a worldwide credibility net. Fourth, God has made of us a worldwide development system. Fifth, God has made of us a worldwide support force. I want the word "us" to be very large; it includes patrons that would never be Guardians. This includes the Guardians who would never live the kind of life you or I live. And it includes the local men and women in the villages of the world who would never find themselves in the blue, but who care every bit as much as we do. This is the support net. Sixth, God has grounded us philosophically. And, seventh, God has made us a comprehensive methodological schemata (these last two I don't know how to say yet, as you can tell). And I'm sure that's not all.

The question is What in the world are we going to do with this that has been wrought? That is the issue. Any sense of value we may have at arriving at this hour turns into nothingness as we face the horrendous decision of what are we going to do with this? In another way, what I'm talking about this morning has to do with precisely that. To win this next year means sticking your fist through the dynamics of the three campaigns. Guess where your fist will come out: in the midst of knowing, doing, and being, exactly where we began. This is what I mean when I say I am not a practical man in terms of popular and common definitions of practicality. I could care less about glazed, heat-resisting, lightweight, low-priced roofs. I could care less about an effective design of global economy. I care not about tripling total village income in two years. What I am concerned about is profound humanness. I am interested in any company and its product only to the degree that it finally ministers unto the possibility of the poorest of the poor of this world experiencing themselves profoundly as human beings. This is true whether it be ferryboats in Majuro, comprehensive cooperatives, or any other practical thing.

We have gotten around to the practical. But, to be honest with you, I am not impressed with the practical. This September we will have been in existence for 25 years. The greatest thing we ever did was not to allow ourselves to become publicly known, never to publicize ourselves in any way, nor to try to focus our attention on what we accomplished. Twenty-five years ago, we looked very carefully at the historical renewal forces in Europe that came after World War II, and every one of them was practically oriented. They were moving into the practical-social, the practical-economic, the practical-cultural issues head-on. But you know what, there is scarcely one renewal force alive today.

At that time we made a decision that was far more significant than we had the intellectual capacity to understand. That was, first, to ground ourselves in the profound deeps of humanness. We used other language in those days, but that is what we meant. Only when we had broken through into the dimension of what it means to be the full and the fulfilled human being were we ready to deal with what books call the practical. That was a long journey. The symbol of the journey that covered years is in the little triangle of knowing, doing, and being. We believe that whatever your cultural conditioning, when you are able to see what this is pointing to, you say "Yes." That's what it means to be human. It has to do with knowing and doing and being. To say it another way, it has to do with profound awareness, with historical engagement, and fulfilled humanness – all three attuned to what is the Mystery. The heart of consciousness is there to seize upon and to understand. Then you can talk about it any way you want, or use any kind of poetry to ground it in your existence or in history's being. But it is first of all an acknowledgment of that reality, and nothing else, that begins the journey of what it means to be a human being.

The second thing we discovered was that one did not really know save he "doed." It has to do with activity, historical activity, with shaping, forming, forging, bending history itself, where you grasp yourself in the service of no other Lord, no other Sovereign, save the Mystery, before which the arena of action could be nothing less than the whole world and the length of history itself. Loving the Mystery and serving the Mystery are but two sides of the same coin.

The third thing we discovered was not a third dynamic, but was the fact that once you intensify awareness and once you intensify engagement, there comes a sense of plethora, a fulfillment, which – though it does not exist in itself as a third element – becomes a reality in the intensification of knowing and doing. Last week I was in New York. I had lunch with the Chairman of the Council of Bishops of the Roman Catholic Church of India. He told me a great story. Some people in his church decided they'd go help the local people. They decided that they would do that by enabling them to intensify and expand their agriculture. So they went to the Ministry of the Government for authorization. The Minister was a Hindu. He said, "Gentlemen, we would be very delighted for you to work with the local people, but from our perspective they need one thing, that is just a tiny bit of hope. If and when you bring that, you will find that all the practical things that you are so concerned about will take shape." That's what I mean by presence.

I have been brutal on you who have been in the front lines of these projects. I have been brutal when I did not see visible change, economic progress, or new housing and the intensification of farming. That is your great power and your great strength. That is the secret of it all, your presence there. What is presence? It is sharing the presence of Mystery itself, which is the hope beyond all hope and itself remaining a mystery. Now, can you understand that the definition of those who care is found in this bit of symbolism, this triangle of knowing, doing, and being? We spent years of our life while people told us we were doing nothing, just philosophizing. What we are about, really, whether we are doing Town Meeting, Social Demonstration, or anything else, is nothing more and nothing less than giving the underprivileged and the privileged the opportunity of experiencing what it means to be a genuine human being, down to the last man and woman on this earth. What is the job of those who care? It is to go out and reconstruct the times in which we live in order that the possibility of humanness may be found there. What is the content of this? Where is it that "all the earth belongs to all the people" finds a new social container, so it is not just a kind of abstract idealism. History is an endless process of rebuilding the earth. But if "all the earth belongs to all" means all the fruits of nature, however they are distributed, belong to every human, then it is utterly important. The decision-making process, the opportunity to participate in deciding not only one's own destiny, but the destiny of history itself, belongs to every person. Up to this moment in history I believe that less than 5 percent of the people who have ever lived have directly and authentically participated in determining the course of history. What an hour!

What about "all the gifts of humanness belong to all?" We throw around the 15 percent and the 85 percent figures so much I feel we may get callused. Most people would not have the slightest idea what we mean when we say 85 and 15. To say it again: 15 percent of us have all the education; we have all the health; we possess the resources and the means of "the good life." I'm saying that what we have also belongs to that 85 percent who don't have what the 15 percent have. Our job is to stand and to stand tall rebuilding the earth, moving in our moment in history toward the common human awareness that all the earth belongs to all.

Now we come to how we do that. First of all are the large ontological maneuvers that are the maneuvers of the void, to use the terms of one Japanese man of long ago.

Second come the historical maneuvers. The historical maneuvers are within the circles of our global campaigns. How many years did it take us to finally come up with this? Instead of 25 years, it seems like you and I have been at it for several centuries.

My point here is that it's not enough to know that all the earth belongs to all. One has to be able to decide, however modestly, precisely how that can become a possibility in your lifetime. For us, it is the *campaign of awakenment* of all people. The specific form of this, right now, is Town Meeting. Second is the task of *engaging every person in the world.* Providing the possibility of engagement to every human in the world is the meaning of Social Demonstration.

In recent days I have begun to talk to myself about the "magnificent seven" revolutions that are happening all at once at this moment in history. One is the *revolution of the third world.* What a revolution. We have noble firsthand members of that revolution in our midst today. We have some secondhand members, and I am one, who symbolize the fantastic dimension of the revolution of the Third World.

The second of the "magnificent seven" is much harder to explain. It is the part of the *technological revolution* that has to do with people. It has to do with the thrust toward globalization of humanity. It is nothing more or nothing less than the so-called international communities of the world. The heart of this is the national and multi-national corporations which are doing the revolution. No matter what your abstract liberal friends may have to say about such corporations, they are revolutionizing the world. And if you live long enough, you are going to see that.

The next, and this may be the first of the "magnificent seven," is the *feminine revolution.* I want to confess to this body that over the years I have not been one who has appreciated the rise of women in history. In this last year when I saw that at least 300 million of the women of the world are a part of the poorest of the poor and spend their total life in a way that is worse than that in which a dog or a donkey lives, I have become a full convert to the women's revolution. Maybe in the long run that will be the most important one that has happened in our time in history.

The next of the "magnificent seven" is the *minorities revolution.* It is the black people of America who enabled other minorities in this country and the rest of the world to rise up and demand nothing less than an equal opportunity to make of their lives what you and I have the opportunity to make of our lives.

The next revolution is the *youth revolution.* It's calmed down now, but don't you think that ever again it will be the same to be a youth. Don't you think that it will ever be the same to be a parent. Women who suckle their existence from their children are going to find their lives changed. And we he-men who have taken such great pride in being the proper father, our hour is also gone.

The last revolution of this type is the *educational revolution.* I don't think we've seen the profundity of that. I think it is going to be the college students in the third world who are going to carry the revolution and require a totally new understanding of what it means to be an educated person.

Now, I've been saying all this only to get to Town Meeting. Profound as these revolutions are, *the profound revolution in our time is the rise of local people.* Though it is still the morning star on the far horizon, save for those who have eyes to see, local humans are on the move. They are going to radically and profoundly alter history in terms of any image that anybody in history has ever conceived.

Social Demonstration, which has to do with engagement, is held with the 24 projects in each of the time zones around the globe. When a human being is awakened, his/her creativity begins to flow. In principle, that creativity will find its own point of engagement. The Social Demonstration assists that creativity in that it is a demonstration of how the most local of all local humans can engage in a way that will affect history. Therefore, for the sake of Town Meeting, you need so many of these demonstrations. But, finally, you have to see that the task for those who are concerned with the three campaigns of knowing doing and being is to emphasize awakenment and not engagement, except in terms of theoretical presentation. If we are concerned with mass awakening of the 4.5 billion people in the world, then we understand the vocation of profound consciousness.

Both Town Meeting around this globe and Social Demonstration have just been set up. Town Meeting in this country had to reach 1500 or we were not talking about anything to do. In principle we have reached that. Town Meeting is set up in this country. Now we have to do it globally. We have Global Community Forum set up. Now let's go do it globally.

This doing is to get ready for next year. A year from now, and only at that time, will the meaning of the being campaign, this pluriform yin-yang, this *interglobal movement campaign* come into being. Now, we have to spell out practically the new spirit mode of the 20th century in a global sense, plus creating a new sociological instrument that will effectively nurture those who care around the world. The latter is going to be the important one. You're not going into the state of Maharashtra and awaken 232 villages into caring if you do not find a social instrument whereby their care can be continually nurtured. In one sense this is what we have been looking forward to. It is not going to be easy, but we won't even dare put our mind to it if we do not do Social Demonstration and Town Meeting this next year.

What's the key to this doing? It is going to take certain qualities in order to do these three campaigns. One quality is just *caring*, caring about the whole world – not about your children, not about your spouse, not about your nation, not about your culture, but caring about humanity. Unless that posture is ground into our quality of character, we are not going to stand long.

The second quality is *courage*. Fundamentally, what I mean by courage is integrity. You decide who you are and spend your whole life being that and nothing else, no matter what the external circumstances are. Without that kind of ontological courage you're not going to win.

The third is *corporateness*. I don't mean some superficial getting together to make the task easier. I mean the awareness that you and I are first of all social beings and secondly individual beings. The corporateness that you exist in, and that other people wonder how you can live in, is simply the sociality that is at the bottom of humanness itself. Without that kind of corporateness you are going to fail in Town Meeting and in Social Demonstration.

The last quality is *creativity*. What I mean by that flows out of all the others. It is not true that sometimes I'm creative and sometimes I'm not, or that some of us are creative and the rest of us are not. Humanness is your creativity. Without guts enough to allow that creativity to be released, there is no doing. That is another way of saying that there is no place you can telephone that will tell you how to go about doing your village. They never install telephones in heaven. (That's one reason I want to go there.)

Down underneath these qualities are decisions. This is the *profound resolve* that's behind the concept of winning. If you do not decide all over again you have only one life to live, you are not going to win. You only go around the clock once. The question no longer is "What is the meaning of going around that clock once?" The question you have to face in absolute solitude is "What in the world are you going to do with that one life that goes around the clock once?"

The second decision you have to make, and you have no choice, is to decide where the *moral issue* is in history. Let's say it is not where we've been saying it is. That's fine. Still, you have to decide it. Once you decide that you have only one life to live, then you are going to decide where *the* moral issue is. There is nothing moral about the moral issue. The moral issue is an ontological reality. No longer do things such as salaries, badges, and degrees have meaning for you.

The third decision you have to make is whether or not you are the *anointed one*. When you're dealing with your own life in the moral issue, it's a vocational decision. There's a chemist, a doctor, a lawyer. When you're dealing with what I am talking about, those things seem quite incidental. The real vocation of life is what you decide that you are anointed to do in history. Then you do it. You alone can decide it.

Now to the last decision you have to make. Isn't it funny, Sun Tzu and the others were right in the arena of winning, and they come down heavy on this. You have to decide all over again about your death. You have to decide whether you are a *dead man or woman*. If you have decided you are dead, Maliwada can't throw you. If you have not decided, it will chew you up and spit you out. If you have not decided you are dead, filling in all of those counties in the United States of America with Town Meetings is going to chew you up and spit you out. You have to decide that you are a dead man or woman. You have to decide whether your death is embraced. You have to decide that you have one life and that it is stuffed into the moral issue and that you are anointed by the powers that be. I'm just dealing with the hard-headed realities of being of service to the poorest of the poor in this world.

There is another category of words which have to do with maneuvers. You can make all the battle plans you want and that is mot going to accomplish anything. You have to learn maneuvers, which gives a context for all your tactics. In the book *The Book of Five Rings,* Musashi says that to be a samurai you carry two swords. One is a short sword that you carry in your belt. The other is the long sword that you wear in a scabbard. When you enter into combat you have them both. The long sword is for maneuvers. The short sword is for the in-fight. To exaggerate just a touch, your long sword gets the maneuvering done so that your tactics can drive home the winning blow. We are going to learn to do that or we're going to fail.

As a matter of fact, battle planning is nothing other than arranging your implementaries within a context of effectivity. There are four principles of effectivity or winning. One is *timing*. The person who has "ants in his pants" has a failure mentality. There is a time to move and a time not to move. The author calls that "applicable timing." There is the timing of life itself. Historical maneuvers have to do with the profound change of our time. Is local man on the rise? Is the way to bring about profound humanness about having campaigns of awakenment, engagement, and one that makes possible the fullness of humanness? Then, in every area and in every task, maneuvers have to be built that have timing in them.

The next thing is that you have to *know your enemy* if you are going to maneuver to win. In our situation that enemy always remains half invisible. It isn't an enemy until it becomes incarnate. You have a hard time seeing that enemy of principalities and powers. Those forces, whether they are in established form or simply in mindset, keep people in darkness, in inertia, and in despair. This is what you are finally attacking.

The next category is *weaponry*. What you've been out to build in this Assembly is the weaponry for the effective doing of Social Demonstration and the effective doing of Town Meeting. The Council will be able to make up its own mind about where and how the forces shall be committed. Your work will be invaluable to that decision-making process.

The last thing is the *deployment of troops*. This is far more complicated than assignments. Generals who let their religious houses go while they pull all the troops out to do some battle have lost, even though they think they've won. Deployment is complicated. The crucial thing is how you get your troops at all times in a position of advantage.

I asked my Bishop brother what he thought held our group together, above all else. He thought for some time and said that he thought it was discipline. That pleased me, but I was trying to get him to agree with what I would say, corporateness. Then I decided that both of us were wrong because corporateness is discipline and discipline is corporateness. And when you put those two together, it's *unity*. In this year of doing I would call upon you to guard your unity. That means guarding any kind of reductionism. Wherever you are you must think blue, guarding against the propensity in yourself and in your neighbor to be somebody. Any awakened person in our group ought to realize that each of us runs our whole, united group. The power is in the center of the table. There is no need for competition. Unity is the key.

Finally, guard against *irrational conflict*. Maybe I can plead a personal statement. I am extremely grateful to all of my colleagues over the last twenty-five years who have put up with all my stupidities, my personal flaws, my personal mistakes, my wickednesses, my stumblings, my down-right sinfulness. In case I never get a chance to do it, I express my deepest gratitude to you. It has occurred to me that if you could put up with my flaws, stupidities, and mistakes, through all these years, you ought to be able to forgive the mistakes and the flaws and the stupidities of each other.

Section IV

The New Form of the Religious

Commentary by John Cock

Talks:

Transpadane Christianity (1974)

Paravocation (1975)

Those Who Care (1975)

The New Movement (1972)

The Two Faces of the Movement (1975)

Six Speeches (1976)

On Taking Care of Yourself (1975)

SECTION IV:

THE NEW FORM OF THE RELIGIOUS

Commentary

By John Cock

Out of Joseph Mathew's compassion for the world, his passion to reform existing religious institutions to care for the world, and his strong belief that everyone is called to live the profound life came his motivation to imagine, design, and experiment with new forms of the religious in his part of the 20th century.

Joe was religious to the core. He was a radical churchman all his life, from his baptism to his last rites. He was raised in the church but had a lover's quarrel with her throughout his adult life: he wanted the church to be her greatness and to give herself on behalf of all, to be mission in the world where innocent human suffering prevailed. No one I've ever met, heard, or read knew how to articulate the message of Christianity as powerfully as Joe. That's why many of us joined with him and the Order: Ecumenical to be about that task. If you wanted to know what "God," "Christ," "Holy Spirit," and "Church" meant in our time, you listened to JWM – how we referred to him in print – for he could get it said in ways that would deeply penetrate your being and call you to a life of radical service.

After WWII, he learned to think dynamically about the gospel and the church from the likes of H. Richard Niebuhr, who is widely considered one of the greatest theologians of the 20th century and was Joe's mentor. After he had held young soldiers in his arms as they died in the Pacific, Joe dedicated himself to the transformation of the church that could speak the *word* with power to the dying and the living. He dedicated himself to creating the new forms of the religious life for any and all humans that could help awaken them, vocate them, engage them, and sustain them on the one spirit journey we all travel.

Where do the dynamics of any faith come from? From the deeps, Joe believed. Therefore he could say, standing in his faith tradition, "When you see this or that activity going on in life, I call that the activity of God, or Christ, or Spirit, or Church. What good are abstract notions? If you can't ground – give examples of – your religious tradition's symbols happening in your life, then you don't begin to understand them." Something like that.

Was he an existentialist? You bet, and one of the best – along with Amos, Paul, John, Luther, Wesley, Kierkegaard, Bonhoeffer – because he understood that the mysterious power that drives us into being and limits us is none other than the power and presence of the one he dared to call God Almighty, made manifest in the events and elements of creation and existence itself. So where is the beginning of the *new religious* in our time – in any time? Joe said, as a thoroughgoing existentialist, at the heart of existence, on the journey, in the experiment of living the profound life. Did he believe in the Incarnation? Absolutely.

Joe stood in the universality of the gospel of Jesus Christ and boldly claimed its truth for every person, without equivocation. Did he try to convert them to the Christian symbol system or the Christian church? Hardly. The word "proselytize" angered him. For him, pure evangelism was about allowing anyone of any tradition to see that at the heart of living is the truth. It was not about abstract and wooden religious dogmas, but about everyday eventfulness that could provoke rage or thanksgiving, a "no" or a "yes." The center of Joe's understanding about anything was the transparent event, coming to us amidst our mundane journeys, over and over. Joe believed this event to be the locus for new religious forms. Is it the Jesus-Christ-Event? Absolutely. Is it the *transparent event* of existence? Absolutely, and for Joe the two are the same.

He was always about experimenting with language that pointed to the way life is for everyone in whatever time. In his deep maturity he spoke the language of anyone: a traditional believer, an angry youth, a Hindu elder, a ghetto bum, a disillusioned secularist, or an out-and-out atheist. Joe took his tradition's gospel to the bottom of consciousness and back.

For Joe, then, the beginning point for new forms of the religious – or what he often called the "secular-religious" – is the understanding that life is good as given and can be lived with thanksgiving on behalf of all. Where did he pick up this understanding that he rehearsed daily? From the liturgical drama of the *old* form of the religious with its emphasis on humility, gratitude, and compassion. Joe was not one to throw out a tradition. Instead, he reinterpreted it through the reality and vision of human life profoundly lived, always on behalf of the other, not on behalf of our own personal fulfillment.

The following seven talks share markings of Joe's articulation of the new form of the religious in the context of the mission, for the profound life is only lived in self-conscious and comprehensive mission, as we heard over and over in the talks of Sections I-III.

In the first talk in this last section, "Transpadane Christianity," we hear Joe say "that authenticity is not exclusive to those of the Christian persuasion. While this may seem self-evident to persons raised in a multi-cultural setting, most of us are not and tend to regard those with dramatically different cultures and values as less than fully human. This, for Joe, constitutes bigotry. Speaking personally, he regarded his deepest and most entrenched prejudice to be 'Christian bigotry,' thinking and acting as though Christians had an exclusive right to authenticity. While Christian mythology spells out the dynamics of authenticity, the capacity for it resides in everyone. The job for the [new religious] is to bring it out." This is the way John Epps says it in the "Introduction" of this book.

The next talk, "Paravocation," comes from one of Joe's many word creations. (You will also have a hard time finding "transpadane.") Joe is talking about the one vocation that all people are called to and to which some respond. He says all people care; therefore, all people understand this calling, at least a little bit. And he lays out the "second vocation" as the one we are assigned to, for example, if a lawyer, the legal division of those who care. This primal vocation is at the heart of the understanding of the new religious. And guess what: the paravocated don't have to live in religious compounds.

Joe's statement, not really a talk, of "Those Who Care" naturally follows the last talk that introduces the image of "TWC." Joe made these remarks during 1976 at a consult to begin a human development project. As you will see, he is speaking to several sectors of society – the private and public and volunteer sectors as they prepare to dialogue with the community, or local sector. The big insight is that in all sectors of society there are those who care and that they form an invisible colleagueship around the world. The indicative question is How does that movement of colleagues become self-conscious and empowered?

Joe gave "The New Movement" talk in 1972, when we as a part of the global spirit movement – what he calls "God's Spirit Movement" – were beginning to make a turn from primarily serving religious communities to serving all sectors of society, especially focused on local communities. Joe also uses other key phrases to point to the "Great Resurgence" of Spirit in our time: the self-conscious "People of God," "the movemental dynamic of the historical church," and the "trans-establishment," who care for both the "pro-establishment" and the "dis-establishment." The telling line of this talk is "You cannot have a reconstruction of society without a resurgence of human motivity," by which he meant a new spirit movement.

"The Two Faces of the Movement," given a year later, depicts what George Walters, a collaborator for this book, says: it's about "JWM's passion for engaging society's leadership in addressing innocent human suffering in the world without putting them all in monasteries" – or it's about the "guild." Joe talks about the two faces as those of the *guildsman* and the *religious*, which are finally but one face, the face of the profound movement of *spirit*, *rationality*, *liturgy*, and *mission*, always with an emphasis on corporateness.

"Six Speeches" is one speech about *learnings from Maliwada*, a village in India. Joe tells the story of three old men falling down three separate wells and finding the common "water table of consciousness"; the second, about *permeation*, or how a movement networks itself to be effective; then the *six stages* of our movement, followed by the *steps at hand* and the *mission ahead*; and the last one, about the *definitudes of presence*, or "the blue," wherein he talks about the corporate saint as that without which the great resurgence in humanness will not come to be.

Finally, "On Taking Care of Yourself" is about the journey of the profound human in mission. Over five days he gave these talks as we prepared for the coming campaigns that would break many of our bodies and spirits. As the good spirit general he was, he talked that week about the marks and forms of radical care for ourselves in the midst of the incredible and impossible mission. This talk "blows the soot out," as Joe would have said, and prepares us for the dark night of the soul and the long march of care, which he tells us will never go away. By design he says the dark night and the long march are the Mystery's citadel for the new religious. If you have had your body or spirit broken, you will want to return to this talk for wisdom and healing.

Transpadane Christianity

Religious Without Being Religious

I have felt with passion that Vatican II was the most important happening of this century. People have laughed when I made that statement because I could never explain exactly what I meant. In Michael Harrington's book on the 60s, *Fragments of the 20th Century*, he said that Pope John meant well with Vatican II, but in actuality he presided over the demise of the Roman Catholic Church. Harrington could not see this, but what he pointed to as "demise" is exactly what symbolizes the greatest happening of this century. In the broad, you and I have had the honor of participating in that happening.

With extreme caution, I told a group of people today that I am proud to have gone through what we have gone through in the last fifty years, and to have become the religious vocationally, in a profound sense. At the same time, I have avoided the pitfall of becoming "religious." If, indeed, we have succeeded in becoming the religious without becoming religious, then it is by the grace of God. We want God to understand that we are aware of that. Therefore, in saying "I am proud," I need to clarify in order to avoid the divine wrath that would keep me from getting to heaven.

I use the word "proud" as the Appalachian mountaineer does when he says, "I'm mighty proud to be here." I am proud to have lived so long as to be part of this historical moment, for, if it is true that we have avoided becoming religious, we might authentically be part of this movement. Only if you have grasped yourself as religious, with some degree of authenticity, can you be prepared for the "at-hand-ness" which is creeping upon this universe and into our lives. We have lived to behold many "unanticipateds" come into being. But the new face that is emerging defies description.

Silence and Stillness

The state of our spirit being at this moment is preparing us for this hour. It comes to me in strange kinds of silences. Since last fall, I have had intense trouble coming to terms with the fact that the dark night of the soul never passes away. It is here for aye. This awareness brings into my being a stillness and a silence. Through the years, many people in our Order have pressed for us to create exercises in silence and stillness. Many times our Daily Office has been criticized for its lack of silence. I have been very afraid in that area. For what the Quakers mean by stillness and silence, as I have grasped it, is not what I am talking about. Nor is it some form of devotional piety where one sits around and does not talk.

Silence has nothing to do with noise or un-noise on the immediate level. There is no way on earth in which stillness or silence can be manipulated.

We have magnificent spirit exercises. Sometimes I have pressed myself as to why we have not experimented under the rubric of being with intensified knowing, intensified doing, and intensified being, or being in being itself. I am not sure if there ever can be exercises in that area. I know that silence somehow fits under those rubrics but perhaps there is no such exercise. Even to consider such exercises has made me afraid because I have sensed the profundity of this dimension of humanness. I was afraid we might be pushed beyond recovery if we stayed too close to this fire.

When I toyed with silence in the past, perhaps I did not grasp what is now becoming clearer. The other day, in a conversation with several colleagues, we were talking about one of our colleagues who had left us. Suddenly I was aware that I was experiencing stillness. There was noise outside and inside the room, but there was stillness. And there was quietness. This has happened to me several times recently. What I have begun to see is what our fathers, and probably the fathers of many cultures, have intimately known: that the sea of being is located precisely in that exercise of humanness which has to do with the quiet, intense struggle to believe what is impossible but unavoidable to believe – that the dark night of the soul, once one has experienced it, is there for the rest of one's life.

I came close to this but did not really shoot at the heart of the matter when I gave the "Transparent Being Lecture." I spoke of the cloud of apostasy that is ever with you, once you have gone to the center. It is the desert one carries forever. It is the darkness one carries forever. It used to be called "hellfire" or the burning one carries forever. I suspect that anyone who speaks of problem-lessness, of ontological joy, of certitude where there is no certitude, and of the most unbelievable of all states, endlessness, knows naught of these unless s/he knows of silence.

What I am trying to say has to do with the silence all of us have been experiencing these past few months. It has to do with the dark night, the intense struggle of coming to terms with the fact that God finally controls. The dark night does not have to do with humanness; it is humanness, which is preparing us – without any solicitation on our part – for the emergence of at-hand-ness.

The other dimension of our spirit state is what I call a vacuum. These past few months I have been floating in a vacuum, though in one sense going a million-miles-an-hour. I have to go back to 1971. When we began to deal seriously with the social dimension of life, we fell through the social into the spiritual. We fell into the Other World. I know now what I did not know then: there is no way anyone will ever discover the Other World in the midst of this world unless, by some stroke of fate, s/he is forced to take with intense seriousness the social aspect of life.

That is why I say no clergyman can ever become a religious. In some way or another we clergy have to discover what it means to be secular. In that sense perhaps my pride at becoming the religious – without becoming religious – can be understood. Perhaps laypersons cannot understand how important it is that I have avoided the pitfall of becoming religious. We have God to thank for allowing us to fall into the Other World. We began carving out highways and pathways through the Other World that let us keep our sanity so we might return with unbelievable treasure to share with all of humankind.

That is why we are clawing with broken fingernails to find our way back to the social. Until we find our way back, we run the risk of tragedy beyond any tragedy: drowning in the realm of the Spirit. This has caused the vacuum. I see it in your faces because it is in your being. But it is a sign that God is with us. When the vacuum goes away, you will not be around to know it in yourself, for you will have drowned in the Spirit. So I am grateful for the profound vacuum I have lived with lately. I believe it is a sign we are preparing for the faceless coming that is at hand.

About the "faceless coming": some will call it this and some will call it that. Some will say it is a new religion and they will be absolutely wrong. Others will say it is what we have called it in the past, the new religious mode, but when it shows its face it can no longer have that name, for that would be escaping a horrifying burden.

Recalling My Bigotry and the Doom of the Church

Today, while working with a group, I began to go back through my life as a bigot, as a man of unbelievable prejudice. The first prejudice I became aware of was religious prejudice. I grew up prejudiced against the Roman Catholic Church, and not only against the Roman Catholic Church but against the Lutheran Church, and any church other than the Methodist Church. The further one was from looking like what I was bred to be, the deeper was my prejudice against them. I do not mean to boast now, but I thank God my prejudice has been cured in my heart. I love the Roman Catholic Church and I would like to stand on a mountaintop and shout that fact to the world, along with my love for the Lutherans, the Presbyterians, the Disciples, and the Baptists.

That was not my only prejudice. I was bred to be prejudiced against Jews. I do not know if that prejudice was religious. It certainly was not racial. I do not know what it was, but I was prejudiced. I became most deeply aware of it when I taught at Colgate University, where some of New York's finest young Jewish men studied. It was no virtue of mine, but World War II made a Jew out of me. I was able to cope with my prejudice when I saw that I was a whole lot better Jew than any of those students were, and I mean that. Thank God, deep healing has taken place.

Then I became aware of my prejudice against blacks, and I would not dare to say that I have been healed in that area. But I witness to God's glory for the ten years I spent in the ghetto. I became an absolutely different human being because I lived there, and I thank God for letting me live in that place. As I look back, I would not have been any place else on earth than in Fifth City, on the West Side of Chicago. Sometimes I become aware of a yearning of mine never to have set foot outside its boundaries.

Later than any other prejudice, I became aware of my cultural prejudice, my understanding that somehow the Western world defined civilization, and that the rest of the world could only be civilized when it measured up to *our* understanding of civilization. I am ashamed to admit to you how old I was before I became aware of that, but that was bred into me as deeply as religious prejudice was. I always refer to my Gatlinburg Experience in 1964 or 1965 as my turning point. Third world peoples were gathered in that Tennessee mountain town where I had been brought in to speak. That is where I met some of the great leaders of our movement from around the world. One of them was a relatively young Chinese man. I asked him where he was from and he said "Kuala Lumpur." I asked him three times to repeat the name. I was too humiliated to say any more, for I had not the foggiest notion of where Kuala Lumpur was, and I was at least fifty-years-old. I immediately went to a map. I figured that since the man was Chinese, Kuala Lumpur must be in the East, so I bypassed Latin America and Africa. Then I stumbled onto Malaysia and discovered its capital, Kuala Lumpur. So, when we say we are becoming global, it means by God's grace I am overcoming what I believe was my second deepest bigotry.

The deepest bigotry I have is my Christian bigotry, which has to do with the faceless coming. It is the retention of 2000 years of Christian bigotry that is in the depths of my being. If by God's grace we had not stumbled onto the contentless Christ, it would have been absolutely impossible for me to have seen this deepest of all my prejudices. What I mean is, not only have I grasped that Contentless Happening as that without which consciousness or consciousness of consciousness cannot finally take place in a person; but I have found myself a defender of creeds, a defender of liturgy, of ecclesiology, and of theology. Only God can open the eyes of a bigot and I believe my eyes are finally being opened, giving me the opportunity to repent for 2000 years of the most fanatical form of prejudice there is.

It was an incomparable moment when in the 19th century people created the images of "ideology" and "relativity." Whether the church knew it or not, the creation of those two images spelled doom for the church. When people invented ideology as a mindset, the 2000 years of the church was gone. Doomed. All the fallen-out-clergy in this room were felled by those two images – ideology and relativity – not that they knew it, but they are knowing it now. This doom for the church is like the doom of the two-story universe, which went away forever and ever and ever. That doom is now becoming not only an intellectual reality but also a sociological reality. To put it specifically, when people invented ideology and relativity, the sociological dimension of the church was finished. Our eternal friend John XXIII presided over the sociological dissolution of the church. Hans

Kung did likewise in giving permission to live in this world of ideology and relativity.

Transpadane Christianity and Transparentized Spirit

However, do not be confused. It is not as if one bright and shiny day ideology and relativity will disappear and we can start anew to build the 2000-year-old church. In this post-modern world God still rules and God's people must ever march. Therefore, we have been given the gift of "transpadane" Christianity. I spent a long time in the dictionary looking for that word. It came out of the Middle Ages, when the Po River divided the civilized world from the barbarians. They called the land of the barbarians "transpadane," meaning on the other side. I am a "con-transpadane" man, a man on the other side. The word "transpadane" can also mean "transparent." What is happening to Christianity is that it is becoming transparentized: transparentized Christianity. Christianity, in going through ideology and relativity, is finding its new essentialism.

The second thing we must ask about after the transparentized Christ is the transparentized God, which also has happened in the Other World chart. And of course that has happened to Spirit: the transparentized Spirit. Our Sanctification Course, or our work with the holy life, is precisely that. One job remains in this scheme of God, Christ, Holy Spirit, and that is the "Church." What is emerging on the distant horizon without a face is the transparentization of the People of God, the leaven that will produce the new sociological vehicle, which will enable people once again to live free and fully.

God is preparing us for the most subtle spiritual experience we have ever had and the most profound repentance we have ever had to make. What is most difficult is that we not only have to repent for ourselves, we have to repent for millions of people – 2000 years worth. Do not be confused, however. I am not saying that a person in the Middle Ages ought to say what I am saying. I stand in the 20th century as responsible for everything that has ever happened in the church. Without letting us in on the secret, God is slowly disclosing to us the form of the face that is, as yet, no face.

Oh, that we should have lived to see such a day!

Paravocation

From Metaphysics to Phenomenology

The 19th century was great for ideology. We were preoccupied with doctrine, not only religious but with the abstractions of life, the rational. We have gone through much since then: life has ground our noses into our own existence.

Since the 19th century spilled over into the 20th century, many of us have stayed up half the night and argued over abstract doctrine of a secular-religious nature. But that metaphysical approach is gone. Not only do you not pay any attention to its going, but you don't hear it going on much anymore. If you happen to get into some kind of religious or ideological discussion, you do not argue on forever. You say, "Well, neighbor, if you would just describe to me your awareness of what is contained in this abstract concept, then we can have a real conversation."

Here we will bracket the problem of whether or not we are dealing with reality in the sense that most people use the term. In our day, reality is what we describe in sensing after our state of being or our awareness. This description is the phenomenological approach.

When we use the word "hope," we are going to take a phenomenological approach and bracket metaphysical issues. For example, belief becomes profound, issuing in trust. Care becomes profound, issuing in power. Then hope appeareth. This is the hope that is the "unhope," the hope that has nothing whatsoever to do with hope. As you stand naked in your contingency, the hope that is nothing appears. You must be careful, for there is no object of belief in what I am talking about. There is just belief, that is, I just show up believing.

Believing, Caring, and Hoping

You abstractionists can live in the metaphysical and bow before all the objects you want, but what I am describing here is simply this, "You believe." You believe in your very contingency, in your very nothingness. You just believe. I do not care what poetry you use to describe it. The turning of belief into profundity is agony beyond which one can scarcely conceive, for it is the process of your own contingency eating itself into every fiber of your being. It is the process by which you experience your own humiliation and your own weakness. You experience not resentment but yourself as resentment and yourself as suffering. Through this process you believe. Belief can only be profound belief when it has gone through that kind of purgatory. Otherwise, it is just one blush of the naïve and the romantic.

You begin to experience yourself as being a believer. I find myself increasingly a believer. It is then that belief has turned into trust. Trust of what? Trust of nothing except being. I believe at this moment, and experience something that is over and beyond. I am describing consciousness, your own consciousness in the sense of intentionality. It is like being is relying on being, and I am in that process. You trust life. You trust death. You trust forgiveness. You trust being. You no longer insist that it has to be this way or that way. You trust the given, out of which arises authentic care.

After the Majuro Consult, one guardian spoke of the five flags of Majuro. He shocked me that day as he spoke about the last flag, the flag of Those Who Care, planted in Majuro. TWC: Those Who Care. When care is turned into profundity, you have gone through the awareness that you no longer have any home, anywhere; that you are rootless, that you were born rootless, and you are going to die rootless; after going through the agony, you experience yourself as sheer ineffectivity; you experience yourself as all drained out. One moment of unlimited care takes your whole life and you are gone.

A colleague told me the other day that he has just been drained out. I suspect that he is hoping for the moment when he will recover. When he does, he may not be clear. But I am clear that he has found a new illusion in which to waddle for a few steps until that illusion, like all others, dies . . . unless he dies first. You experienced that you are not only unfulfilled, but that you and I are never going to be fulfilled. Do you see the amount of spiritual energy you could save in fighting with your wife if you could just grasp this? Not only are you not fulfilled, but if you care, you never will be.

It is in the midst of the purging of care that one becomes aware of power that is somehow not your power. I am not talking metaphysically. I am trying to describe what happens to you. When Leah Early talked about the Majuro miracles, you almost felt power was emanating from her. She was creating in me a miracle while she was describing something in Majuro that she called a miracle. It is as if being the power of being is what being is, and you are in the middle of it. I call it strange power.

It is precisely in this trust of being and in this power of being that the hope that does not let you down exists. It is the hope of all hope. However, all you can see is the residue of hope. You can never see hope. If you hope in something, it is not the hope beyond hope. It is the hope in something.

Somebody here wrote recently that hope is something good because it motivates you. No! The hope beyond hope is not a functional category in any way whatsoever. It just is, but it does have residue. Hope is like the Spirit. You can't see it, but when the wind blows, the leaves tremble and you can feel the wind brush your cheek. So it is with hope: it leaves, but it leaves with us its residue.

Paravocation: One Vocation with Two Manifestations

It is the residue of what I call "paravocation." "Para-" means alongside. I don't mean that. It also means beyond and before. When hope appeareth, paravocation is. It is like the trembling of the leaf when the wind goes by. What I mean by paravocation is the awareness that you were sent. It is the awareness of your destiny. It is the awareness of fatedness about life, about belief, about care, and about hope. From now on, all of your doing and all of your being is paravocation.

There are strange things about this paravocation. Suppose I am a lawyer. No, I am a TWC assigned to the Legal Division of Those Who Care. I am a businessman. No, I am a TWC assigned to the Business Division of Those Who Care. I am a clergyman. No, I am a TWC assigned to the Clergy Division of Those Who Care. I am not describing some rational concept that I want you to believe in; I am trying to describe the way it is when the hope that is beyond hope appeareth. You know something then. You sense a kind of oneness.

Rationally you can reflect and you see that there is only one vocation for a human being and that is to be a human being assigned to some division or other. Nobody cares much about how you do in that division, in the first instance. They care about your paravocation. I never made it in the Clergy Division, although I am still trying. I have not given up, but I would hate to have you measure my life only on that division I have been assigned to.

Finally, there is only *one vocation*. There are not great divisions between us because some are this and some are that, or some have done that much and some have not done that much in their second vocation, their assigned division, for example, the Legal Division. What excites me about this is talking about the People of God, but not as if that is some concept. It is at the moment you experience the People of God that you experience the fact that this vocation is corporate. Mark you, in the Legal Division some compartmentalization takes place and there is such a thing as individual success. But in paravocation we are a body of which our gathering in this room is but a sign and a signal.

I would like to deal with what happens to your operation in your division when you do not say, "Now I am going to have a paravocation," but when paravocation happens to you. I believe you begin to deal with what happens to your second vocation when paravocation happens to you. How you begin to function in your second vocation is exciting. Society gives you a check list of what a lawyer is, of what a doctor is, and so on. There is no checklist for a paravocation. It is just "I care."

There are authentic, profound, social groups and dynamics that involve paravocation. You are clear that whenever you perceive a radical reconstruction of human settlement in the cultural dynamic, before that happened there was an awakening of the profound deeps of consciousness itself. The civilization of India at the feet of the Buddha was that kind of profound spiritual breakloose. Such a breakloose always leaves a residue. The residue I am talking about is the trembling of a leaf that you cannot see. You cannot see the hope that appeareth as it passes by. But I believe that the Town Meeting is the deposit of the hope that appeareth. I believe the Town Meeting is not something in and of itself. It is the deposit of hope, the hope that appeareth. Today it is Majuro and tomorrow it will be Korea, India, and Africa. It is the trembling. It is the passing by of hope.

For the first time since we have been together, all of us have been under direct assignment. Nobody assigned us. The job just appeareth. When I look around this room as a whole, I am overwhelmed. What a fine group of people you Guardians are. I bet you think you decided to come here. Or you think somebody got you to come here. No. We are a deposit. We are the tremble. Way down deep underneath is the hope. It has nothing to do with the way we feel.

If what I say is true, then by golly, history had better watch out. If what I say is not true, then history can relax, unless the hope that appeareth has trembled in some other place.

At the top of the triangle before you, in line with the *trust of being* and the *power of being*, is the *presence of being*. What you have just experienced in the last few minutes is a state of being that humankind through the ages has named "presence." Where the presence is, hope beyond hope is.

Those Who Care

The Invisible College Exists

People ask me, "Who is the Institute of Cultural Affairs?" and I say that we are a not-for-profit global group concerned with community development and methods of effective action. Then they say, "I don't mean that. I mean, who are you *really*? What makes you tick?" That's a hard question, but I give them the answer I noticed in your book, on that first thin page: "we are *those who care*."

More than that, we are part of those around the world who care. As I travel the world I'm finding more and more people who just care. I don't mean care about familiar things, simply things that are close. I mean those who care about the world and what's happening in it. Like you, they care about the past journey, not just of their own people, but of all people. They care about creativity. And they care about the future.

We just care. We don't know any more than anyone else, and we don't have any easy solutions to anything, but we care. Some economists call this the "invisible college." There are people around this world who are not formally related but are people who care – and therefore are an invisible fellowship.

All over I find people who care. But I also find people who don't seem to care. I have to deal with government people quite a bit these days. Walking into offices I sense persons who care or don't care. Last week I went to see Mrs. Gandhi's Chief Minister of her cabinet. He cares. That encouraged me, for if she died, he'd be Prime Minister. And Mrs. Gandhi cares. I went to another cabinet minister and sensed he doesn't care.

I am also extremely encouraged that those who care around the world are finding out that other people care. That's fundamental to this week's planning consult.

Spirit Precedes Practical Matters

My point is this: when I got up this morning, I asked a serious question about us as a group gathered here. We are teachers. We are planners. We are social workers. We are business men and women. Then I said, "Now, who are we *really*?" I decided that none of us would have come to something like this week-long consult if we were not either self-consciously or un-self-consciously part of those who care. Today we are going out to the local people of this beautiful island, because in some way or another we care. If you don't mind, we're going to postpone the overall orientation until tomorrow morning so that we can get right out into the villages. When we bring back some of their responses, we'll have a context for what I've just been saying, that people everywhere care.

Action Generates Context

This time in history calls for action and so we start with action. This first day we are concerned with the latent operating vision which is present in the minds of local people on this island of Jeju [South Korea]. You don't mind going directly to work, do you? All of this is because we care. And don't be surprised when you find out that the villagers care as much as you do, or probably much more since it's their home.

Just remember, we all are *those who care*.

The New Movement

What the Church Has Recovered

We have been on the way for fifty-five years. Somewhere toward the end of the 1950s, certain people in the spirit movement – God's spirit movement, not ours – began to sense that a radical alteration was taking place within the forces of renewal. It soon became clear, as we symbolized it, that forty years in the desert in the effort to renew the church had passed and that the theoretical job fundamentally had been accomplished. That was 1957. Then it seemed as though it would take about a decade to shift from the emphasis on the theoretical recovery of the church to the practical. In 1967, according to our symbolic timeline, that decade was concluded. We are now five long years into that aspect of church renewal which has placed the emphasis upon the practical. To arrive at our symbolic figure of forty years of practical renewal, that is, to the year 2007, we have thirty-five more years to go. And there are some of us who have promised ourselves and God that church renewal is going to be accomplished. It has taken the forces of renewal these five years to think through the practical march toward the great reconstruction of society and the great resurgence of humanness, which will be the practical recovery of the People of God. This summer becomes, therefore, a serious turning point in the 20th century renewal of the church and the world.

As you look back across these fifty-five years, it is clear that in terms of what the renewal forces beginning about the middle of World War I intended to accomplish, the church has been renewed. When I look back over the fifty-five years and the people involved, most of whom have already shed their blood one way or another, it is pretty clear to me what has really happened. First of all, the church has recovered the centrality of the Christ Happening in the human journey. Secondly, the church today has a fresh operating image of itself as mission in the civilizing process. It is hard for some of you young ones to realize that only twenty years ago the church did not have the foggiest image of her practical function in society. And the third thing that has happened is the recovery of the universal quality of God's people. It has been a long time, maybe several hundred years, since the church really believed that she was ecumenism itself. The church knows nothing about Japanese churches and American churches and Australian churches and Indian churches and black churches and youth churches and white churches and female churches, for the church is one.

The next thing the church has recovered, and I scarcely know how to put this, is that to be a person of faith is to be disciplined; that to be a person who has been sent as the church to bear the burdens of this world means discipline. In the past, the church has understood that a person of faith is to be consumed with discipline. The church has recovered that in our day. There is not a soul in the room who does not know that to be the People of God in the next thirty-five years will require a kind of discipline that would have frightened the daylights out of you ten years ago. The church knows again that to be the church means rigor.

Lastly, church renewal forces stumbled upon the Other World that is always in the midst of this world. That breakthrough of the consciousness of consciousness has brought a fresh radicality to humanness. Sometimes I think it has been more that 500 years since we have known anything about the Other World as a reality in the midst of the concretions of this world. And perhaps this is the glory beyond glory of church renewal, for even Jesus Christ opened up to history the realm of God, the domain of the divine.

Church Renewal Has Been Accomplished: The Great Turn

I am well aware of the fact that it is going to take even more than thirty-five years to enable every last human being to understand what you and I are talking about, but that too shall come. Therefore, there is no more need for the forces of renewal in the church, since their job has been accomplished. This does not mean that the church does not have a long road ahead as she concretizes this renewal in the social forms of operation, actualizing her function, her task, her mission in civilization. And to accomplish that, she is going to need the assistance, as never before, of the revolutionary forces within her very body. But the movement that is required at this moment is something quite different.

I am reminded of a movie I once saw of a wagon train. It got stuck in what appeared to be a blind gulley that ended with a sheer cliff. So the drivers got them into a circle and made camp, and some of them kept the fires burning while they sent their scouts on ahead to see if the canyon was blocked, and, if it was, to discover some other route. It occurred to me that the movemental dynamic within the historical church always has to be the scouts of the wagon train. Somehow, I have a deep appreciation for all those pastors and laypeople who have kept the home fires going in the established church, so that those of us who were called to scout out the future might have something to come home to, and something to scout on behalf of.

Now another scouting expedition has to be sent out. What the church needs are demonstrations in the concrete arenas of society of what it means to be mission in the civilizing process. Therefore, a new movement within the church is called for. It is going to look different, because it will emphasize the practical. We must build within ourselves the concrete illustrations of what it means to be the church, to be mission to the civilizing process, and always at the local parish level. That is what lies ahead. This is the *great turn* that we are on now.

But you also have to look at the secular. I am convinced that already there is breaking loose in the civilizing process at large a new bubbling of the radical deeps of humanness. This has been brought about by many revolutionary forces: the black revolution, the youth revolution, the non-Western world revolution, the feminine revolution. But within all of those revolutions, the movemental church has played a role, the results of which are not nearly so clear now as I believe they will be within even ten years.

Let me say that a different way. I am sixty-years-old. In my whole life, the trough of the wave has been apparent. I have lived my total existence in a world which understood itself as going to pieces. Think of that. You can almost see yourself hanging on with your fingernails. But now there is a turn. The world is moving to a crest where a brand new perspective on life is slowly coming into view. We are beholding things we could not have dreamed of ten years ago. There is a bubbling within my existence that I have wanted all my life, but never dreamed I would live long enough to experience. It seems as if all around me showers of blessing are falling. It is not that they were not falling before, but in my moment in history you could not grasp that they were showers of blessing. Now this is changing.

The Great Resurgence at the Heart of the Great Reconstruction

As you look ahead for this new movement, one of the interesting things is that you can see rather clearly what your goals are. Twenty years ago you could not perceive your goals. Day after day you were putting one foot out in front of the other without any idea where the next one would go. That is what it means to be in the movemental dynamic of the church during the past fifty-five years. This upward turn, this moving toward the crest, means that you now can perceive clearly what has to be done. What that does to your own spirit deeps is almost beyond description. I am pointing to the fact that it does not make it easier. In one sense, it makes it far more difficult. When you look across the decades ahead, you now see that the goal is the *great reconstruction* of society, whereas in the past the goal was the renewal of the church. The church is renewed. You must now be concerned for the renewal of the world, and that means you become the demonstration to the church of what the church has to be if it is mission to the civilizing process. That is the great reconstruction. That is the goal that lies ahead.

But there is also another goal, the flip side of the first, which I call the *great resurgence*. I like that word "resurgence" because it is a secular word. I also like it because one of its meanings is "resurrection." By *great resurgence* I mean the release of a fresh sense of motivity from the deeps in every person. Resurgence also means "revival," but I do not mean by that the kind of revival Protestants have called the Great Awakening and which went to seed in the last part of the 19th century.

I mean something closer to what happened in the 26th and 25th centuries B.C. in Egypt, when a people who were nothing experienced a strange outbreak of human motivity. Almost overnight (really during the course of two centuries) that great civilization of the Nile was built.

I am talking about that moment in which we reach outside the church to secular folk and find a way in secular language and secular style to release the "last fat lady" to her deep, long-confined feeling for the wonder and awe which is the gift of consciousness. That kind of revival is coming, which is more than the Great Awakening ever dreamed of.

You cannot have a reconstruction of society without a resurgence of human motivity. They work together. You will only have that new social vehicle at the moment that a new deep spirituality is broken loose. Those are the visions ahead for the next thirty-five years. And do you know something? I do not have the slightest doubt that the movement forces will realize those objectives. But you have to remember one thing: no man, no group, and no movement ever renews the church or the world. God alone renews the church, and God alone creates revivals, and God alone restructures the human adventure. But God never renewed the church nor the world save a body of people decided that God's world was going to be renewed. And that is what happened at the beginning with the renewal forces: a body of people decided the church was going to be renewed. However, when God decides to renew something, on the other side of bodies of concerned people deciding to renew it, what comes out is never precisely what was intended by those who began the renewal. And that is just as well.

Being the New Movement

There is one more point here. Those who set out to bring into being a new social vehicle and a new spirituality have to be that new world even as they begin the task. Do you think Bonhoeffer could have done what he did if he had not already become what he intended to do? I have got to be that new social vehicle now. What does it mean for me to think globally, to live globally, to resolve globally? I have got to be that new outbreak of the Holy Spirit now, or it is not going to happen. You are not playing games here. Either you are out to renew the world, or you are not. And many there are who will fall by the wayside, for this is a long march.

The long march can only happen when you know where you are going and when you are clear about the price of going there. Then it becomes a long march. Therefore, you and I have to decide all over again tonight and this month whether we are going on the long march, knowing that it is not for five years or ten, but for twenty long years. Many of you in this room are going to be older than I am now before you even get near the end of the march. Some of you are going to be dead. Some of you are going to fall along the way when the going gets even tougher. And, of course, some of you are not even going to start.

The Practical Aspects of a Revolution

I had to give a talk not long ago in which I felt pressed to say rather concretely what I felt were the essential ingredients in bringing off the practical aspect of a revolution. There are many self-styled revolutionaries who never intend to practically bring off the revolution. I told them about where my own spirit struggle was most vicious and most wracking. I used the imagery of the Psalmist when he feels that he is surrounded by mad dogs on every side. Well, I feel surrounded by mad dogs, but they are really hyenas. They all have grins on their faces. The say, "Joe, you don't really intend to do it, do you? You don't really intend to accomplish what you're talking about. All of those triangles last year, you know, you meant to just keep them there in the abstract. You don't mean to be practical. That's where you get hurt. You want to remain an intellectual abstractionist." That is what their grins say. And again and again I have to swell up my shoulders with a strength beyond my power and say, "You go to Hell. I *do* mean it!"

When I laid out what I thought was essential to the practical aspects of revolution, I said that you first of all need a practical vision. You are not going to get anywhere if you do not forge a *practical vision* of that reality you want to bring into being. That is what finally captures people. That is what you did last summer. A practical vision always has to be a fundamental reinterpretation of society. Last summer you worked that out with the dynamical processes. It has to be a statement of the imbalances that are present in light of that theory. It has to be a clear statement of your own vantage point, your ideology, if you please, and a clear articulation of those *underlying contradictions* that stand between what is and what you intend to bring into being. Then there have to be what last summer you called *strategic proposals*. And with those has to come a hint of how they are going to be accomplished. You already have your practical vision. You hammered that out last summer.

The second crucial thing for a practical revolution is what I call the *tactical system*. This summer you are going to build those tactical systems. I do not know what they will look like, but one thing I am sure of: only a naïve liberal would believe that you will work out some kind of tactical system for each one of those triangles. If you make a frontal attack, you will be dead 500 years before there will be any serious change in society. What you have to look for is what somebody has called the "whistle point." That is, if you have a mountain of snow, and you find exactly the right places to stand and to direct the sound of your whistle, and you get the right whistle, a whole avalanche starts. Your tactical system does not itself do the job, but it gets the snowball rolling whereby, in principle, every last soul on this planet is a part of the social revolution. Those of you here are going to be working on the tactical system this summer.

This third thing that has to be for a practical revolution is what we have called an *operational design*. If you had the best tactical system in the world and you did not have any forces to do the whistling, you would not have a revolution. Half of you are going to be concerned with the training of forces, the disciplining of forces on a global scale. You are going to work out designs for specific engagement. And the concern, as you well know, is both for the local parish and for a global movement.

Spirit Training

The last thing necessary for a practical revolution is *spirit training*. If you and I do not find a way to build a factory that can produce spirit people, there is no hope for the tactical concretizing of any model, any strategies, or any tactics. We have to start by unlocking the spirit in ourselves. This summer we are going to be engaged in that. We are going to attempt to discover, not intellectually, but with our being, the contours and topography of the Other World, of the radical dimensions of consciousness right in the midst of this world.

Somebody has said that a movement moves on its singing. We are going to sing this summer and we are not going to sing the kind of songs that we have been singing for the last fifty-five years. We do not live in that kind of world any more. The Spirit is flowing. Just think for a moment. Up to now we have been walking around the edge of the abyss. On the long march we have to walk right across that abyss. If you do not waltz across that abyss, you are not going to get across it. So we are going to learn once again the meaning of the waltz.

But you are also going to have to learn marches as you never have before, because that terrain is rough and those marches consume long hours. If you do not learn once again to count cadence, one, two, three, four, you are not going to make it. And not only that, but on a long march you have to tell yourself fresh stories, day after day after day. This is where the new form of folk music is going to have its role. You are going to learn to sing folk songs and sing them in a new way. Lastly, you will learn that to keep your stamina you have to have diversion. You will learn to sing popular music again. You will learn to whistle those tunes which you spent your lives saying “no” to. And since some of you are not going to have the courage to do that, you are not going to last long on the march.

We have got to experiment as a movement with new means of internalizing discipline. I have never cared one bit for any kind of external form of discipline. But it has to be there because I can only learn to be a disciplined man if I have external structures. But that is not what I mean by discipline. What you are out to do is to discover and to build a discipline down inside. I think we had better experiment with some kind of sign of chastity. We should experiment once again with vigils and watches. And perhaps we should experiment again with fasts. I would even like to see us experiment with a grand ball. Some of you are not old enough to know what the old Aragon Ballroom meant, but it is right down the street from this building in which we gather.

I think that the mood of this summer has got to be serious fun, and I mean the kind of giddy fun that I experienced with troops during World War II the night before we had to go ashore. We sat around. Nobody could sleep, of course, and we tended to have sort of silly fun. Well, this summer has got to be that kind of serious nonchalance. Those of you who were here last summer know that you are going to work, and work hard. But in the midst of that work we have got to have fun. Not for the sake of fun, although that is all right, but for the sake of the march, of the next twenty years, the next thirty-five years.

Symbolizing the New Movement

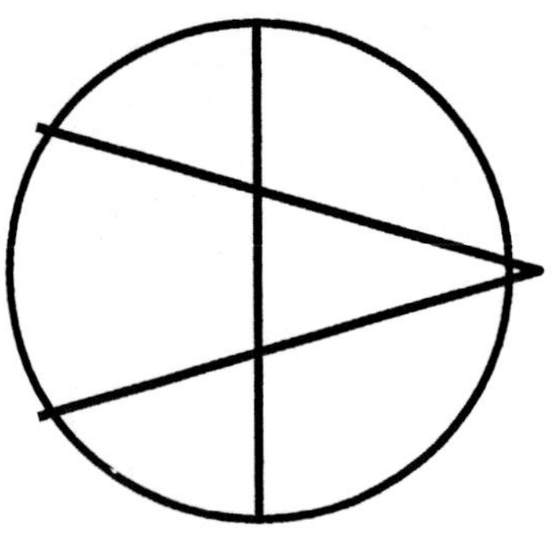

Figure 4-1: The Wedgeblade

And so, I call out of history, out of existence, the old movement and call into being the twenty-year march, the new movement. And for me, this is the sign: there is the wedge blade; that is the old movement. The globe is put over it, divided into the pro-establishment and the dis-establishment, and we are both of these as structural revolutionaries. But outside the circle is the trans-establishment, which alone enables one to stand in both camps at the same time, yet transcending both.

This leaves only one thing: the decision, my decision and your decision. You have a month to make that decision. As you go into this month to make that decision, while you build that about which you are making the decision, go with God.

The Two Faces of the Movement

I have been concerned in recent months with the First Epistle of John, with Peter's First Epistle, with Colossians, and with Ephesians. This is from Ephesians. In the third chapter Paul says,

> I kneel in prayer to the Father from whom every family in heaven and on earth takes its name, that out of the treasures of his glory he may grant you strength and power through his Spirit in your inner being that through faith Christ may dwell in your hearts in love. With deep roots and firm foundations may you be strong to grasp with all of God's people what is the breadth and length and height and depth of the love of Christ and to know it though it is beyond knowledge. So you may finally attain unto the fullness of being that is the fullness of God himself. Now to him who is able to do immeasurably more than all we can ask or even conceive of; by the power which is at work in us, to him be the glory in the church and in Christ Jesus from generation to generation evermore. *Amen.*

The Spirit Movement

In this time of the *great turn*, church renewal can no longer be. In the beginning there were centers of renewal, projects of renewal, and experiments of renewal. Now there are none. From time to time somebody opens up a new center. I am extremely clear that if I go by that center in a year or two, it will not be there. This is no longer the hour of church renewal in the sense that centers or even institutes conceive of.

I remember in Austin, in 1953, that James McCord, who has been for some time the President of Princeton Theological Seminary, was on our board. We had been in existence for a short time and at a board meeting he suggested, "You have been experimenting long enough. Let us stop experimenting." I did not have much courage in those days so I didn't say anything, but I died inside. I did not have the foggiest idea of what was ahead, or how you would go about getting to that about which you did not have the foggiest. I knew he was absolutely wrong. But now, if James McCord were to rise in the room and say that the day of experimenting is over, in the sense of centers and projects and institutes, I would have to say, "Yea, verily." There is a long way to go before the church, which is renewed, is renewed. But centers, projects, and institutes, as they were formulated in the past, are not going to help much anymore.

What has actually happened is movements have begun within the renewed church which will carry out that renewal. I find it very difficult to point to this and that. So I went to Lord McLeod, the founder of the Iona Community and the grandfather of the renewal institutes, centers, and experiments. Lord McLeod has been a friend and colleague of ours from the very early days. He came to see us in Austin and in Chicago.

Whenever we are in his part of the world we make every effort to bestow upon ourselves the honor of sitting in his presence. I saw him on this last trip. He had been to Australia and visited the Sydney House. Lord McLeod was extremely pleased and somewhat overwhelmed at what he discovered in that House. It was in Australia that he first made the statement which more recently he put in a document presented before the Synod of the Church of Scotland. He stated that at this time in history there were just two possibilities for the church. One was the charismatic movement and the other was the Ecumenical Institute.

That rocked me because we had a movement and then we had an institute. What he was pointing to is not the Ecumenical Institute. He was pointing to a movement. I remembered we had called ourselves the "spirit movement." What we meant by that was that human spirit was being released in our time, and it had nothing to do with us. We were clear that this was God's spirit movement and not some kind of movement we were doing. We pointed concretely to the profound activity of the Holy Spirit in the 20th century, both within and outside the church. What we meant by the term "spirit movement" was the Holy Spirit Movement.

I put two and two together and realized that this is what the charismatic people are doing. Then I became aware that there is a great chasm between this spirit movement and that spirit movement. I believe with all of my heart that if a movement comes within the church, charismatic or otherwise, it is God's movement. I believe that what people mean by the charismatic movement is not the Pentecostal movement in the world, though there is a relationship. The charismatic movement is a short term fad. This does not mean that God is not making use of it, nor that it is not attempting to get something out in the open which is deeply experienced by humans. But in its current form it will not last long. It is as faddish as sensitivity training, through it is widespread. It may be, however, that you have not heard the end of the Pentecostal outbreak, particularly as it has occurred in Latin America. Something could happen in other places and in established churches that in the future might be pointed to as a Pentecostal movement. To criticize this is not my intent. I am after clarity on who we are as a spirit movement, by looking at what we do not stand for and at what we are, unavoidably.

Lord McLeod must have seen a kind of astonishment on my face. Also, he must have grasped a rational dichotomy between the terms charismatic movement and Ecumenical Institute. So he hastened to try to solve that problem by saying, "Now, let's see. What is it you emphasize? It is the liturgical, isn't it?" Then I was astonished. After I recovered I said, "Yes." But if that is the first thing someone says then I say, "No, that is not adequate." So I came up with four qualities of this movement that we are, and yet God's movement that we are a part of, for it is way beyond us and anybody we know. I tried on for size, but the word is ruined, the "missionary movement" or the "mission movement," if you are talking about movements within the church. There is another great word: *diakonia.* We are the "deaconate movement." That means humble service. It means the church in service. Yet that doesn't get hold of it all. One time I thought you could say we are a "profound movement," but others would not understand "profound" the way I mean it. Your colleague from England used the term *"radical movement."* In England there are two movements, the charismatic movement and the radical movement. The word radical points to radical humanness. You couldn't just say that. Anyway, here are four qualities.

The Four Qualities of Who We Are

First of all, we are a *spirit movement.* In the sense that we are concerned about profound humanness, we are concerned about the radical relations to the divine activity in history. We wish to push the very bottom out of spirituality. Here we merge with the charismatic movement in its conscious or unconscious concern about the deeps of humans, which rational and structural frozenness has denied to us in our moment in history. We are interested in the deeps of the Spirit. I tried to say to myself which one of these we are more interested in. I don't see how I could be more interested in anything other than this breakloose of the deeps of humanness in our time. Now, let us skip over to my fourth one. These are the extremes.

We are a *rational movement.* Sometimes I am astounded at our concern for the rational. We go slowly and sometimes it irritates me. It seems like we ought to have been where we are now four years ago. Last summer I thought we had it. Yet we have required of ourselves, as we have moved every step, that everything we do is grounded in the deeps of humanness. We ground it in history, inside and outside the church, in the temporal domain of the time in which we live. Then we require of ourselves internal consistency in that grounding. Here is where we part company with the charismatic people and with those who do not grasp themselves as a vital part of the establishment, both the civil and the ecclesiastical establishment. We are revolutionaries and we must die revolutionaries. But we are structural revolutionaries.

Another way we stress the rational is that every new inch of understanding we gain into the unfathomable interior deeps, we attempt to articulate in every manifestation of humanness. This sets us apart. We are interested in how this breakloose manifests itself in what it means to be a woman and a man, in understanding the family, the nation, community, and in understanding the methodologies whereby you alter history itself. To us there is no part of life that is not related to the interior deeps of what it means to be a human being. We intend, within the limits of our ability, to manifest that on behalf of all of humankind. That sets us apart. I would want Lord McLeod to believe that though we may not have the mind of a Thomas Aquinas, we are deeply related in every part of our being to the vision which he articulated for his time, relative to the whole world of humanity.

We are a *liturgical movement.* The efforts toward renewal in the Eastern Orthodox Church basically have been concerned with the liturgy. Our group would stand shoulder to shoulder with them. We believe that the one great drama of history, that the curtain of time has never been rung down on, is some form of that drama with which we begin everyday, the liturgy. I am convinced with a passion that if I did nothing all the rest of my life but to see to it that the liturgy went on in my lifetime, that would have been a mission, a mission for the well-being of humankind. Without that there is not any eschatological revolution at any time in history.

I need not point out to a group like this the relationship of these insights to our almost fanatical concern for the local church. For the first task of any local church is to keep in being that drama. Generation after generation that liturgy has been kept in history. That liturgy brought the good news to this old man who once was young and heard it. Instead of pastoral counseling in a parish, instead of going out to psychologize people, we pick up the altar and carry it to people. Does that communicate? We pick up the altar and carry it to the last person in the parish.

The last thing I would say is that we are a *mission movement.* By "mission" I mean taking that altar to all of civilization, which means catalyzing a new social vehicle. This is our task. We are perpetual revolutionaries working within the structures of society to keep them always moving toward the future. That is carrying the altar, if you please, into history. For I believe that any radical revolution in history has happened only when there was a recovery, regardless of what poetry you use, of that relationship to the unfathomable mystery that the altar symbolizes and that the liturgy holds before history, whether history likes it or wants it or not.

The Two Faces of the Movement

We still do not have a name. Certain things become clear, clearer than they used to be, about who I am, about who we are. Two pictures do it for me. For some time I have been aware that any person who assumes the horrible, burning, consuming responsibility for humankind is elected to be the religious in history. The Christ figure is the figure of that. Next to him is the old king. I decided he is a guildsman. I understand now I am not only a religious, I am also a guildsman. I am not sure what a guildsman is, but I have two pictures. We saw a movie last week, "The Seven Faces of Dr. Lao." I read the book a long time ago, but I looked at it with a new set of eyes. When I read the book I was that woman having her fortune told by the one who was doomed to tell the truth: no more love, no more money. This time I was Dr. Lao, the circus man, the magician.

The only difference between us is that Dr. Lao had seven faces and I have only two. One is the *face of the religious*, and that is before God. The other is the *face of the guildsman*, and that is before the world. I have another figure. As I grasp myself the rest of my life I am going to wear the sign of the religious. For me it is going to be the cross. Then I am going to wear the sign of my other face, the face of the guildsman. It is going to be the wedge blade. The circle represents space, and I intend to stand in the midst of unlimited space with my life, for the rest of my life. The wedge blade represents time, and I intend to be on the edge of time and the center of space.

At the end of this Research Assembly, in the year of the guild, you are going to tell me what a guildsman is. But I know that a guildsman is the person who stands with his/her being at the center of space forever, and forever on the edge of time. I intend to wear this symbol so that hopefully I will never be lost again. I will have that which tells me of my face before God and that which tells me of my face before the world. And I believe that for the first time in our history we will be prepared to tell Lord McLeod who we are.

The Six Speeches

Grace be unto you and peace from God our Father and the Lord Jesus Christ. Amen.

I knew that other people would tell you all about Maliwada before I got back, and so I want to do something else on Maliwada, under six points. I have six talks, and each one has six things in it. The first talk is the *learnings from Maliwada*, the second is the *flags of permeation*, the next the *six stages*, then the *steps at hand*, the *missions ahead*, and the last one is the *definitudes of presence*. Though I will quickly talk about all six, really I'm only interested in talking about the first and the last.

Learnings from Maliwada

I have an appreciation for rural people in India I don't know how to articulate. The only ones in India I'd really known before were the ones stretched out on the sidewalks of Calcutta, who had come for whatever reason from the land to the city that was not capable of supporting them. You can imagine my impression, not that I wanted it. It was just there, of rural people in India. I got the shock of my life – rural people of India are proud human beings. They are competent human beings. Most surprising of all is their poise. I finally had to hide from people to keep from going into their huts and drinking buffalo juice out of their graciousness, but you know when they got you inside those mud huts they had a poise that you would not believe.

The next thing I was impressed with was their intelligence. Out of that intelligence flows creativity with forthrightness that is incredible. This underscored for me what we have said was a basic image in Sub-Asia – in India, in the culture of Hinduism – namely, selfhood. And guess what: local people of India have selfhood!

I've been beaten by the forces of history into confessing that local people are on the rise around the world. The deep current of history in our time is that local people are on the move. And if my image of local people in India could be so profoundly changed, then why should I not believe in the possibility of local people in every nation of the world? This is why I am not grumpy after this trip.

I fell in love with some old men in Maliwada, and some old men fell in love with me. At times I was a little irritated. I wanted to talk and I couldn't talk. Then after a while I knew why the Lord never taught me Hindi, or Marathi, because he wanted me to look deep into the eyes of the local people of India and to permit them to look deep into this local man's eyes from the United States. I don't know whether they embrace in India, but I know just as well as I know my name that if I ever go to Maliwada again, I can see an old Muslim who is going to reach out his arms, and then I'm going to reach out mine, and we're going to embrace like a couple of Frenchmen. And when I see an old Hindu man, I don't know whether they do this, but I know he's going to reach out his arms and I'm going to reach out mine and we're going to embrace like a couple of Frenchmen. This I know.

What am I trying to say? Well, golly, I had fun, tiring fun. I tramped those gullies for miles with some of those old men looking for a precious resource, water. And then I beheld it. Early I stumbled into a dam that nobody seemed to know was there. It had been washed out, the people said, 700 years ago (others said 300 years ago). I came finally to believe that it was from 300-700 years ago. Next I walked down a long, long gully about twenty feet deep and about twenty feet wide, and dry. But in the monsoons it was full. Then I stumbled on what I was looking for. I knew that one time that place was a Garden of Eden and now it was arid, and they cry for water, water, water. I stumbled on it. They had built a series of earth dams with rock in the center, then channeled the water and stored it. They used it both directly and indirectly because it kept the water table high, which they touched when they dug wells anywhere from twenty feet to seventy feet. That's the way they kept their wells full. The only question I asked is, "What was it that happened 300 years ago?" and if I live I'm going to find out. You know those dams had been washed out before. Guess what the people did before; they rebuilt them. What happened? What happened?

When we talk about the fundamental principles of Fifth City, one of them is the profound human issue. If you do not know people's past, you never get at the profound issue. The basic contradiction in Maliwada is just two things – just two things – one is they don't have cobblestones on their streets, and the other is they do not harness the water. How do I know that? Can you imagine every morning when you get up, being before the glory of that unbelievable Fortress, which points to a civilization highly developed while our ancestors were running around in bearskins, and Maliwada in the deprecated condition it is? Can you imagine being a Maliwada person? Can you imagine, with your psyche, getting up in the morning, going out of a mud hut, and looking up to see that Fortress? You see the glory of the people that were there before. And then you look at the filth in the street, and the lack of education in the village, and the lack of bread to eat. What happened 300 years ago?

My point has to do with those old men. They have these big dug wells, some of them twenty to thirty feet across, others six to eight feet across, and in my imagination, I was afraid of falling down those wells. As a matter of fact, vertigo came over me, and I looked in one of those things and thought if you don't get out of there, Mathews, you're going to jump in. I was walking with those old men and we were spread out, all three of us, an old Muslim, an old Hindu, and an old Christian. We were walking in the fields and simultaneously each one of us fell down a separate well. There we discovered a table of common consciousness. Whatever that was 300 years ago, or less, or more, they had lost their profound consciousness. We three fell down into consciousness again. The greatest story of Maliwada is the story of the recovery of profound consciousness, right before our eyes. Those wells we fell down were our own historical poetry. I fell down through a well in Christian poetry, another fell down through a well in Hindu poetry, and another through a well in Muslim poetry. And when we hit the common water table of consciousness, we didn't need to speak Hindi or English together. We just looked into the deeps of one another's eyes.

We were doing theology, theology that has significance beyond the power of this moment to describe. Some of you will live to write it, but remember when you do that you will be writing empirical theology. You are going to be describing events that happen before you write them or you wouldn't have anything to write about. You are going to articulate how Jesus Christ is Lord of all in ways the world has never dreamed. When you hit the table of profound consciousness, which is the transparentization of your own poetry, you discover that, lo, we are one in Christ Jesus, empirically. You are going to write about what has already happened. It has happened in your own life; you are the manifestation of this happenedness. You are ready to move shoulder to shoulder with the Hindus and the Muslims of the world in ways that a few years ago I could not even have dreamed of.

In the heyday of RS-I, we were concerned with lives being changed within 44-hours. We were concerned not with whether anybody agreed with us theologically or methodologically but with lives being changed. In this community of Maliwada during the consult, I saw lives changed, profoundly changed, and I am skilled at recognizing a profoundly changed life. I did not say, "The Lord Jesus Christ" or "In the name of the Father and the Son and the Holy Ghost" once. Instead, I did it. I beheld the power of the gospel in presence. I mean my presence – no, not my presence, but the presence of the blue. And by that I mean our presence. You weren't there. But you were there. You're just stuck with this: the presence that God has given you is yours to use, but it's been mixed with George's presence and my presence and those who wear the blue around the world. I'm mixed up with you, so that where I am there you are and where you are there I am. And there's nothing you can do about that. The presence of the blue changed lives in Maliwada. And it didn't take one single theological utterance. But theology was being "do-ed" all over the place. That's the story of three old men who fell down three wells. And that is one of learnings from Maliwada. If I look unusually mature to you today, you understand I have grown a bit since you last saw me, due to Maliwada.

Flags of Permeation

My second talk is about permeation. Whenever you go rapidly into the future you go rapidly into the past. Have you ever noticed that? You remember the word "permeation"? That was long before we knew about the big bend, the big turn. You people from Texas would be delighted to know that when I first began to think about this summer, I was thinking about Big Bend country in Texas. The turn to the world: the word "'permeation" was the beginning of that.

In India we chose to go through the Minister of Education, who is Mrs. Rowe, and she brought her husband along. She paid us the honor of coming to the hotel rather than having us go to her office. We gave her the Maliwada five-year-plan document, and then we said, "What we want from you are two things: one is your permission to take over the school in Maliwada and make it into a rural demonstration primary school for all of India." She said, "You have it, I will take it off the formal list of schools and designate it a separate demonstration school so you do not get trapped in the education bureaucracy." And she said that she would put her good office behind that project. Second, we said, "We want somebody with your clout to make us an appointment with the Chief Minister." She said, "Well, it will take three days," so she took the document and went home. Overnight, she and her husband read it. She must have come loose at the seams, because the next morning around 9:00 we got a call from the Chief Minister's office saying that he would see us immediately. We had a great time. There is a picture of us giving him the document. We had five or six things, one of which we were scared of: "Will you permit us to promote money from other governments for our work in India, such as Australia, Holland, Great Britain, Germany, and the United States?" He said, "Yes." And he said that if there is any trouble with the Indian government, "I will take care of it, and you work through me on that." Then, I asked him, "Well, what about visas? We have been having visa trouble in India. If we want to send a farmer to Maliwada or if we wish to pretend that someone is working in Maliwada while he is in Delhi, how do we get the visas?" And he said, "I'll take care of it."

The same morning that we got that call, we got another call from the Governor's office of Maharashtra state, Governor Young, a Muslim. He invited us to come to a state luncheon. While we were in Maliwada, the Governor came to Arangabad and suggested we take about twenty minutes. It took twenty minutes to tell our story, then he started talking. He talked for an hour on the rural situation in India and his interest in it. Later, we received a telephone call from his office asking us to come to lunch. We went to his mansion to a huge state dining room with waiters in gorgeous uniforms, twenty of them. I suppose there were thirty-five in all around the table. One of the people, the Prime Minister of Mauritius, which is an island off Madagascar, Malagasy, was George Reves, with his ministers. We all sat at the table. I sat beside the President of the university system in the state. As the Governor opened the meal, he said, "Mr. Prime Minister," he was talking to his guests, "I'm going to ask Mr. Mathews to tell about his work. I think you would like to hear it and I want everybody else to hear about it, too." I said, "Now?" And he said, "Yes, now." I took about five minutes and spun about Maliwada before the whole group, and when I finished Governor Young said, "Now, Mr. Mathews, I have given you a passport to Mauritius." Then he turned to the Prime Minister and said, "I want you to give him his visa." And the Prime Minister said, "If you could do in our country what you described you are doing in India, you can come tomorrow, and you will have the full support of my government."

What is behind all this? I want to repeat: we, by wisdom and energy that is not synonymous with ours individually or collectively, are at the right place at the right time with the right service to humanity. I think of the past when we went to see people about courses and about this and that. You first of all had to sit there and sell yourself. And if you succeeded on that, then you pulled out your product and sold that. Now they could care less about you. The product sells itself.

There is a picture of a young man standing with Mrs. Rowe, the Minister of Education. The young man's name is Rowe, too. He was the printer. Your colleagues lived with him night and day for about sixty hours to do the finest printing job that their company had ever done. Another way of saying what I am trying to say is that God is raising up in high places and low places, west and east, people who care. I believe it is the presence. It is almost that they don't know they care until you walk into their office with a document. Something is happening in this world.

Six Stages

This next speech has to do with *six stages to date*. The first stage I call the Christian Faith and Life Community. What a man was that Jack Lewis! He did a great thing with Lyn and me: he forced us to go to Europe the first nine months we were there to look at all of the lay centers. Out of that trip we got the beginning of the substance of the Faith and Life Community. On our trip we organized the lay centers in a pattern. There were those that were interested in the liturgy, like Taise; those who were interested in social mission, like evangelical academies; those who were interested in education, like the YMCA colleges in London and the Church in the World in Holland; and those who were interested in community, like Iona, with George McLeod and like Agape in Italy. This gave us our first vantage point, so to speak: come and worship, come and study, come and live, and come and mission.

That was the beginning of our getting hold of our mission back in the Christian Faith and Life Community, and our interior life. My point is this: from the very first, even when we didn't know exactly what we meant, we said we are out to renew the church for the sake of renewing the world. That is one of the brightest things that we ever came up with, even though we were wet behind the ears. And we criticized the Academy, which was the most powerful church renewal movement, because they were going directly into social action, by-passing the theological issues. That is the reason why ten years later the academies developed what they call "the 10-year malaise," from which they have never recovered and in which they are going to die. Most of them have. I thank

God that we went the way of the theological as the ground upon which we did the social. I look upon that as stage one.

The second stage was Fifth City. We had a great deal of pain during the time when we left Austin and traveled to every major city in the United States trying to figure out where is the place that we could best launch what we had in mind. Fortunately, we hit the Ecumenical Institute in Chicago. But you know that when we went to all of those cities, we went to the slums. We sensed in the early days a call to the ghetto. I believe that we are ghetto people. I believe God knew exactly what he was doing. He intends that we always be ghetto people, that we be out to serve the poor, not in some charitable sense, but to relieve the suffering by giving to humankind a new sense of community in the historical process. We were one year in Evanston before we were able to get to Fifth City. I do not think of our coming to Chicago, I think of our coming to Fifth City. That was stage two of our work.

Stage three had to do with RS-I. I can remember the time when we covered the nation with it. Then we covered the globe with it. Now we were in Fifth City. That was our basic junction, and without that we wouldn't have moved anywhere, and we would not be ready for this day.

Stage four, and many of you were there that day, just four small groups of us went out to start religious houses. It was Los Angeles, Boston, Chicago, and Atlanta. And then across the world we built the framework without which you would not be doing human development consults like in Maliwada.

Our fifth stage was development. I don't mean raising money. We learned as nobodies to walk with kings. Without that painful discipline we could not be here. All of us are doing development. I blame this on Amy in many ways. She is the first one who said to me, "Joe, our group has got to become sophisticated," only she didn't use that word. She used the word "gracious." Very few of us were hippies. Even as old as I am, we were rebels. If you didn't have an ounce of that in you, you wouldn't be here.

Steps at Hand

Now, the sixth stage in our history is not social demonstration. This is but a symbol of what I am talking about, and I'll come to that in a minute. I want to talk for a minute on the *steps at hand* relative to social demonstration before I come back to Town Meeting.

I have to tell one or two stories first. We've done Oombulguri, Kwangyung II, Kawangware, and Maliwada. We have Majuro coming up. Then there is Fifth City. God only knows what will happen at the consult in Fifth City. The Isle of Dogs is going to come off, and it is going to be something. You should see that old Harbor Master's House that the Port of London Authority have given us to use free for eight years as our living quarters. We are going to have to learn all over again how to do Fifth City. People who are out there doing primal community ought to have all six ears focused on the Isle of Dogs.

The day after tomorrow every religious house in the world is going to be doing a social demonstration. I'll come back to that in a moment. In December, when the North American Priors were here, they asked to do one in each one of the areas in North America. That means Montreal, Edmonton, San Francisco, Houston, New York, and we already have Fifth City going in Chicago. Where are the other places in the world? We have to do one in Cebu. We have a fantastic opportunity to do one outside of Jakarta. We could flip the Centrum over into Jakarta and permeate the government and get their permission. We have to do one there. I am hopeful that this is the time we could do one in Pakistan; that would be in Lahore, if we did it. With great pain I pass by Tehran. There has got to be one in Lusaka. And we ought to do one in Berlin next year, and one in Caracas. I think this will be our means of doing Latin America, which we have long postponed. This has nothing to do with the fact that we could do one tomorrow in Alaska and in Samoa or Fiji, or even better, Tonga. There is no place that you couldn't do one. If I were the people in Taiwan I'd be screaming. In fact I'm the kind of idiot that would start one whether the outfit permitted me or not.

The most shocking thing was the invitation we received from Bishop Samuels, who is Mr. Coptic Church. Bishop Samuels and Bishop Theophilus and Mrs. Armend invited us to stop by on the way back from India to discuss a social demonstration in Cairo, Egypt. We were invited to this one by the power itself, on the upper Nile, outside of Cairo. The name of the village is Bayad. I had to call it "El Bayad." There is a monastery right there. When we finished and sat down I said we would need a place for our people to live in the village. They said they would see that one is built. I said that if one is built we want it to be the model house, the kind of new house that we want to build there. And this means no animals inside. Anyway, they are going to supply seed money which would include our travel to Egypt, and the people over there running interference for us with the government for visas and so on. Then I wanted to know how soon. We could go in there tomorrow. If we do not live out of a failure mentality, when we set out to do eight of these in one year we will do eight. It would be very easy to say, "My God, we have worked so hard doing seven. That is enough." The eighth probably ought to be Cebu, and my guess is that they have already started one in Cebu. Or it ought to be Cairo, El Bayad.

The Missions Ahead

I've got two more speeches to give, and one of them has to do with a syndrome that has developed, or the *missions ahead.* We are not doing town meeting, we are not doing social demonstration, although these two are the mighty forces. Without doing social demonstration you could not do town meetings. For you are not about to get there if you do not have government support, and they would not give you government support for town meeting, but they would give it for social demonstration projects. Then town meeting is the first step of replication. Do you see that? We have already written that into the Maliwada report. Some years ago you remember we had a great image of going to the masses. You are not doing town meeting, you are not doing social demonstration, you are going to masses. You are going to the "last fat lady." For years we were going to the last fat lady in abstraction. That is what we were out to do. The time has now come when we have the means to do it for real. In these years ahead we are going to be doing town meeting, preaching missions (we will have another title for it, I'm sure.), social demonstration, social methods school, and it is going to be all one syndrome. When it is mixed together and spinning it is going to spell Primal Community Experiment or Local Church Experiment.

Definitudes of Presence

My last speech has to do with the *definitudes of presence*. Did you read that article in *Time* magazine on "Saints" in December? It had Teresa's picture on the front. I was excited when I saw it. To think that *Time* magazine at that time of year would do that. I read the thing and it was outrageous. I am not blaming *Time*, I am just blaming history, or something, but you read it with fascination. There have always been saints and there always will be saints, but there is a new something coming into being. You can really smell it in the article. One thing I believe is that in the past you grasped the saint in terms of interior qualities. From now on you can't look at it that way. It has to be an external service. I believe when they interpreted sainthood, they interpreted the qualities behind external service rather than the service. This is going to flip the idea of sainthood. I'm trying to shove corporateness. Then you see that corporateness was there in the beginning. One of the glories of the early church was that they were called "saints." Why? The church grasped itself as caring.

But it was corporate, and I am very clear on that these days. I know in all humility that it is *the blue*, and I don't care how much of a donkey you are in that blue. The blue, it is the presence of the blue! You know these days I am very little concerned about going to heaven. Lord Buddha came back and kept working until all people were saved. But I've decided I'll just sit down outside the gate and wait for all the blue. Then when all the blue get there, we will get up and walk in together. That is what I mean by presence. It is the presence that heals and creates new possibility in history.

On Taking Care of Yourself

During Summer 1975, Joe gave five talks to the global Priors on "taking care of yourself." I have cut and rearranged them considerably to make them into one talk – still leaving in some repetition for emphasis, because Joe repeated himself often when making a talk. Here he passionately encourages us to take care of ourselves as we prepare for the mission before us. ~J. Cock

Grace and Peace be unto you from God our Father and the Lord Jesus Christ. Amen.

I. On Taking Care of Yourself

I want to talk about taking care of yourself. For a long time I have believed it is necessary to have crutches – not psychological crutches but spiritual crutches – in order to make it through life. Yet, you must tailor and build your own crutches. This is what makes the subject difficult to talk about. Nonetheless, a couple of general things can be said. Standing at attention to your life is something we do not like to do, and no one can take care of you; you must take care of yourself. It has not been easy the last two years. We have lost some. We are scarred in ways we were not two years ago, but as a whole we're pretty fit.

How do you take care of yourself? My mind goes back to an art professor I knew at the University of Texas. He was the first person to get through my skull that there was such a thing as experiencing your experience. Actually, experiencing your experience is the beginning of profound consciousness. Think of the innumerable happenings, or hunks of life, that have come to you since this day began. How many of them have slipped by and are gone forever because you did not stand at attention before them? That is experiencing your experience, or consciousness about consciousness. To begin to take care of yourself is to take seriously the experiencing of your experiences; that is, taking seriously the fact that you have only one life. It's your life. Stand present to every bit of it.

For me, this requires certain oddities. I have decided not to tolerate anyone waking me up in the morning. I have, before being and God and my own existence, decided that I will take care of getting up every morning. I don't always make it, and it burns me up when I don't make it; I even appreciate it, on those days, for someone to come by and tell me that "Christ is risen!" all over again. But I intend for those days to be rare. I can get myself in decent condition to meet my fellow human beings in fifteen minutes. But I get up forty-five minutes before I have to leave. Why? I want to get myself spiritually dressed. For me, taking care of myself is getting myself ready to stand at attention before everything that happens that day.

I would not permit anyone to pass me in the morning without my saying "Good morning!" to them. Why? Not because someone is walking by me but because that other person's walking by me is *my* life. My spiritual ablutions in the morning serve no other purpose than to get me on tiptoe so that when I turn the corner coming down the stairs on the first landing, the people will see a human being coming down the stairs. And when folks see me early in the morning, even though I may not feel very chipper, they encounter someone strutting like a drum major.

Another thing, you can't take care of yourself unless you get hold of what you're despairing over. If you don't get hold of it, then down inside of you it will begin to eat away at you. This is where emotions come in. God did not give you emotions because they tingle you. I don't think God is much interested in tingling. He gave you emotions so you could experience your experience. If I feel terrible, if I feel like a failure, my job as a person, as a self, is to find out why I feel this way.

For instance, if you make me angry, it has nothing to do with you. It has to do with me. And if you delight me, it has nothing to do with you. It's *my* delight. Perhaps I wouldn't have had the delight were it not for you, but once I have that delight, it's mine. I have to appropriate it and live it.

II. The Substance of Taking Care of Yourself

There is another way I could have introduced this subject. You and I dread the experience of the self-conscious dark night and the self-conscious long march. If we as a group went out of existence today and were remembered for only one thing, it would be for staking out the netherworld, the netherland. You may think I'm naïve, but for the first time I understand how the Starets have their power of seeing through something. They may not use these words to express it, but they understand that every so-called problem anyone ever had is simply the experience of humanness itself – nothing other than the dark night of the soul and the long march of care. That is what consciousness is.

I have decided that I am going to pull everything that happens to me through the dark night. I finally realized that every situation literally is a container of spiritual meaning. If the word "spiritual" is too religious for you, then try "transparent meaning," or the "meaning of consciousness itself."

How do you take care of yourself? What if a beloved one dies? I have two choices: either I can respond temporally or I can respond transparently. In Joseph Campbell's book on schizophrenia and the Spirit, he says when you enter the Other World, either you learn to swim or become a schizo. However, it has occurred to me that even if you can swim, you become a schizo. The only difference is, if you have learned to swim, you're in charge of being a schizo rather than letting it take charge of you.

I always say to myself that I lead a double life. I have this life that has relationships to various human beings, and it is a very, very particular life. But I have another life, the one of looking through to the transparent meaning of life. A different world entirely. But the Other World only exists in this world – yet it's another world. And it's universal. That statement is not abstract Platonism. It is an empirical statement. In the Other World are humiliation, weakness, resentment, and suffering. In the Other World are dislocation, burned-out-ness, ineffectivity, and unfulfillment. They are all there. If I were at all adequate in articulating this, you would hear your fathers in the faith say, "You can't touch me. Not even the death of a beloved one can destroy me."

If you have not been catapulted into the profound depths of consciousness, you do not have to talk about taking care of yourself. The normal structures of society take care of you pretty well. Once in a while somebody flips out of them and has to receive special treatment, but most of us make it to the grave without that. But once the deeps of consciousness have opened up, and you have dared to walk into those portals of consciousness, until the day you die you are vulnerable in a way that you cannot even describe. You had better take care of yourself.

The secret of it all is to experience your experience. That is underneath all the wisdom and insight about the devotional life. Taking care of yourself begins with standing at attention, and that involves at least four things.

The first of them is checking on your *spiritual attire*; that begins in the morning, as I said earlier. I should think that the thing you would fear most would be appearing spiritually nude at anytime.

The second thing that is involved in standing at attention is the *external environment*. I would not dwell my days anywhere else than in a place where I chose what unconsciously addressed me. I might make terrible mistakes, but I would not choose to expose myself to any environment which did not address my profound understanding of my own selfhood.

The third thing is what I call the *crutches of integrity*. One of the crutches is humor, being able to laugh at yourself and knowing when you have to get other people to laugh at you.

The last thing that has to do with standing at attention is *afterbrooding*. I cannot stand myself when I get angry. When I get angry I try to stop myself immediately. And then I try to remember the point before which I was not angry, and after which I was angry. Then I start pushing, and the moment I begin to grasp why I am angry, then I forget the whole thing. There is no sense of guilt; that is not what I am after in doing this. I am trying to spot what I am angry about. You know that you are never angry about what you think you are angry about. When I have located the real reason for my anger, then I can deal with it. Afterbrooding is dealing with your responses to life.

To take care of yourself you must grasp the substance of it. That substance is the dark night of the soul. Today's new transcultural human being is discovering the essence of being human all over again. And that essence – that which we all hold in common – is the dark night of the soul. It is about the netherworld, for in substance I do not encounter you. It is as if you are not there. Only the Mystery I encounter in you (and I could not encounter it except in you) is before me.

"Attention! Here and now! Here and now!" It is being a person of profound deeps in every situation, for the rest of your life, to the glory of God. And do not forget the rest of us. If you do not care for yourself, if you collapse, we have to carry the whole load.

III. Meditation as Taking Care of Yourself

If you don't learn to be a detached human being, you are lost. You must clearly participate in each situation without losing your soul to any situation. This is done by meditation.

What is meditation? I call it grounding myself in history. I take extremely seriously what I relate myself to in history. This also has to do with my meditative council. You use your council to ground yourself, to give yourself a place to stand that will enable you to detach yourself. If I didn't grasp that I was marching with the league, with the community of saints, I could not endure the profundity of consciousness I have. I would be a candidate for suicide.

Meditation has to do with Satan, who has to do with the relationship we take to our relationships. Meditation has to do with grounding. You never collapse because something external happened to you. You only collapse in relationship to that other relationship you take to what happened to you. To put it in secular language, you only collapse when you get into a dis-relationship with consciousness. External happenings have nothing to do with my consciousness. Whether or not you like me has nothing to do with my consciousness, nor does whether or not I like myself. When you begin to see what I am talking about, you become aware that you have no excuses ever again. You have nothing to blame anything on. It's all about the relationship you take.

All of us are in exactly the same boat as we experience our profound experience. I have not had a different experience for as long as I can remember. I am always trying to pick up my humiliation and my weakness, my resentment and my suffering. In the deeps of consciousness, that is the way it is.

Back to the meditative council: it is in your minds. You do not dialogue outside of that council, in principle. Meditation is not contemplating sin. As a matter of fact, when you are looking directly at sin, or for sin, you could no more find it than you could find the proverbial needle in a haystack. Your own sin is disclosed to you, and the best you can do is to see it out of the corner of your eye.

The only way we can deal with the category of sin concretely is to understand that it has to do with depth consciousness. Sin is the refusal to be consciousness. It is your rebellion against who you actually are – contingent, humiliated, and weak. To use theological language, sin is only rebellion against

God. That happens when you refuse the resentment you are, when you refuse the suffering you are, when you say, "I have had enough of this," which means, "I am going to do my best to get myself out of the profound depths of consciousness. I have had enough of it." The tragedy is that once you get that mud on your feet you never get it off. If you have actually fallen into the deeps, what you have ahead of you, if you flee from your profound consciousness, is zombie-ism. Sin is the refusal of being unfulfilled. It is the refusal to endure drained-out-ness. It is the refusal to not have hope. Do you see that this is precisely the point and the only point where, to use the images of the Persians, Satan attacks?

Meditation is not something you go aside to do an hour a day. I am extremely suspicious of that. Meditation goes on constantly. It is constant brooding. Finally, meditation is that goingonness with whatsoever meditative council you have that enables you, when you have collapsed into a heap of shaking palsy, to pick yourself up and walk tall. This means that meditation is our continuing the profound decision to live life in profound consciousness with gratitude.

IV. God Will Take Care of You

I have tried to say four things: first, taking care of yourself means you experience your experience. My father was a nut on chewing food. He would sit there and almost count the times we chewed before we swallowed. It burnt me up as a kid. That came back to my mind last night as I was thinking about experiencing my experience. Second, taking care of yourself has to do with the dark night of the soul, and third it has to do with meditation. Now, fourth, it has to do with God taking care of you.

If you want being to take care of you, then you decide you've got to ask for it. You have to give yourself into the hands of being. When you hear that song "God Will Take Care of You," remember that he'll not do it unless you ask. And that is done by standing on tiptoe, at every situation and in every life circumstance.

Lots of things have hurt me. One time someone said something to me that implied God didn't know what he was doing. That statement flagrantly violated my understanding of what it means to trust being. Every situation – not all, minus one – but every situation (for one who has asked being to take care of him) becomes being taking care of you – even unto death.

Maybe I've got to clarify this word "God." It's a faith statement. At this point I am experiencing the overagainstness that I am trying to talk about as sovereign. To be a male is just one thing. I could go on with the fact that I am sixty-four, I am not twenty-four. These days every time I come upon myself, I am sixty-four. People ask these days What does it mean to trust? What does it mean to trust God? I am talking about taking care of yourself. Whatsoever else it means, it means that you self-consciously in every given situation acknowledge God's sovereignty.

We were in a group of people four months after my son John died as a youth, and someone made a statement that made me feel that John ought not to have died. I cannot describe the explosion that went off in me! Do you know what the explosion was? I went through hell to maintain the faith posture that I am not simply the subject of fate but God is my merciful father.

Do you hear what I am talking about? I believe that when you understand the sovereignty of God you never again have any excuse about anything. I am talking about trusting God, not in some abstract way, but in the concretion of your life. If you can ever blame anything on anything, then you are not hearing what I mean by trusting God. I am talking about taking care of yourself. You get up one morning and you forget, and you say, "This is a hell of a day." That is sacrilege. That is not trusting God. This is the day God gave you. You let go one day and you will not notice it, but the next day when you get up you are exactly that much shorter than you were the day before. You do it two days in a row and you are that much shorter. You do it three in a row, and then pretty soon you are there like a heap of shaking palsy. You let one go and the trouble has started.

What do you mean when you say God cares for you? To get this in secular language, being cares for being. Being could care less about deeds and could care less about knowledge. Have you noticed that? Everything passes away. Or, maybe the best evidence is this fine body I have. One of these days they are going to stick it in a six-foot hole and then it will not be here anymore.

So, what is my being? I do not want to deal with it in abstract philosophy but in concrete experience. The way I experience my being is to know my knowing and to do my doing. I am talking about the experience of the intensification of knowing and the intensification of doing. By *knowing my knowing*, I mean standing present to my knowing. I used to say to a particular colleague, "You and I must do something." The night before we would sit down and make a model and then lay it aside, and the next night make another one. What you make models for is to bring them into being, and the way you bring them into being is to appropriate them in your being. That is knowing your knowing. This is why abstract thinking is finally not helpful. This is what the existential dynamic of our time has taught us. What is my being? Knowing my knowing. I do not want an idea that I am not. This is what I mean by integrity.

Secondly, being does not care anything about our doing. It is the difference between doing a job and sticking the one, God-given life you have into ironing a white linen handkerchief. The cross is not something that happened two thousand years ago. It is at the heart of being, which means you and I can stick the one life we have and one death we have into the least of all deeds. That is *doing your doing*, which is being. What I am trying to say is being takes care of being. This is what I mean by endlessness. What does it mean to take care of yourself? Very simple. You know your knowing and do your doing, and being always takes care of being, or being takes care of the rest.

V. On Being the Son of God in Meditation

In the tenth chapter of the Gospel of John, Jesus stands up and says, "I am the son of God." That jarred me into seeing that precisely in the aliveness of the dark night of the soul, precisely there and only there, one sees the heavens open and hears the voice saying, "Thou art my beloved son." But the Jews cannot hear what Jesus hears as he says, "I am the son of God."

I wish for one second that I were not quite so short. But, anyway, I will stand tall before you and say, "I am God's son." I am proud, as I hope you are proud this day and every day, to be a son or daughter of God. I hope always when I feel the pressures of living that I will not forget to throw my shoulders back. I hope I do it so you can see it. When you see me, remember, I am a son of God. I am not what you think I am. I am not what I think I am. I am not what anybody thinks I am. I am what God thinks I am. Therefore, I say I am a son of God. This is the heart of meditation. Knowing this is what it means above all else to take care of yourself.

Meditation only takes place in a concrete situation. That is to say, only when you get the tragic news that four young people you care about are suffering does meditation take place. A situation that pries loose profundity of consciousness itself occasions meditation. Meditation does not have to do with sin; it has to do with redemption. It does not have to do with the past but always the future. Any situation is toward the future.

Secondly, meditation has to do with being the guardian of profound living. Meditation has to do with the angels and the saints. They only talk ontologically. If some voice says you were a naughty boy, that is fine, but that was not the talk of the angels and the saints. Meditation deals with the deep truth of our lives.

Next, meditation is the endless dialogue of life. Meditation always operates, but only when it is triggered. In one sense, meditation is always going on; the disciplined person only brings self-consciousness to it. This dialogue of life floods us constantly, but we dam it up. To meditate is to get out of the way and let it rush by.

Meditation is bringing to self-consciousness who your meditative council is. If you don't know anything about Luther, then Luther can play only a very small role on your council. Why should I read the lives of the saints? It is obvious. Like them we have been captured by the Mystery, enslaved by the Mystery.

Two times this morning I almost did something ridiculous. I was sitting in my cubicle when I almost stood up and said, "I am *too* a son of God!" I believe you say this to Satan – not for the world to hear. Like Jesus, I am the son of God, consecrated and sent into the world. First, he was consecrated, then he was sent, and where? Into the world. That is who I understand myself to be, when I meditate, when I become really self-conscious about who I am.

Who am I? *I am the believing one*. I don't believe in this, that, or the other thing. I am just the believing one. That is my consecration. It is like that hymn, "Make me a captive, Lord, and then I shall be free." Sometimes I get all messed up inside and feel that God requires of me that I be this or that, or I do this or that. Until the day I die, I am required to be only the believing one.

And *I am the caring one*. There are many times when I don't want to be a believing one and when I don't want to be a caring one. Earlier this morning I was wishing I had never heard of caring. But I am the believing and caring one, because *I am the elected one*. That is the category of being which has no substance. It is the depth of knowing that you were sent to believe and to care.

All this is what I mean when I stand up and say before Satan, "I am the son of God." I mean I am going to be what I am sent to be, the one who believes and the one who cares, even unto death.

So you see, the purpose of meditation is to get you to say before yourself, the world, God, and Satan, "I am God's son," or "I am God's daughter."

Now, you won't be surprised that as I finish I will stand up as tall as I can, throw back my shoulders proudly, and say one more time, "I am God's son." How about you?

Men, repeat after me, if you will: "I am God's son!" . . . Good.

Women, repeat after me, if you will: "I am God's daughter!" . . . Good.

You now know the essence of taking care of yourself. So, take care of yourself. Remember, taking care of yourself is to discipline yourself constantly to experience your experience by standing at attention in every here and now. Secondly, taking care of yourself is to discipline yourself constantly to participate in the double reflection that is meditation. Third, taking care of yourself is to discipline yourself constantly to appropriate the double paradox that depth consciousness is to live to the hilt the dark night and the long march. And taking care of yourself is to discipline yourself constantly to surrender into being's care forever, remembering you are God's son, God's daughter.

And remember, finally, you only take care of yourself because you're called to care for the world, to the glory of God. *Amen.*

Postlude

By George Walters

Bending History

The 21st century has brought us a whole new collection of challenges and possibilities, many of which Joe would hardly have imagined. Bending history, however, remains the same challenge. It is not about fixing the past but shaping the future.

I recently had a conversation with a colleague about the potential for being of service to the thirty poorest nations in the world. He was visibly excited about the prospects, as was I, and as we talked he began to speak about "giving back" from our potential wealth.

Without a pause to reflect, like a voice from someone else, I said: "No! It is not possible to give back. Once it is taken, it is taken; and those who gave up their wealth that you and I may have it, we can never return it to them."

He was shaken and fumbled for words to respond, sure that "giving back" was the right thing.

"What about atonement?" he asked.

"Penance, maybe," I said, "but there is no atoning. "

"So what do we do?" he asked.

"Change the future, which is all anyone can do," I replied. "Change the future. We cannot fix the past. It is just the gift we are given. We can only change the future."

I was shocked at myself. I still do not know where those words came from. I think they were more of an address on me that they were on him. I was rushing to catch a plane. We parted. There were tears in his eyes, tears of gratitude, that he no longer had to atone for that which he could never atone for; he no longer had to live out of guilt for what he had been, what he had gained at the expense of others, not maliciously, just by virtue of the way life is. He showed up as one of the "haves"; others showed up as "have-nots." Now what? I fell into a deep silence the next three hours of my journey, trying to comprehend what had just happened.

Primordial Truth

Beneath this conversation is the primordial truth embedded in the *word* that Joe, the radical churchman, tried a thousand ways to articulate, to demonstrate, to expose in every situation, in every culture, and in every human being he encountered. It went something like this:

> Your life, as it is, is utterly received. You can take that life and expend it on behalf of others, or horde it for yourself. It is your choice, your freedom, your responsibility. And whatever you choose to do, or not do, either way you affect the future. You either just let future happen as it happens or you *bend it.*

What Joe Imagined

Recently, Betty Pesek shared with our writing group one of Joe's last talks, given to our group in Chicago after he had discovered he had a malignant tumor in 1977. I remember sitting spellbound in that room listening to him speak, listening to a man who had his death in his hands, as he calmly and firmly painted imaginal pictures of what he saw the future to hold, and the consequent imperatives. I have chosen a few paraphrases from that talk in the hope that they help interpret what those images might mean to us now.

Premise: Joe believed that the task of the historical church was to pronounce the *word* that awakened human lives so that they engage with others in serving a suffering world. This is a perpetual humanizing task that never ends. Every era presents its new challenges and possibilities. Structural change is the key, as it blends with universal change and makes further human change more possible.

Social Change: Social change can only occur with massive transformation at the local community level, where local governance releases the power of local people to shape their futures. At least 2 million communities must be so awakened and engaged to catalyze this re-humanization of society, to start the snowball effect. Joe believed no little group like ours could do this alone, but there had to be a way. Multiple forces – many unknown and unconnected to each other, from many cultural and religious traditions, but all clear on what they were doing – had to catch this vision and engage themselves to make it happen. Our principal task today is still awakenment, then others can do the structural work and get the credit. That it gets done is all that matters.

Unity and Harmony: The understanding that "God is one" (see Teilhard de Chardin's *Building the Earth*) is the key to releasing profound humanness. Humanness is founded on forgiving one another. Retribution against those we disagree with demonstrates an inhumanity that history cannot tolerate. World wars like the one Joe came out of, cold wars, civil wars, cultural conflicts, and even gang wars in local communities all point to the need for a radical new understanding of what lies beneath our cultural and religious diversity. Those deeps must be exposed. We must finally learn to forgive one another.

Resurrection Presence: Those who would be the church today must no longer wait for a resurrection but *be* the resurrection presence now. This is the role of the laity through their engagement in secular vocations and their capacity to see the resurrected life of the Other World as a normal everyday phenomenon within this world and act out their faith in care through whatever they are doing – doctoring, lawyering, waiting tables, digging ditches, clerking, teaching – all vocations can build the new earth. Through such vocatedness the world is renewed, as are the religions of the world.

Spiritual Mode: Spirituality today is no romantic mysticism, but a radical empiricism where awakened and engaged radical selves offer illumination to those around them – acting courageously, seeking and dispensing wisdom from all quarters, getting things done, embodying reality, taking spiritual and physical care of themselves, and committing to being a presence that empowers others to act out their own selfhood through care.

Intellectual Frame: The new intellectual is not some "smart" person, but rather one who knows what s/he knows and does what s/he does without apology. This is being theological in our time, where one does what he knows. This is being the church in our time. This is being a child of God.

Sociological Care: "Care" is at the heart of the new religious order that is coming into being, where spirit prowess is at the center of worship, study, life together, and mission. A gracious, simple, neat, organized, and disciplined community, home, or workplace may be the most profound manifestation of this orderliness that is a portent of what is to come. This new order form may not look like an organization. It may be loose knit and somewhat fragmented. But the connectivity that glues it together is most apparent: care. When and wherever care is manifest, all the traits above become visible, whether it is a meeting in a hotel lobby, a workshop or training session at the UN or in a local community, a gathering in your home, a few old colleagues at a baseball game, transformed space in your workplace, a late night conversation on the phone, a transformed institution, or non-profit structures caring for others – there are no bounds to the forms. But always remember that profound care is at the center.

Casting a New Shadow

Action without thought is foolish and thought without action is in vane. We who assembled this book, and the greater we of thousands of persons who contributed one way or another to it, no longer stand in the shadow of our former teacher, mentor, and colleague. He would not permit it. We now cast our own shadows, whoever and wherever we are. The wealth of wisdom collected in the Joseph Wesley Mathews Archives, from which this project was drawn, constitutes a call to us and others who would do more in-depth and focused research and writing that further releases and empowers those who would bend history today. This book is but a taste of what is there for those who have the eyes to see and the will to explore.

A thousand volumes may be written that take the writers and readers beyond Joe's wildest dreams. Indeed, if you explore the lives and read the writings of those who learned from and used the wisdom of this community that Joe founded – over the past twenty-seven years – this can already be seen to be true. If this book has one central truth which sums up Joe's thought, it is:

> You are received. You can bend history.

The Call

Somewhere in some village, on some academic campus, in some ghetto, in some law firm, at the top of some corporate empire, in some church pew, there are awakened persons for whom this book – and others to come – will be encouraging and empowering. There are those who long for a renewed church/ renewed religions and transformed community/transformed world who may discover in these pages that they themselves are the key to that happening. We hope this book will serve as a call to them and thousands of others to be the next generation of those who bend history as they care for all the earth.

The Archives

By Betty Pesek

Joe felt that his efforts to give shape to the resurgence of the Spirit in his time might be a contribution to others who had a similar passion – love for the church, deep faith in God, and gratitude for the presence of the *word* in their lives. His legacy is far greater than the eighteen file cabinets filled with his papers, writings, talks, reflections, tapes, and other pieces of research. These file cabinets, however, stand as a symbol of his life's work that affected so many people in so many places.

I maintained Joe's personal files from 1967 to 1977. At the time of his death in 1977, he asked his wife, Lyn Mathews, and me to protect these works and keep them separate from the Ecumenical Institute and Institute of Cultural Affairs archives that were maintained by others. His papers and works were personal, like his clothing. Many documents that he had a hand in creating for EI and ICA are also in these files and have his personal notes and asides hand-written in the margins. Joe told me that whenever anyone wanted to borrow his papers to make a copy and not give out his original documents. This I have done as many have used these resources in the twenty-seven years since his passing.

Joe also asked Lyn to decide where the files finally reside. He had an intuition that his collected works might be helpful, and wanted them to be available to others to further the efforts to which he had dedicated his life. Lyn and I had numerous conversations with Bishop James K. Mathews, his brother, and approached several institutions. Conversations continue.

During Joe's life, we did not have the advantages of modern technologies for maintaining documents and images. It is mind-boggling to me that the entire room filled with the file cabinets, plus numerous additional materials in the personal possession of others, could be contained on a single hard-disk, 3x5x1 inches. The *Bending History* editorial guild has actually begun this process, digitizing and OCR processing the many papers and resources needed to publish this book. This may be the secret to finally finding an institution to host these works, since entire libraries are now managed this way for online research.

I feel deeply that Joe's archives should serve the suffering world, as he did.

Table of Figures

List of References

Bergson, Henri. *The Two Sources of Morality and Religion.* New York: Greenwood Press Reprint, 1975.

Bonhoeffer, Dietrich. "Freedom," *Ethics*. New York: Macmillan, 1965.

Boulding, Kenneth. *The Image*: *Knowledge in Life and Society*. Ann Arbor: University of Michigan, 1971.

Buber, Martin. *I and Thou*, trans. R. G. Smith. New York: Scribner's, 1958.

Bultmann, Rudolf. "The Crisis of Faith," *Rudolf Bultmann*: *Interpreting Faith for the Modern Era*, ed., Roger Johnson. London: Collins Liturgical, 1987.

Campbell, Joseph. *The Hero with a Thousand Faces*. Princeton, N.J.: Princeton University Press, 1972.

Camus, Albert. *The Myth of Sisyphus and Other Essays*, trans. Justin O'Brien. New York: Vintage, 1991.

——. *The Stranger*, trans. Matthew Ward. New York: Vintage, 1988.

——. "The Adulterous Woman," *Exile and the Kingdom*, trans. Justin O'Brien. New York: Vintage, 1957.

Castaneda, Carlos. *Journey to Ixtlan*. New York: Simon & Schuster, 1972.

Cock, John P. *The Transparent Event*: *Post-modern Christ Images*. Greensboro, N.C.: tranScribe books, 2001.

Cummings, E. E. *Selected Poems of E. E. Cummings*. New York: Liveright, 1994.

Gogarten, Friedrich. *Christ the Crisis*. Richmond: John Knox, 1970.

Golding, William. *The Inheritors*. New York: Harvest, 1955.

Hammarskjöld, Dag. *Markings.* New York: Alfred A. Knopf, 1964.

Harrington, Michael. *Fragments of the Century*. New York: Saturday Review Press, 1973.

Hesse, Hermann. *The Journey to the East*, trans. Hilda Rosner. New York: Noonday Press, 1970.

Kazantzakis, Nikos. *The Saviors of God*: *Spiritual Exercises,* trans. Kimon Friar. New York: Simon & Schuster, 1960.

Kierkegaard, Søren. *The Concept of Dread*, trans. Walter Lowrie. Princeton, N.J.: Princeton University Press, 1957.

——. *Fear and Trembling* and *The Sickness Unto Death*, trans. Walter Lowrie. New York: Doubleday, 1954.

——. *Concluding Unscientific Postscript to the "Philosophical Fragments,"* trans. David F. Swenson; ed. Walter Lowrie. Princeton, N.J.: Princeton University Press, 1941.

Lawrence, D. H. *The Complete Poems of D. H. Lawrence*. New York: Penguin, 1977.

Mathews, Joseph W. *The Christ of History*. Chicago: *Image*: *Journal of the Ecumenical Institute*: *Chicago, Number 7, June 1969.*

——. "The Time My Father Died," *Motive* magazine of the Methodist Student Movement of the Methodist Church, January-February Issue, 1964, and printed in *i.e.* (newsletter of the Ecumenical Institute: Chicago), August 1964.

Musashi, Miyamoto. *A Book of Five Rings*, trans. Victor Harris. Woodstock, N.Y.: Overlook Press, 1974.

Niebuhr, H. Richard. "The Responsibility of the Church for Society," *The Gospel, the Church and the World*, ed. Kenneth Scott Latourette. New York: Harper & Brothers, 1946.

——. *Radical Monotheism and Western Culture*: *With Supplementary Essays.* New York: Harper and Row, 1970.

——. "Toward a New Other-Worldliness," *Theology Today*, April 1944, Vol. 1, No. 1.

Nietzsche, Friedrich. *Beyond Good & Evil*: *Prelude to a Philosophy of the Future*, trans. Walter Kaufmann. New York: Random House, 1966.

Otto, Rudolf. *The Idea of the Holy*. New York: Galaxy, 1958.

Phillips, J. P. *The New Testament in Modern English.* New York: Macmillan, 1958.

Sartre, Jean-Paul. *Being and Nothingness*. New York: Washington Square Press, 1966.

——. *No Exit and Three Other Plays.* New York: Vintage International Edition, 1989.

Schweitzer, Albert. *The Quest of the Historical Jesus* : *A Critical Study of Its Progress from Reimarus to Wrede.* Baltimore: Johns Hopkins University Press (reprint), 1998.

Smith, Adam. *The Wealth of Nations*. New York: Modern Library, 1937.

Smith, Huston. *The Religions of Man*. New York: Harper and Row, 1958.

Stanfield, Brian. *The Courage to Lead*: *Transform Self, Transform Society.* Gabriola Island, BC, Canada: New Society, 2000.

St. John of the Cross. *The Dark Night of the Soul & The Living Flame of Love*. San Francisco: Harper, 1995.

Teresa of Avila. *Interior Castle*: *The Mansions*. New York: Sheed and Ward, 1948.

Teilhard de Chardin, Pierre. *Building the Earth.* New York: Avon Books, 1965.

Tillich, Paul. *The New Being*. New York: Scriber's, 1955.

——. "You Are Accepted," *The Shaking of the Foundations*. New York: Scribner's, 1948.

——. *Systematic Theology* I. Chicago: U. of Chicago, 1951

——. *Systematic Theology* II. Chicago: U. of Chicago, 1957.

——. *Systematic Theology* III. Chicago: U. of Chicago, 1963.

——. *The Theology of Culture*. New York: Galaxy, 1964.

Editorial Guild

M. George Walters: IT Professional – programmer, knowledge management, maritime, banking industries. Served with O:E[9] with his family in USA, India, Malaysia, Philippines, Ethiopia, and Belgium. Resides in Florida, USA.

Betty C. Pesek: Archivist of Joseph W. Mathews files; human relations. Assistant to Dean Mathews, 1967-1977. Former English teacher and speech therapist. Editor of book on ICA/EI/OE stories. Resides in Illinois, USA.

George R. Holcombe: pastor, consultant. Seminarian where J. W. Mathews taught. With O:E in USA, Australia, India, Malaysia, Hong Kong, Korea, Marshall Islands. Professor Emeritus, Wesley Seminary, Philippines. Resides in Texas, USA.

John L. Epps: writer, consultant, teacher. Served O:E in research in Chicago and operations in Southeast Asia. Founding member of International Association of Facilitators and Malaysia Facilitator Network. Ph.D. in systematic theology from SMU. Based in Malaysia.

John P. Cock: writer, spirit journey guide and blogger, earth guardian. Served with O:E with his family in USA, Australia, Indonesia, Malaysia, and India. Author of five books. Resides in North Carolina, USA.

[9] The Order: Ecumenical (O:E), the covenanted global community of self-supporting volunteers who operated through the program arms of the Ecumenical Institute: Chicago (EI) and the Institute of Cultural Affairs (ICA). Today the ICA International works in some thirty countries.